NEGATIVE FEEDBACK

BY
EDDIE LANCASTER

For more information
e-mail allaggro@btinternet.com

First Kindle edition April 2020

Cover design by Eddie Lancaster

Chapter 1

Jasper Skinner leaned back from his elderly laptop and sighed deeply. The time it took from switching it on to actually being able to do anything was increasing day by day. Just lately, he usually had enough time to boil the kettle, make a coffee and sit back down before the antivirus software had even begun scanning the hard drive. But rather than investigating the delay, he had simply incorporated it into his daily routine. This deliberately relaxed approach to life was skilfully crafted to shield him from any unnecessary stress. With a great deal of dedication, debt-free, tax-free and carefree had progressed to feckless, jobless and penniless.

His ninth-floor flat in Derek Robinson House looked out over the less-than-scenic railway line and a partly demolished factory opposite which in recent times had become a 24-hour recreation centre for all things unsavoury: the place to go if what you were planning was illegal, unethical or possibly grounds for divorce. With time to kill, he watched with amusement from his balcony window as two teenage kids pushed a rough-looking moped onto the factory plot. They happily roared around on it, dodging stray bricks and various piles of debris on what appeared to be an improvised race track, until one ducked down behind the handlebars to gain speed, lost control and clipped his mate before crashing heavily. It was a few seconds before either of them moved, during which time Jasper considered calling the emergency services. Eventually the kids got up, laughing, and spent five fruitless minutes trying to restart the bike. Then they wisely decided to head home to do the repairs.

The laptop gave a final beep at last, allowing Jasper to make the few clicks required to see his overnight eFlog sales. Vintage audio cassettes weren't breaking any records lately. He had initially experienced moderate success with classic car enthusiasts who bought them to listen to via the vintage stereo equipment in their cars. But he had soon realised that they didn't want to buy just any old tapes. They wanted cool rock bands' music from the 1960s or '70s to play as they drove along in the sunshine, posing with the hood down. Or the soundtrack from a famous film, like Grease or The Graduate, that connected with their car. What they definitely didn't want was Val Doonican or Des O'Connor, and quite frankly Jasper's entirely dismal sales reflected this.

Four overnight orders – not bad! Three compact cassettes and a Carpenters' Greatest Hits 8-track. A grand total of £32.50. Not a king's ransom, granted. But when you're dining for one at the expense of the tax payer, a reasonable top-up of his Jobseeker's Allowance. He printed off each order, like he always did, and laid the corresponding tape on top of each printout, ready to pack. As he did so, his eye caught something red flashing on the screen:

Feedback last 30 days

28 positives

0 neutral

1 negative

Negative feedback?! What the fuck?! Jasper swiftly clicked open his profile and read the accompanying comment.

Tangled in my player 1st play, seller unresponsive, avoid!!!

Jasper's cheeks burned with indignation. Seller unresponsive!? That was never the case! He promptly answered every message or enquiry, whether good or bad! Surely he couldn't be expected to play through absolutely every tape he sold? Admittedly, he had done at the very start of his enterprise, when he'd first hit on the idea after returning from his Uncle Bert's house clearance with a large cardboard box of assorted cassettes he'd liberated from under the stairs. But it was a very time-consuming process, and there is only so much Herb Alpert & the Tijuana Brass that he or his neighbours could stand.

Early on, he had tried playing two cassettes at once, which had unwittingly exposed him to a classic CIA brainwashing technique. That became apparent when he spent the best part of a morning crying in the lift as he tried to remember which floor he lived on. Since then he had relied on a brief visual examination and a quick twist with a ballpoint pen. If he had the time, he sometimes rewound them to the start. But the ever-present pressures of his complex social life made that a rarity these days.

So, granted, a rogue cassette may have sneaked through. But how was he supposed to know that?! Still raging, he checked his emails and the questions that customers from eFlog had sent. No complaint case against him had been opened and there were no messages of any kind. Angry enough to leave bad feedback but not organised enough to go through the correct channels? Clicking on the sales details of 'supergriff', the complainant, he noted that he had purchased Benzo Breakdown by Meryl Mental on compact cassette a month previously. So he'd had a whole four weeks to advise Jasper of a problem. This was getting much worse. The man was a juggernaut of injustice and someone needed to stop him.

Unluckily for 'supergriff', Jasper now had a window of opportunity on his hands due to his Approved Hospital Visitor status recently being revoked – yet another example of someone making rash claims about his honesty. His special visitor status had been taken away after he was apparently overheard asking a terminally ill patient if he had ever owned an 8-track cassette player and where his interests lay in the musical world. Another couple of clicks revealed that 'supergriff' only lived across town and currently had a few items for sale. Judging from his sales listings, it seemed he had a history of failed outdoor hobbies.

Jasper scanned down his listings, looking for the possibility of an inexpensive revenge purchase that he could then slate in retaliation. But as he lived in landlocked Oldbury, a small grimy town on the edge of Birmingham with an obvious lack of rolling green hills and foaming surf, neither a surfboard nor a hang-glider would be any use once the joy of vengeance had evaporated. Not to mention the cost. He was angry, but not angry enough to be delirious.

After briefly toying with the idea of an Escape from Colditz-style launch from the top of the block using the hang-glider, and dreaming about the resulting YouTube video of his final seconds of life before he disintegrated on impact like a dropped kebab, his attention returned to reality. His cup was now empty and further deliberation would require another grim own-brand instant coffee to engage his brain fully. Just as the world's slowest kettle came to the boil, the doorbell rang.

Well, actually it played 'White Christmas'. It wasn't Christmas, it was February. But Jasper had never fully got to grips with the various tune settings. The doorbell was one of those novelties that appeared charming at the point of purchase. But then you progressed to wanting to smash it off the wall when it randomly played ten seconds of 'Edelweiss' at 3 am. Striding up the hall, he knew who was there before he opened the door.

"Morning, Sweet Cheeks," said Annie, striding past him and into the kitchen.

"Why don't you come in?" said Jasper, with more than a hint of sarcasm.

Annie and Jasper made a strange couple, if 'couple' was indeed the right word. He was a sickly-looking specimen of thirty-two. Average height, pasty complexion, built like a pencil with a shock of red hair. Annie had once, unwisely, likened his lovemaking to being romanced by a bottle of skimmed milk. This led to a major exchange of views in which Jasper informed her that she was a woman lingering between retirement and death.

Annie was, as you would expect from this snapshot of the relationship, a little older and plumper than her sometimes partner. Aged fifty-two, she was a woman who existed almost entirely on a diet of biscuits and chips, equally enjoying both the deep-fried and the oven varieties. This gave her the silhouette of a portable cement mixer, and with her acidic viewpoint on life, her fat ankles and her badly dyed blonde hair, she had all the allure of a volatile overfed ferret with a 'bite now, ask questions later' policy. Many relationships are based on mutual attraction. Jasper and Annie's relationship was entirely the reverse. Their lack of attraction to other people was the catalyst for their union. Annie helped herself to a cup from the drainer and made them both a coffee.

"So what's wrong with your face?" she inquired.

"Someone left me negative feedback on a sale."

"Why?"

"Because the tape got tangled in his player."

"Seems fair enough to me…"

"Really? So you think that having an issue with an accurately described product, expertly wrapped and instantly dispatched doesn't obligate him to inform the seller that there's a problem before leaving feedback?"

"Has he asked for his money back?"

"Well no, but that's not the point. The issue is about good manners and etiquette. Plus, his feedback damages the reputation of my business."

"You sell second-hand cassette tapes online. You're not a master baker. One dodgy French Fancy isn't going to destroy your entire empire and cease production."

"It might if it had a mouse turd in the cream tit on top. Besides, it's the injustice of the issue, not the money. He says I was unresponsive, but I haven't heard anything from him!"

"So you're raging because of this massive crime against communication?"

"Well, business is slow enough already. I don't need a slur on my feedback profile to make it any quieter."

"Well if you'd have taken my advice, you'd have started selling vinyl!"

"As I told you before, Business Woman of the Year, I'm aiming at a niche and previously untapped market. Plus, you can't play a 12-inch single in a moving fucking car!"

"So what are you going to do? Carpet bomb his road, send your ninja monkeys to kill him in his sleep?"

"I'm still thinking about it"

"So are we still going to Asthma Club?"

"In spite of the fact that neither of us has, or has ever had, asthma?"

"Because the clientele is interesting and the free biscuit selection is epic!"

"Granted, it's far better than the assortment at the Diabetes Club, but then I suppose it would be, as sugar-free biscuits are as tasty as tofu trifle. Well, you can if you want, but I'm going to see Bernd."

"Why would you go to see 'Burned Toast' in preference to a plate of free biscuits and a go on the blowy ping-pong thing?"

"Because Bernd is a product of the Cold War and the man I need to speak to in such difficult circumstances…"

Bernd Tost lived in a flat on the very top floor, which he referred to as the Eagle's Nest. He was Germanic in a 'Dad's Army' sort of way. He looked German and he had a Germanesque accent. He liked bread and salami for breakfast and put Maggi soup sauce on everything. He ate chocolate-covered marzipan. Sometimes said Vs for Ws and did a great number of other stereotypical German things. Except that he never talked of home, his family or how or why he came to be in England, particularly why he had chosen to settle in a small grimy dump in the Black Country. If you could choose anywhere in the UK, why in God's name here?

In his early sixties, just under 6ft tall, a slim build and with greying blonde hair, Bernd was a total enigma. He had lived in the block for many years and had always possessed assured wisdom. Not the type that tells you the right answers to put on a tricky benefit claim form, but the type that encourages a measured response to a marital fidelity problem, like dialogue and reconciliation rather than putting a balaclava on and smacking your love rival with a sawn-off scaffolding pole and then getting an actual scaffolder to say that you were definitely in the pub. No, Bernd was considered by most people in the block to be a go-to source of temper-calming knowledge and reasoning.

After drinking as far down a cup of cheap supermarket instant as anyone dares, Jasper and Annie took the lift to the top floor to seek Bernd's wisdom. Annie was still miffed about missing Asthma Club, and she didn't feel that a visit to the Eagle's Nest was an adequate substitute. But as she was loyal to her man, skint till Thursday and only he possessed the required bus fare, she decided she'd tag along to see what transpired.

As always, the lift stank of piss and disinfectant, the balance of which altered by the hour. The closer to midnight, the less you could smell the piney freshness. Thursday onwards it always got worse, peaking on Sunday, whereas Monday to Wednesday it was bearable. Bank holidays were really bad and Christmas often passed with a pallet to stand on, which was particularly helpful if you were going out for the night and had suede shoes on. Otherwise, standing on your tiptoes, lake stepping and the 'fuck it, I'll use the stairs' approach were useful workarounds. One particular Christmas, Jasper had thoughtfully provided a sturdy pallet, and in the spirit of the season had inscribed it with 'Merry Christmas to Derek Robinson House, love from Jasper'. By

Christmas Eve, he wished he'd used a waterproof marker. To add insult to injury, his name was the first casualty…

Jasper knocked on Bernd's door and the man himself opened it. Bernd had a dress style that was stuck in the early 1980s punk era, which would have been fine when he was in his mid-twenties, but looked more than a little odd on a man of his age, particularly when the punk movement in question was the German one, rather than the common-or-garden home-grown British variety. It involved wearing T-shirts of bands most people had never heard of with lots of black and lightning flashes. Today's band was Sweinhund Mutter, or Pig-Dog Mother if you will. You didn't need to sample their wares to know it wasn't for you. A bit like frogspawn mayonnaise…

However, always a man to take something from current trends, he had a small footballer-style ponytail on the top of his head. It would have been fine if it were not for the fact that he was going bald at the crown, which gave the ponytail the look of a limp dick hanging over a toilet seat when viewed at the wrong angle.

"Ah, Herr Skinner," said Bernd, holding out his hand. "To what do I owe the pleasure?"

"Hello, Bernd," said Jasper. Annie just muttered and smiled weakly. "Need a little of your genius, mein Freund."

"Come in, come in. Tea and maybe a little strudel?" Bernd winked at Annie, who instantly warmed to the whole mission when he elaborated on the nature of strudel. A further explanation of "flaky German apple pie" from Jasper sealed the deal to dispel any lingering doubts.

They settled around Bernd's dark German-looking table, drinking his dark German tea that was sweetened with little glassy cubes of German sugar, and ate the strudel. Jasper explained his serious issue with supergriff's feedback and sought a remedy and Annie tried not to laugh. Bernd for his part listened intently without interrupting except to ask Annie if she wanted any cream with her second slice of strudel. She said she didn't as that would be greedy, but truthfully she did. She was also beginning to find Jasper's eFlog problems more than a little boring and longed for the excitement of Asthma Club. Plus Bernd didn't look like a man who paid much attention to 'best before' dates, if she was honest. When Jasper had finished, Bernd sat back in his heavily carved wooden chair at the head of the table and turned his international man of mystery dial up to twelve. Then he pulled open a drawer in the table and took out a stubby little onyx pipe. He packed it with a little of his favourite herbal cannabis, Himmler's Hemp. Then he lit it and drew it in deeply.

"So you say that this man lives not far away?" Bernd enquired thoughtfully.

"Other side of town," said Jasper.

Annie was incapable of answering as she was hoovering up the remains of Jasper's strudel. Waste not, want not, and all that…

"Then I think I may have an offer supergriff can't refuse. Or as we used to say in the old firm, we already know your name and where you live…"

"So you'll help us?"

"Us?!" spat Annie Strudelcrumbs.

"It would be my honour," Bernd said darkly, staring at Annie. "But first I must vacuum the carpet and think my thoughts. Then I will be in touch in due course."

Walking down the stairs to avoid the growing urine lake in the lift, Annie loudly voiced her doubts about Bernd's ability to deliver on his promise. But Jasper dismissed these as he was now fully engaged with the project. No more would he suffer the irritation of one-way criticism. Now he would be taking the fight to the enemy, whoever the enemy turned out to be…

Chapter 2

David Arthur Griffin, known as 'Griffo' in the pub and 'supergriff' on eFlog, was a larger-than-life character. A keen member of his local gym, long-time classic car enthusiast, occasional rugger fan and louder than a mynah bird with an ass full of chilli sauce. If Griffo was in the pub, you knew as soon as you got to the car park. His dulcet tones carried on night air like a wet fart through a convent prayer meeting. If he was holding court, you listened. You didn't talk or interject. It was purely a one-way thing. A verbal machine gun set to automatic with seemingly limitless ammunition. Consequently, if you knew Griffo, you either liked him or hated him, as indifference wasn't an option. Either way, your opinion held no relevance. That's the way Griffo lived his life. From the cradle to the grave, from boy to man, whatever he said was right. So it would be no surprise to anyone acquainted with Griffo to know how he behaved on eFlog. If he had a problem with an item he had bought, he didn't want his money back and he certainly wouldn't want to contact the seller. He couldn't care less about the money (as even by Sutton Coldfield standards he was loaded), and of course the seller's opinion on the issue was totally irrelevant. So why would he invite it? He simply left his feedback and moved on. No inquest, no excuses, no apologies.

Griffo was a self-made man. He started out as a YTS carpenter working for the local council. He had steadily moved up the ranks until his total self-confidence and steamroller-style charisma could take him no further, whereupon his eye fell on the emerging UPVC window market and he left the council to go it alone. Now he headed up his own white plastic empire modestly named Awesome Home Improvements. The business boasted four directly employed fitting teams ("NOT subcontractors!", a phrase he liked to include in the rant he usually used to seal a deal), with Griffo coordinating the whole thing from his showroom on an exclusive trading estate on the edge of Sutton Park. He had pushed windows, doors and conservatories for the first 10 years. Then, in response to a changing market, he had sold orangeries to people with too much money who already had a conservatory and needed a reason to pull it down to usurp their Jonesy neighbours. So Griffo, as he would happily tell you, was "minted". Of course, it goes without saying that his wife, Kirstie, was gorgeous, his massive house was impressive and his cars were some of the smartest. But the one thing that lingered from Griffo's old life was his love of a freebie. As a wise man had once said to him, "Griffo, you'd push in front of a five-year-old to get a free ice cream!", just before Griffo knocked him spark out. If it was free, he was in. Have you ever wondered why the ketchup in cafés is in sachets these days? Bosha! Griffo is the reason. Half a bottle, six sugars, ten napkins, three plastic spoons. A one-man gluttony experience…

It was Wednesday, and in the world of superior home improvements, Wednesdays are quiet. People think on a Wednesday; they don't act. So Griffo was at a bit of a loose end when the phone rang and a foreign voice asked for David. Griffo listened politely for once, answered the caller's questions, laughed in the right places, made soothing noises, sighed, thanked the caller and said he would be there. He was a trappy git, but when he smelt money, he knew when to shut up.

Across town, Bernd replaced the receiver and sat back. Jasper burst into applause, and even Annie looked impressed. Once Jasper had provided him with supergriff's email address from the eFlog sale, it had been a simple matter to Google his name and see what came up. As David Arthur Griffin had a truly massive digital footprint, they soon learned that:

He had a home improvements company.

He had once lost a dog called Gyppo.

He liked to sell cancelled orders for cash on Gumtree.

Fortunately, there were no little Griffos!

Subsequent searches based on other information gleaned from these links revealed a Facebook page with privacy settings that, unwisely, allowed everything on it to be seen by anyone. In the world of casual stalking, this was a gift! By searching the page, they learned that Griffo (as they now called him) had eventually found his dog. He liked his Mediterranean holidays. His wife had an ample cleavage (they spent more time on this than Annie was comfortable with) and they both loved eating out (the couple, not the cleavage). A couple of days' further reflection on these findings (and possibly the cleavage) had led to Bernd summoning Jasper and Annie to the Eagle's Nest, where Bernd had laid out his master plan prior to making the phone call.

Now the German community in Birmingham isn't a massive one. But if you add in the other German-speaking expats such as the Swiss and the Austrians, it gets a little bigger. So it was a simple matter for Bernd to remember an old acquaintance that ran a restaurant not far from Griffo's house in Sutton. The Goulash Chalet was a Bavarian-themed eatery that specialised in a wide range of meaty stews, spicy sausage and peppery sauces, all served by staff wearing traditional Bavarian outfits. Steins of frothy beer, piped oompah music and a plethora of German antiques and signs completed the picture.

All in all, a restaurant so German it once declared war on the British steakhouse across the road owing to a staff-poaching incident. This led to a scuffle between the owner, dressed in Lederhosen, and the duty manager of the steakhouse that spilled out into the street. A group of football fans who had been waiting outside for a table in the bar, sensing that national pride was at stake, immediately joined the fracas as they could see that the duty manager was taking a fierce beating from what looked like a massive Pinocchio. In short, the police were called and had to separate and arrest what appeared to resemble the entire cast of the Sound of Music (the rest of the waiting staff from Goulash Chalet) plus a fat, drunken England team. Obviously, no goulash was sold that night and the duty manager eventually switched branches. The waitress who was poached (amongst other things!) by the duty manager returned to the Goulash Chalet to reclaim her blonde pigtail wig and resume her tired relationship with the owner.

So that Saturday evening at 7 pm, the three members of the newly formed Negative Feedback Retribution Squad (NFRS) stood in the dark in the shoppers car park in Sutton Coldfield. The tailgate of Bernd's elderly BMW 3 series estate was open, and the plan was once more being repeated. Annie, as you would expect, was in it for the food. She wasn't too sure if she was going to like goulash after Jasper had described it as herby meat stew. But if it came with a side order of chips, she would force it down.

"So have you got everything?" said Bernd, checking his watch. In his head, he was Kurt Steiner in The Eagle Has Landed. To everyone else, he looked like an underfed old punk in an ankle-length imitation leather coat.

"Yes…" said Annie, eyes skywards, tiring of the

Secret Army routine.

"Zynchronize vatches," said Bernd, upping the German accent a bit for effect.

"You're not doing anything to my vag," said Annie.

"He means check your watch against ours," said Jasper.

"I haven't got a watch."

"Then check your phone!"

"Well, if it's wrong, I'm not altering it…"

Jasper and Bernd compared watches and agreed that they were as synchronised as it was possible to make them. With that, Bernd shut the tailgate and strode off.

"You could try to be a little bit nicer to him," Jasper scolded.

"He's weird and bossy"

"You'd be weird and bossy if you'd been with the Stasi," countered Jasper.

"I don't give a shit if he's been with Huggy Bear. He looks at me funny."

"Huggy Bear?"

"The black bloke with the big hats and the massive cars."

"Stasi, not Starsky you dopey bint. The East German Secret Police."

"Not very secret if he told you then, are they? Did they have a big punk following, then? And if you call me a dopey bint again, I'll drop you on your arse and go home. All this because a bloke didn't like your poxy cassette."

With that, she huffed off in the direction of the Goulash Chalet, with Jasper following in her wake carrying a large holdall, like a scolded five-year-old with slapped legs.

Bernd stood at the door and looked around the coffee shop. Just as he had expected, he spotted the owner of the Goulash Chalet sitting in the corner nursing two cups of coffee and two packets of overpriced crappy wafer biscuits. His old foe looked nervous, but there was really no need to be. These were different times, and they were no longer childhood enemies. All that had gone before was forgotten, and what remained wasn't worth mentioning. The owner rose to shake his hand. The ice was broken and they began to chat loudly, as Germans tend to, which no doubt you will know if you've ever tried to sleep on a sunbed anywhere in the Mediterranean.

Annie and Jasper had settled their differences by the time they were waiting to be seated at the Goulash Chalet. Well, actually, Jasper had capitulated and Annie had negotiated a free choice on dessert as reparations for their spat. The waitress came over, looking slightly flustered. Her blonde pigtail wig was obviously making her a bit warm as she went in and out of the kitchen with plates of hot meat.

"Table for two, please…"

"Any preference where?"

"Here, just to the side of the door would be fine."

"Are you sure? We have some nicer tables further in," said the waitress, concerned about the extra traipsing this would involve for her. Her night was going to be busy enough with the owner out and the other waitress 'apparently' on light duties.

However, it was important that Jasper could see both the car park that lay to the front of the building and the whole restaurant floor if their plan was to work. He was more than a little nervous and didn't want to fail Bernd, as he was pretty sure he would have an unpleasant method for dealing with incompetent operatives, and he didn't want to find out what it was.

"No, this one will be perfect," said Jasper as he clambered into the booth and put the large holdall down beside him. Annie slid into the other side with slightly less ease. She wasn't a big fan of fixed table seating as short legs and an ample waistline could lead to friction burns at table height across her belly. But she managed it with aplomb and smiled at the waitress, who passed them two wipe-clean menus and informed them that the soup of the day was Green Bean with Baked Egg Custard Islands. Annie made a face that she often pulled when confronted with foods that weren't chips or biscuits, and the waitress smiled weakly, leaving them to read the menus.

Jasper checked his watch: 7.20 pm. Just as he did so, a silver Mercedes G Wagon entered the car park, with 1980s music blaring from it, and parked facing the road. The occupants, a couple, were both spray-tanned, dressed from head to foot in white and dripping in jewellery. They looked like sun-kissed extras from a beach-based George Michael video, but at the same time utterly ridiculous because it was February.

The couple climbed from the car. Griffo walked round to the rear and with some difficulty lifted out an air tank, a wetsuit, a pair of flippers and a mask. Jasper instantly recognised the cleavage which he made so obvious that Annie gave him a kick under the table to break the spell. Kirstie wobbled in her heels across the car park and held the door open as Griffo struggled through it.

The weary waitress viewed them with some amusement, then strode across the restaurant to greet them. She prided herself on being a true professional as she had once held a supervisory role at a Jimmy Moniker restaurant. Sadly, due to Jimmy's rather ambitious overexpansion and the country getting bored with Parmesan shavings on everything, she found herself working in this dump. So she totally ignored the ridiculous collection of musty-smelling crap that Griffo had lugged in with him and guided them to a four-seat booth in the centre of the restaurant, lingering just long enough to ensure that it was big enough to take both them and their stinky cargo. She handed them their menus, told them about the soup and beat a retreat. The moment Griffo's arse was on the seat, he was off on one. Like a big, tanned silverback gorilla, he began to hold court. The other occupants of the restaurant, a man on his own, a young couple (who gave the impression they were on a first date) and what looked like a very tame hen party, seemed unimpressed. This was Sutton Coldfield, after all. The home of the extrovert 'done well' Brummie. They'd all met loud, self-made men before…

"What do you fancy, babe? Go on, treat yourself." Griffo sniggered.

"What's asparagus?" inquired Kirstie. "They seem a bit keen on that in the starters…"

"It's a thin soft vegetable. Looks a bit like pale celery…"

"Let me stop you there, babe. You lost me at vegetable!"

Both Griffo and Kirstie laughed like drains. His booming baritone laugh shook the roof, while hers was as shrill as a power drill. It was worst sort of opera, the really annoying free kind.

"Why don't we try the Bavarian Sharing Platter. Looks to be all cooked meats, sausage and cheese. We could take it home for a butty if we don't eat it all."

Again they shook the place and everyone in it with guffaws and shrieks. The waitress eyed them from her post by the kitchen door. It was going to be a long night, and this pair were just going to make it longer. Eventually, Griffo and his vegetable-dodging spouse made it through the menu and Griffo clicked his fingers to attract the attention of the waitress. *This dickhead is going to get something extra in his sauce*, she thought as she glided over.

On the other hand, Jasper and Annie had ordered a simple selection of no-brainers from the menu. He had just let her choose, as she was the picky one and he really wasn't. After all, it wasn't the food he was here for; it was revenge! From their booth, he could see Griffo enjoying his last supper. Wolfing down massive portions of everything while the cleavage just picked and moaned.

"We could have gone to the Shahlah for a curry." She sighed. "This is all so bland. It's like dinner at your in-laws. All vegetables and gravy…"

The waitress was also watching them, quietly

seething. Not because they were rude about the food or because their continual laughter was giving her a headache, but because they really had no idea how to behave in a restaurant and above all they were vulgar. She would never have had to put up with this at Jimmy's!

Damn his balsamic vinegar obsession, his shitty rocket garnish and his John DeLorean business plan. The useless Cockney twat…

Meanwhile, back at the coffee shop, Bernd and the Goulash Chalet owner were parting as old friends. They had talked and laughed about the old days. The passing of time had rounded the corners for both of them. They shook hands, and the owner apologised for having to go but said he needed to get back to the restaurant before it got really busy. In all honesty, it was rarely busy. In fact, near to failing would have been a better description. Despite a regular clientele over the years, costs were continually rising. Imported food was more expensive and Brexit hadn't helped. Like everyone else, the owner was waiting to see what would happen and what it would mean to the world of meat stew and pickled cabbage. He rose from the table, and with one final "Wiedersehen" and a wave he left the building, like a fat Bavarian Elvis.

The scene in the kitchen of the Goulash Chalet was not a typical one this evening. Of course, as you would expect, there were pots and pans of various stews and sauces on the hob. Plus lots of clanking of utensils and shouting between the chefs. But the other waitress was sitting on a chair by the swinging kitchen door, and she was pissed in both senses of the word. It had started that afternoon when the owner had announced he would be out for an hour or so that evening as he had plans to meet an old friend for coffee. Theirs was not just a working relationship, so she had asked whom he was meeting. When he wouldn't tell her, she hadn't taken it well. In fact, she had taken it so badly that she had got stuck into a bottle of peach schnapps from the bar and had eaten more Black Forest gateau than is generally accepted to be wise.

Now she was unsteady on her feet, maudlin in drink, and had to be firmly instructed by the other waitress to stay in the kitchen. She bitterly regretted her time over the road at the steakhouse (though it had been exciting at the time!) and worried that the owner was looking elsewhere for love. When he eventually appeared through the back door of the kitchen, she rallied slightly but wisely decided to stay on her chair by the swinging door. The owner knew only too well that she was a handful when leathered, so he let her be. He had enjoyed his evening with his fellow countryman and didn't want his mood shattered by another clash with a bladdered Heidi look-alike. He was just having a quick word with the chefs when the other now totally overworked waitress burst through the swinging door and marched right up to him.

"There's a customer asking for Mr Tittenkopf," she said. "I told him I don't know anyone of that name, but he won't have it and he's getting a bit annoyed. Can you come and speak to him, please?"

At that precise moment, the owner's mood instantly changed and a fireworks display began behind his eyes. The reason was that the bald, fat owner of the Goulash Chalet had simply heard the waitress say the word 'Tittenkopf'. Had Jimmy's Italian been Jimmy's German, she might have known that the customer was asking for a Mr Tit Head. Amusing as that might be to the average person, when you are a bald, fat German with a rather large sebaceous cyst right on the top of your head, it's not so very fucking funny! Especially when the insult is delivered in your own language and you thought it was a well-kept secret.

"Tittenkopf?!" he repeated icily. "He definitely asked for Mr Tittenkopf?" His temper was building.

The Goulash Chalet owner Franz Bols had endured much piss-taking over the years about the nipple-like lump centred on his cranium. When he used to have hair the piss-taking was bearable, but when the alopecia totalis took every hair on his head due to the stress, it was not. His head did in fact (as he admitted himself during image therapy) look like a massive breast with a face. Despite the best efforts of several doctors, the cyst always returned. So in order to hide it, he had taken to wearing a traditional Bavarian Trenker hat. He wore it constantly, both indoors and outdoors. Eventually the people in his hometown just called him 'The Hat', which was a big improvement on 'Tit Head', in his opinion, the cruel but entirely accurate name that he had endured since high school. So when he finally moved to England, he began a new life. He wasn't Tittenkopf any longer. He was just the German bloke who always wore a hat, which he much preferred.

"Yes, I gave him the bill, and he wanted to speak to Mr Tittenkopf. Then he said it very slowly for me several times, like I'm the stupid one."

"Which one is he?" Franz barked as he peered through the round window of the kitchen door.

"The one all in white with his wife, sat on the middle table..." said the waitress, wisely neglecting to mention the musty assortment of diving gear in the booth beside them.

"The focke!!!..." exclaimed Franz, grabbing a massive ladle from the rack above the hob, booting open the swinging door and marching over to Griffo's table.

Surprised by the sudden explosion of activity from the kitchen, Griffo looked up from his coffee and the twenty-seven accompanying complimentary chocolate mints he had 'acquired' just minutes earlier.

"Are you Mr Tittenkopf?" he inquired innocently.

"Who the fock told you to call me that?"

"You did, when you rang me…"

"I rang you? When?"

"When you enquired about the scuba gear…"

"Scuba gear? What focking scuba gear?"

"The scuba gear that you agreed to pay £200 for and a free meal if I delivered it." Griffo waved his arm at the collection of rubber beside him and began to think the rather rotund Franz was perhaps a tad delusional about it being the right size for him.

Franz was now out of control, incandescent with rage and getting worse by the second. "I didn't agree to buy anything, and the meal certainly isn't focking free!" he bellowed. He was now even angrier than he had been when he had found out his girlfriend preferred the more 'hands-on' management style over at the steakhouse.

By now it was dawning on Griffo that there might be a problem. As he eyed the ladle, good sense told him that hitting a man sitting down was a lot easier than hitting one standing up. So he tried to stand, which isn't easy when seated in a booth, particularly when it's half full of mouldy scuba gear and you're a greedy freeloading gorilla. That's when Franz, sensing the need for an immediate escalation of hostilities, caught him smack across the bridge of the nose blitzkrieg fashion with the ladle. Instantly, Griffo's snout exploded like a fresh jam doughnut. He howled with pain and desperately lunged for the ladle. But Franz was light on his feet for a fat tit head, and a nifty sidestep saw the perma-tanned window king miss him entirely and land face first in the adjacent booth, smearing blood and snot across the fake-wood Formica table.

Franz now saw his chance and was about to land the killer blow to the back of Griffo's head with his massive culinary utensil, when Kirstie intervened by jumping on his back and jamming her false fingernails into his eyes. The scream of pain that emanated from Franz was enough to alert his still-tipsy 'waitress with benefits' in the kitchen. Seeing Kirstie through the little round window riding her man like a sun-kissed cowgirl and being more than eager to save their relationship (and possibly her home and job), she flew through the swing door and across the restaurant like a bodice-clad cage fighter. Fearlessly, she whacked Kirstie in the side of the head with her clenched fist, but Kirstie swiftly responded with a Zumba-style Bhangra kick to her chest. An excellent retaliatory move, perhaps, had it not been for the fact that Franz's tag partner was full of peach schnapps and rather rich chocolate cake, which she promptly projectile vomited all over the other three participating parties.

Meanwhile, Jasper and Annie had been enjoying the unfolding fracas from their table by the door. Obviously, the ladle and the vomit were a massive unexpected bonus. No one could have foreseen that. The whole thing had so far totally exceeded their wildest expectations. As an observer, Annie had been tasked with the job of recording the action for

Bernd on her camera phone. But as the level of violence had quickly escalated, she had stood on her seat for a better angle. A welcome consequence of this was the opportunity to jump easily across to the door for a speedy exit when the action dictated it.

Now, at last, came Jasper's moment of glory, his sole reason for walking God's earth for the last two weeks: sweet revenge! As the puke rained down, drenching Griffo, he lay still, stunned. He punched the play button of the old ghetto blaster he had taken from the holdall and Meryl Mental's 1980 number 3 breakthrough punk single 'You Never Tell Me' blared out from the speakers…

You like to criticise
I hear about it all the time
The constant moaning
Your endless boring whine

But you never tell me!
You never tell me!

Regretfully, the only part of the whole adventure they hadn't planned properly was the final escape. Now all the attention in the room switched to them, as the four combatants quickly began to grasp their side of the situation individually.

1.   Griffo realised he had been set up.
2.   Kirstie realised Griffo was a gullible pillock.
3.   The waitress now realised why Franz never took his hat off or put the light on during sex.
4.   Franz realised that, in fact, Bernd was still a bastard after all.

While he was amid the absolute mayhem, Meryl was cranking out the end of the third verse…

So now I'm leaving
You far behind
Haven't bothered saying
Just hope that you don't mind?

Coz you never tell me!
You never tell me!

"Time to go!" shouted Jasper belatedly, only at that moment realising that Annie was already half out of the door. Angry words came to his lips, but remembering her earlier threat, he wisely swallowed them. Franz, who was, of course, the stool pigeon in the whole episode, now realised that without swift action he stood to lose the money for four meals that night. Two he could almost bear, but four was taking the piss. Through sore and bleary eyes, he began to free himself from the scrum, slipping on pungent alcoholic chocolate puke as he did so. Unfortunately for him, Jasper had already got his hand on the door handle and was making good his escape.

Across the car park and past the silver G Wagon they ran. Annie was looking a little out of her comfort zone at speed, and Jasper thought that she resembled a character from the 1970s game show 'It's a Knockout' from behind. He then made a mental note never to tell her for the sake of his own health. Just as they reached the road and were faced with a direction dilemma, there was a squeal of tyres. Bernd's utterly knackered BMW estate came to a slithering halt in front of them. They flung open the doors and dived in. Jasper shouted "DRIVE!!!!" in a way that he immediately regretted because his throat hurt straight afterwards. But wheelman Bernd was way ahead of him and accelerated away as the disgusting boke covered Franz and the Goulash Chalet quickly disappeared behind them. It was only at that precise moment that Jasper realised that in his panic about leaving he had left Bernd's prized vintage ghetto blaster on their table… DOH!

Chapter 3

The three occupants of the speeding BMW were unaccustomed to such success. They whooped, laughed and recalled every detail of their role in the mission to each other as they returned to the rather less elegant side of the city.

"Did you see his face!"

"God that must have hurt!"

"Did you smell it? Ugh!!!"

Eventually, after reviewing the footage in a quiet side street, they roamed back towards Oldbury town centre. The night was still young, and the adrenalin was pumping. But due to Bernd's attire and their combined financial situation, a club was out of the question. Even a visit to the pub was quite beyond their means. Anyway, the only clubs in this part of Birmingham were full of old ladies playing bingo, even if it was Saturday night, since the Goose and Goslings had become an all-you-can-eat Pan Asian gluttony experience a few years back. The local availability of music and dancing, with a fight on the way home, had been drastically curtailed. Most of the other larger pubs had long been demolished to make way for tiny designer housing developments. So even the possibility of gatecrashing a birthday party with a free bar in an upstairs function room was long gone.

Now was the age of the micro-bar. Craft beer and artisan gin now ruled supreme. Gone were the days of lager tops and snakebite, as these were enlightened times. Now ales like Nobnudger, Colon Shredder and Tastesofdabog were the ones to be seen drinking. As the flavoured gin market grew too, a liquor-infused one with Sugar Puffs rolled in Harpic was fast becoming a possibility. So Bernd wisely suggested a coffee.

Megabean in Oldbury had late-night opening till ten on a Saturday. As he had a full loyalty card and a tenner, it would be his treat!

They strode into Megabean Coffee looking like three unpaid extras from 'Tomorrow's People', took a table by the window and sat down. Annie was tasked with the job of going to the counter, as Jasper didn't like ordering and there was still some traditional sexism alive in their relationship. Bernd gave her the cash and the loyalty card and told her firmly that under no circumstances was she to get any biscuits as he needed the change. Annie bounded to the counter and attempted to attract the attention of the person serving, but she was actually more interested in talking to her colleague, who was out of sight in the kitchen. Stupid move, as Annie was not a woman that you should ignore under any circumstances. When you sit low on the ladder of life, any challenge to your validity as a person must be addressed. Annie was feeling useful for the first time in a long while, and some beverage bringer wasn't going to steal her thunder.

"Excuse me."

Nothing… The conversation about what the male supervisor had supposedly said to her earlier continued. That how, if she told 'her Kevin', he would come down and knock him out. He was only talking to her like that because she didn't fancy him, and it had always been accepted practice that any damaged cakes could be eaten by the staff…

"EXCUSE ME!!!"

The server couldn't ignore her this time and turned towards her, instantly switching on her smiley pseudo-American service face, which looked a bit like the headlamps popping up on a TR7 when you flash them.

"Hello, guys, what can I get you?" said the server, grinning past Annie at the table where the 'men' were sitting.

Bad start, thought Annie, who was very sensitive to any male superiority situations apart from being sent to order stuff, which often presented her with the opportunity to freestyle the order in her favour. Put in simpler terms, buying cake with Jasper's money without prior consultation.

"Before we start, are you called Cliff?" Annie enquired, her hackles rising.

"Err, no, I'm Mel…"

"OK then, are you an American Mel?"

"No, I'm from West Brom," said Mel, the coffee woman quickly sensing she was on a sticky wicket with Mad Question Woman.

"So then call us folks, people or even peeps. But not guys!"

"Why not guys?" countered Mel, who considered guys to be a cool and current collective form of address.

"Because as we've just established, you're not a 1960s pop star or an American!" said Annie through gritted teeth.

"Hello FOLKS, what can I get you?" said Mel pointedly.

"Three flat whites, please."

"Small, regular or large?"

"Medium, please"

"We don't do medium. Just small, regular or large."

"Mel, I'll ask you once again. Are you an American?"

"No, I'm still from West Bromwich."

"Then may I suggest that your 'regular', occupying the traditional position between small and large, is in fact an old-fashioned, pre-American bastardisation of the language we invented and exported worldwide…. MEDIUM! So why not call it fucking medium, rather than regular? Which is a word better employed to describe the bowel movements of an eighty-year-old soft fruit enthusiast!"

"OK, small, MEDIUM or large?"

"Sorry, changed my mind. Small, please…"

Mel considered retaliating in response to the expertly delivered verbal humiliation that she had just been on the wrong end of. But because she was already looking at a written warning over the CCTV footage of 'broken' Sticky Toffee Muffin-Gate, she wisely thought better of it. She took the proffered loyalty card and £10 note from Annie, quickly gave her the change and told her that she would bring the coffees over. She actually wanted to throw them at Annie from the counter, but she knew that wasn't going to help her case. Annie triumphantly returned to the table, where she gave Bernd the change and sat down.

She quickly sensed that Bernd really wasn't at all happy. Jasper had taken the opportunity to confess about the ghetto blaster, and he wasn't taking it well. The Blaupunkt KCR800 was one of the first things Bernd had bought on arrival in England. It was a treasured relic that reminded him of the old days in the glorious Fatherland. It had never occurred to him that they might be stupid enough to leave it behind during the escape phase of the plan. Jasper soothed him by making empty promises to get him another one from off the internet, and eventually Bernd calmed down.

Mel eventually took the coffees over and the handover passed without further enquiry as to her singing ability or indeed her nationality. If nothing else, Annie was firm but fair. She realised that as the customer, she naturally possessed the upper hand. So it hadn't really been a fair fight, but she had enjoyed it all the same.

The conversation had now moved on from mislaid audio equipment. All three readily agreed that they had not only enjoyed the execution of the plan but also the rather meticulous planning that had gone before. Annie found further motivation in the fact that she had a free feed. Not that Bavarian food was her chosen cuisine, but then biscuits and chips wasn't a current restaurant concept as far as she was aware.

"It's the fact that we struck back, rather than just taking it. Little people get kicked every day..." ranted Jasper.

"Do you mean jockeys?" said Annie.

"Jockeys?"

"They're usually little people, and horses kick!" said Annie, enjoying her joke enormously.

She was bang on with the sarky wordplay tonight, and deliberately misunderstanding for comedy effect was her chosen speciality. Bernd gave her a complimentary grin to show he enjoyed the gag. Annie admitted to herself that she was warming to the dodgy German weirdo. However, Bernd proudly never admitted to anything, not even under torture.

"We used classic guerrilla tactics, ambushed them, then we ran. Too dangerous to stop and fight. Just look for the enemy's weakness, then exploit it," lectured Bernd, who was now growing into his role as the poor man's Kurt Steiner.

"There must be loads of people just like me, getting a kicking every day and having no way of getting their own back," enthused Jasper, whose cash cogs were finally starting to turn. "We could advertise like the A-Team and take on jobs. Righting wrongs by making the wrongdoers look totally stupid."

Annie laughed. "Advertise exactly where? In the Oldbury Grumbler? Next to the plasterers and gardeners?"

"Online, of course. Facebook maybe? That costs nothing, and that way we can keep it local. No point pulling a job in Cornwall if the petrol to get there costs more than we're getting. A thirty-mile radius of here should do it. There are just under six million people in the West Midlands. At least some of them might be so utterly pissed off that they would consider hiring a team of ingenious vigilantes."

"Or desperate enough to hire us instead." Annie laughed again.

"I think Jasper has a point. We have footage of our first job. We just need to upload that to YouTube and then we can prove to prospective clients the mayhem we can create."

"So how much will we charge?" asked Annie enthusiastically. She liked the idea of getting paid to eat.

"We will consider each assignment on its individual merits, carefully weigh up the personal risk, then just ask for as much as we think we can get away with," said Jasper, who based his whole eFlog empire on that one simple rule. If you have it and they want it, reasonable prices are for mug sellers.

They left Megabean Coffee in high spirits. Jasper had promised that he would work out the text for an advert. Bernd had promised to acquire a spare mobile phone. And when Bernd was in the toilet, Annie had promised Jasper something quite special for later. But we won't go into that now...

Later that night, Bernd lay in bed and for the first time in a long time he thought about home, the people he had left behind and the reasons he had done so. Sometimes he looked at the profile pictures of some of his family and friends on Facebook. They were much older now, and some had passed. Life in the East hadn't been easy prior to the reunification of Germany. Bernd's was just one such life, for a variety of reasons...

Bernd Helmut Tost was born in Leipzig in 1954. His parents, Sabine and Deiter, ran a small café and bakery in a backstreet of the city. Bernd was their second child – they already had a daughter, Frieda, who had been born in 1948.

It was a difficult birth even by 1950s East German standards. Sabine had tiny, size 3, feet, and consequently, Deiter had always called her Engel Zehen (Angel Toes). As any gynaecologist will tell you, this doesn't bode well for easy labour, because when it comes to childbirth, you want feet the size of a circus clown for speed of delivery, foot size been directly related to pelvic dimensions. In essence, the smaller your feet, the more it's going to feel like you're pushing out Jimmy Krankie.

This was further complicated by the boy-child Tost possessing a truly gigantuous head, which was by far the biggest the midwife at the birth had ever encountered. It resulted in a labour so long the midwife slept standing up in the waiting room during lulls in the whole grisly process. But finally, Bernd made his way towards the light and the little family was complete. Unfortunately, his tiny-footed mother later saw more stitches than a new girl on her first day at the parachute factory. And it was a good while before she could serve someone a jam and cream horn without having PTSD flashbacks.

Sabine and Deiter were upstanding members of the community who ran their business in a way that reflected their socialist beliefs. They declared all their earnings to the authorities and always paid their taxes promptly. They didn't allow tittle-tattle in their establishment, nor did they serve critics of the state. Anyone who made mischief regarding party members or indulged in scandalous gossip had to buy their baked goods elsewhere. This would have broken your heart if you had a sweet tooth, as their cakes were famed throughout the city and people often caught two trams just to buy them. Streuselkuchen, a sweet, buttery crumble, Mohnkuchen, poppy-seed cake, and sweet, soft pretzels of every kind were all very popular. But the real reason people flocked to Sabine and Dieter's little corner café was their Bienenstich, a sweet custard-filled almond cake that was both chewy and creamy in equal measure. The sort of homecoming gift that East German wives knew might mean that the electric blanket would be switched on early.

The little bakery only had a few small tables, and on Saturday it was often standing room only. The aroma of strong coffee from communist Cuba mingled with the smell of the fresh cakes to tempt the tastebuds. Little Bernd worked to help his parents as best he could. He ran between the tiny tables delivering the cakes on small cardboard plates with 'Tost Bakery' printed on the edge in French blue. When the customers had finished eating and drinking, he cheerfully collected cups, coffee pots, spoons and cake forks and carefully carried them to the kitchen for his sister to wash, sharing any tips with her that he'd learned along the way.

As Bernd grew older, his father taught him his secret recipes, and after school, he learned to make the café's range of cakes and bread. Bernd was not the most academic of students, but he was good at art and showed a strong talent for music. For his 10th birthday in 1964, his father bought him a second-hand acoustic guitar from a local pawnshop. From that point, Bernd spent any free time he had learning folk songs from the radio and pop songs from the West when his parents were safely out of earshot. By 1968 he was fourteen and was growing his hair longer and playing with a group from school. They practised Western pop songs heard on 45s smuggled over the Berlin Wall that they bought at flea markets from shady dealers.

Then, in 1976, it happened! The punk explosion began and the shock waves were even felt in Leipzig. Bernd's music changed and so did his friends. They customised army clothes with safety pins and wore ripped donkey jackets. Secretly watched music shows on West German TV and copied what they saw. Now he was a twenty-two-year-old punk, and that's where it all began to go wrong for Bernd in the Fatherland…

Chapter 4

A breakfast meeting had been called by Bernd for that Monday morning at the Eagle's Nest. He knew that if he didn't strike while the iron was hot, his feckless colleagues would soon return to their familiar routine of illness clubs and free refreshments. Little did he know that Jasper was still massively enthused and even Annie was more than a bit keen on the whole thing, even by her standards. She could sense the opportunity to do something useful with her life and to earn a few quid at the same time. She was bored of cheap biscuits and crappy multipack crisps. A new chocolate-covered, cream-filled, premium brand life awaited her.

Now sitting around Bernd's table, each member of the NFRS felt they were on to something big. Just like the A-Team back in the 1980s, each member had their own specialist skill to offer.

Naturally, Bernd was Hannibal – the ever-planning, cigar-sucking leader who always knew just what to do in any given situation. As long as it didn't require physical strength, getting up early or prolonged exposure to strong sunlight, Bernd was your man.

Jasper was Faceman – the ladies' man smooth operator who secured the missions and lied to everyone who needed lying to. Possibly a bit lacking on the physical attraction side of things, but then this was the Black Country. People there are bred to be useful rather than pretty…

Annie was of course Mad Murdock and Mr T rolled into one. A five-foot-tall combination of the most appalling stupidity backed up by extreme violence. Admittedly, she'd never used a welder or flown a helicopter, but it was unlikely to come to that.

Breakfast at Bernd's was always going to be odd by British standards. He made no concession to the fact that he no longer lived in Germany. So he had pushed the boat out slightly with a cooked meat selection of salami and smoked ham, dainty little vacuum-packed rolls fresh from the oven and tangy German mustard. Knowing that Annie was most likely going to baulk at cold processed meat for breakfast, he had thoughtfully included a small pot of chocolate spread as a back-up. He would have got a pain au chocolat, but sadly there was only one packet of them left in the shop and it looked like an elephant had sat on it.

Annie was relieved when she spotted the chocolate spread, as her normal early morning intake was a cuppa and a handful of digestives. She happily made a pig of herself with little rolls slathered in chocolaty goodness. The adverts on the telly never mentioned the shitloads of sugar in it. They just concentrated on the hazelnuts, skimmed milk and cocoa, so she naturally regarded it as a health food.

When they had finished eating, Bernd declared the meeting open (he had feared a repeat of the strudel crumb explosion from the last time!). From the drawer in his table, he took out a rather battered smartphone and dropped it in front of them.

"This has a fresh SIM card in it, fully charged, and it's ready to go!"

"Wow," said Annie. "That's had a hard life…"

"Yes, I bought it from Clive the Claw. It's his old one, he got a free upgrade…"

Clive was a rather bad-tempered amputee who also lived in Derek Robinson House. He was called Clive the Claw because of the old claw-style metal prosthesis he had instead of a right hand. Many versions of how Clive had lost his hand were in circulation. Jasper's favourite was that he had put his hand through a glory hole in a public toilet during a 'misunderstanding' regarding loo roll. The outraged occupant grabbed it and smashed it to a pulp with a tin of rice pudding.

Annie favoured the version in which Clive worked as a butcher on Halesowen Market. Following a rather animated disagreement with a customer regarding the quality of the ingredients in his chocolate orange pork sausages, he had an epileptic fit while using the meat grinder that was brought on by the anxiety of the confrontation. He was Clive the Stump for a while after that, as the story goes…

"No wonder it's knackered then. He's rough with everything. He broke his own nose brushing his teeth once," exclaimed Jasper.

"It's a pity they don't upgrade his right hand. He might be a bit happier then," joked Annie.

"It wouldn't make any difference, he's left-handed," replied Jasper, laughing.

Jasper then stood up, and, reaching into his back pocket, he pulled out a folded sheet of paper. Remaining standing for effect, he began to read: "Do you feel that you have been treated unfairly? Are you frustrated by your inability to get revenge? Does your blood boil with the injustice? Then call the Negative Feedback Retribution Squad. We can help you redress the balance in your favour. Bizarre scenarios created to embarrass unpleasant people. Click the link below to see our last caper."

Then he sat down. No applause came, but then Annie said, "Brilliant!" Bernd was always a bit slow to absorb flowery English as you didn't hear a lot of it in those parts, but eventually, he smiled and simply said, "Wunderbar!"

The rest of the morning was spent creating a profile on Facebook for their new enterprise, which was surprisingly difficult when you don't want your photo on it, for obvious reasons. But after finding a photo of three laughing chimps with water pistols on Google Images, it all fell together easily! Then it was just a simple matter of adding the advert to the local buy-and-sell pages on Facebook.

Not surprisingly, nothing happened for a few days, as prank-playing vengeance fighters clearly have a niche market. Jasper carried on selling his cassettes online, and both he and Annie returned to their busy illness club social schedule. They excelled at every one they attended (well Jasper did, Annie was in denial about belonging at Obesity Club!), particularly their Stop Smoking Group. Everyone was impressed by both their willpower and their lack of tetchiness. They didn't even need the patches, gum or vaping – they just went full cold turkey, not to mention that they reported no weight gain whatsoever!

Susan the health worker, who ran the group, was astounded. Nonetheless, Annie nearly blew it when she was asked what brand she used to smoke. She was panicking because she patently knew nothing about cigarettes as she had never smoked in her life. Then, recalling a school trip to a war museum at school, she blurted out "Black Cat". This caused quite a stir, as Black Cat cigarettes had their heyday in World War One. Jasper quickly butted in and said that she bought them in bulk from a Turkish lorry driver and that the brand was still widely sold there. "That's why her teeth are so yellow," he said, elaborating in an effort to back up the lie. "They're filterless!" Although Annie had been saved by his quick thinking, she was less than impressed with his qualifying follow-up. The ride home on the bus afterwards was a quiet affair. He also noticed that the toothpaste in her bathroom changed to a whitening brand soon after.

Then, a week on Wednesday, it happened! Bernd rang them to say that he had a message from a lady who might indeed need their help. He had messaged her back and arranged a meeting for the following day. Jasper privately felt he could have gained more detail, but decided that as Bernd was the espionage expert, he'd keep shtum. So on Thursday morning, all three took the bus from Derek Robinson House to Waynrose's supermarket in nearby Blackheath. Bernd had wisely decided that the bus was the safest means of transport in terms of anonymity. Jasper thought that this was Bernd's training at work. Bernd knew it was nicked from a documentary he had watched about a cat kidnapper. Annie simply thought it was a fucking liberty as it was still February and freezing...

They arrived at Waynrose's ahead of time. It was an odd location for one of the country's most expensive supermarkets to select. A bit like a luxury jewellers deciding to open a store in Mogadishu. Nevertheless, it helped the local police officers, in as much as at least they knew where all the local shoplifters were based. The NFRS trooped in past the checkouts and up to the café seating area. At one time, the café had had a door that led directly into it from the street. Soon the management realised this was like the Silk Road for anything that had resale potential in the local pubs. So it was permanently locked except for staged photo shoots in the local press. Many foil-lined 'bags for life' went in the bin that day.

Annie got the coffees without incident. Then she went into the main store and bought a value pack of Jaffa cakes, which they shared under the table. The staff of the café were well aware that people did this and honestly didn't care. After all, they were bought on the premises, so what was the problem? But Annie had realised that by employing this ruse she could get two extra Jaffas, as the other two dorks obviously weren't counting.

Then she breezed in! She stood out in both the gloom of February and their humble surroundings in a three-quarter length white coat, a designer dress, her hair up and flawless make-up. In a room full of tracksuit bottoms and all-day breakfasts, she was a princess. And the fact that she thoroughly checked her plastic seat before sitting down bore this out. Annie didn't think she looked like the type of woman that would be interested in a second-hand Jaffa cake, so she rammed the remainder of the box in her pocket for later. Jasper ran to get her an Americano, and when he returned with the coffee and a wide range of sugar, sweeteners and stirring implements, Annie made a note to take issue with him about it afterwards. The slimy tosser! Then their first-ever client began to tell her sad story…

The previous November, Melissa Murray had been looking forward to a 5-star winter holiday in Dubai with her then-boyfriend, Travis. She had left nothing to chance as it was their first holiday together. Travis was a solicitor, and this was her chance to settle down in style. Melissa worked on the perfume counter at House of Major in Birmingham. She had met Travis when he came in to buy perfume for his secretary's birthday. As they were chatting while he was choosing the perfume, she had discovered that he was single, minted and not terribly experienced with women. A bonus was that his secretary was in her fifties and favoured Dawn Mist, which told Melissa she was no threat to her whatsoever, as it was a fragrance popular with menopausal women with too many cats. After three months of fairly intense courtship, she had raised the idea of a last-minute holiday, being careful to bring it up when the lesser Mediterranean destinations were closed for the winter. Travis, taking the bait, had booked online for Dubai, so she had bought elegant swimsuits, sensuous sarongs and exquisite evening dresses, along with a wide range of 'get him up the aisle' lacy nothings and battery-powered friends.

Unfortunately, the day they flew out, Melissa impulsively decided on a sunbed session in her dinner hour. Because she had spent so much on her outfits and bedroom accessories, she didn't go to her regular solarium. Instead, she decided to use a cheaper one in the arcade opposite Argos as they had an introductory offer on and she could get a sandwich with what she would save. Win, win! Speaking to the owner, she chose a new high-pressure bed and was assured that fifteen minutes would give her the results she was looking for. Soon Melissa left the solarium and went back to work with the last of her jobs ticked off.

That evening, as they queued to check in at the airport, Melissa became aware that her peachy bottom was a little tender. Though she just put this down to chafing from the rather racy lace underwear that she was wearing. During the long flight, she squirmed and wriggled and swapped from cheek to cheek, trying in vain to escape the discomfort. By the time they were in the private taxi transfer to the hotel, her ass was on fire. It was burning as if someone had sprayed muscle heat spray on it, then rubbed it with sandpaper – several times!

On arrival at the sumptuous room, which had a jacuzzi, a round bed and stunning views of the marina, she locked herself in the bathroom. Looking over her shoulder at the mirrored tiles, she could see that her backside was the colour of an African sunset. Her underwear clearly wasn't the problem – she was sunburned! The owner of the salon had misidentified her skin type and the amount of time that was appropriate for her to tan. Now she was on a dream holiday with a rampant solicitor, half a case of sex aids and an arse the colour of a baboon's!

Needless to say, as she went on to explain, her holiday was ruined. Travis spent the holiday mostly on his own, while she lay on the bed face down watching TV and rubbing aftersun lotion into her bum cheeks every three hours. To add insult to injury, her prospective meal ticket took a shine to a shy dental hygienist that he met playing poolside Jenga. So she and Travis had returned from their holiday as friends and, apparently, the exotic underwear shop didn't offer refunds for unused equipment.

When Melissa had spoken to the salon owner, she had denied all knowledge and implied that Melissa was mistaken. She recalled that they had just had a casual conversation and that the tanning decisions she had made were of her own choosing. When she saw a solicitor, they advised her that these actions were very hard to win. Besides, she could not sue for the lifetime of luxury living she would now miss out on. So that's why she now found herself gently sobbing in Waynrose's Blackheath, with Bernd eyeing her cleavage and Annie watching Jasper trying very hard not to…

All three thanked Melissa for coming and said that they would gladly take on her case, realising after she had left that they had neglected to agree on a fee or expenses. Annie had been particularly touched by the whole saga, as she had felt the rough side of mankind a few times before meeting Jasper, so her pleasure would be getting retribution for a sister. He was by no means perfect, but he folded easily in a row, couldn't count biscuits and was easily manipulated with the suggestion of sex, three excellent qualities that Annie had consciously sought in prospective partners in recent years.

During the bus ride back to Derek Robinson House, they took turns suggesting mission scenarios that might work. Bernd's tended to be too complicated and Annie's were way too violent, but Jasper's were agreed to be about the best. So it was decided that Jasper and Annie should take themselves into Birmingham the next day on a reconnaissance mission. Based on the fact that Jasper would look a little out of place in a tanning shop due to his sickly complexion, Annie decided she would be better suited to making enquiries about sunbed sessions as she took a tan a fair bit better. She often bragged that she could get a tan from the light in a fridge. *If that was the case, she should look like David Dickinson from all the fluorescent tubes in the chip shop*, thought Jasper.

The Bella Della Tanning Salon was typical of its type. The window was decorated with stickers of palm trees on sunny beaches and used words like deep, tan, tropical and exotic. The woodwork of the window and door had been badly painted orange by someone who was clearly in the grip of St Vitus's dance, as there was paint everywhere there shouldn't be. All in all, it had the look of a low-rent enterprise that might vanish as quickly as it had appeared. There was a bench conveniently situated opposite the arcade from where they could see a steady stream of tan enthusiasts entering and leaving the premises. No shortage of customers, but how many might have trouble sitting down later was another thing.

During a couple of walk-bys, they noted that only one woman appeared to work in the shop. Judging from the description they had from Melissa, it seemed this was the owner herself, Della. She was quite thin and had a deep-mahogany tan, which contrasted sharply with her jet-black hair. Her clothes were fashionable and gave the impression of someone who was doing very nicely, thank you!

It was decided that Annie should go into the shop and enquire about a course of tanning sessions just to scope out the lie of the land. Jasper was to wait outside. He thought that he might have to rush in to save her if her cover was blown. Admittedly, unless Della had a crystal ball or Bernd was a double agent, she was probably going to be fine.

So in strode Annie with her phone sticking out of the back pocket of her jeans so that the camera lens could record video footage. It probably looked a little odd, but this was Birmingham city centre. Odd, mental and off your tits were daily occurrences.

"Hello. Welcome to the Bella Della Tanning Salon," said Della with a warm smile.

For a woman with badly painted windows, she's mad for the corporate greeting, thought Annie, as the interior of the shop was just as shabby as the exterior. From the poorly fitted orange carpet to the hastily painted woodchip wallpaper, this wasn't giving the health spas anything to worry about.

"Alright!" Annie replied. "I'm interested in some sunbed sessions. I'm going on holiday in a week or so and I don't want to be as white as the Michelin Man on the first day." She immediately regretted mentioning the Michelin Man, as although he was clearly white, it really didn't conjure up a pretty picture of what she might look like disrobed.

"Where are you off to then?" Della enquired.

"Barmouth…" said Annie, panicking. She clearly hadn't learned from the Stop Smoking Group about getting your cover story straight. She suddenly realised that Della might be wondering who in their right mind would strip off on a beach in Barmouth in early March. But once again it was Birmingham city centre and you get all sorts, so it was fine.

"Nice," enthused Bella, riding it out like a pro. "Well, we can't have that. It's all very easy. You simply decide how much sunbed time you need in terms of total minutes and I will give you a card with your pre-paid time on. You come in when you want to, for as many sessions as you think you'll need, and that's about it. The lotion is provided in each cubicle, so no hidden costs. Simple as that!"

"How many sessions do you think I will need for my skin?" asked Annie, bearing her arm to show Della.

Della moved forward and, being careful not to touch, she made a big deal of looking studious, as if she knew exactly how long a big arm of ham took in the oven.

"I would say, based on your skin tone and my years of experience, three ten-minute sessions. But it's entirely up to you."

Now it was Della's turn to lie. She didn't have years of experience. In fact, until a couple of years ago, she had worked for the council delivering meals on wheels for the elderly residents of Bartley Green, a job she had been happy to do for five years. She liked the old people she met and they, in turn, liked Della. That is, until one day when, as she was leaving an old gentleman's house, she tripped over his oxygen tank and damaged the ligaments in her knee. She accepted it as an accident, but when her union rep came to visit, he encouraged her to claim against the council for "failing to ensure her safety at work". To be fair to her, Della wasn't keen. But she filled in the form as he advised and, lo and behold a few months later, the council settled out of court to the tune of £15,000. So Della decided to buy five second-hand sunbeds and plunge into the world of tanning salons. So far, she was enjoying herself and making decent money. No more tramping in the rain, no more concrete steps and no more smelling like school dinners after a day driving her van. Now she was a successful businesswoman with a tan like a long-lost Bee Gee!

Annie suddenly remembered the phone in her back pocket. Sensing the conversation was coming to an end, she began to do what can only be described as 'arse around' to obtain the required footage for her co-conspirators. Della, by now well used to all sorts of madness, just looked on, smiling, then offered Annie a pricing leaflet as she did 'The Bump' with an invisible dance partner.

When Annie got back to Jasper with the leaflet, they viewed the footage on her phone. Although it was a little wobbly, you could clearly see five cubicle doors off a short corridor, lots of posters for skincare and tanning products, plus a multitude of bottles and sprays arranged on shelving stands in the reception area. Despite its lacklustre image, the Bella Della Tanning Salon was a busy little enterprise. Customers constantly came and went in the time it took for Annie to demolish a Steak Bake and a can of Coke. Jasper had a chicken and salad sandwich on brown with a bottle of water. Annie marvelled at how anyone could eat brown bread when it clearly tasted of mouse piss and sawdust.

Back at the Eagle's Nest, they showed the leaflet and the footage to Bernd. Next, three of the most gifted minds in Oldbury started to hatch a plan, which didn't say much for the rest of the deep thinkers in the little town…

Chapter 5

Jasper stood outside Mucky Barry's flat on the fourth floor and banged the letterbox. No answer. So he banged it again. This went on for about five minutes until, eventually, Mucky Barry answered the door, rubbing his eyes. Attired in brown nylon Y-fronts with magnolia detailing, a faded Flash Gordon vest and bottle-bottom glasses, he smelled like he looked. However, if you had a query of a technological nature, then Mucky Barry was your man. He wasn't, however, ideal baby sitter material…

Naturally, when in Barry's company, you simply addressed him as Barry, not Mucky Barry. The Mucky prefix harked back to the long-passed days of the video recorder. During that period, Mucky Barry had been the block's premier supplier of adult video entertainment, famed not only for the quality of his merchandise but also for the wide range of subject matter that it covered. Barry was no prude. If you were prepared to rent it, he was happy to supply it. Girls, boys, animals, rubber, leather, SM, role play, orgies, domination – the list was endless.

Of course, as a serious businessman, Barry made a point of watching everything he stocked to ensure standards were kept high. So if you were a first-time renter, he would politely inquire as to your particular penchant. Then, like a good wine waiter, he would guide you to viewing material that would suit your palate. He had learned long ago the value of product knowledge after an unfortunate episode with a 'best man' who had sought his help with 'after the pub' stag party entertainment many years ago. This was back in the days when a stag party took place on the Friday night before the wedding and eyebrows couldn't easily be restored via Photoshop.

Anyway, the best man worked in a bank and had heard of Barry through a friend in their local wine bar.

More reserved than Barry's usual clientele, he was unable to adequately express his exact requirements. So Barry had hedged his bets and supplied him with a tape on the day of the stag party that he hadn't had a chance to review yet, telling the best man it was a mix tape of fifteen-minute shorts on a standard three-hour tape.

"Nothing too tasty, a bit of this, a bit of that. Proper family viewing." He laughed.

So picture the scene late that Friday night. A horde of expectant young stags gathered round the telly, chock full of Carling Black Label, doner kebab and sexual frustration. The palpable tension, scatter cushions on laps, all ready to go. However, twenty minutes into the tape, during a two-boy, one-girl scenario, one of the male actors takes it upon himself to 'swap teams' midway through the action and leave the young lady 'watching from the sidelines', so to speak. Imagine the resulting uproar as a living room full of firmly hetero bucks loudly expressed their displeasure to the 'best man', who had been confidently stoking anticipation for his under-the-counter rental all evening in the pub. Sadly, views were expressed that made the next day's nuptials a slightly awkward affair. Matters were not helped by the fact that he still lived with his mom, struggled with women and was strongly suspected of being a 'bit busy' himself.

Of course, those days were long gone with the arrival of the internet, which provides easy access to all manner of debauchery. Barry was still involved with technology, but now it was computers that filled his waking hours. He was Oscar Goldman of computers. If it had a hard drive and it beeped, he would make it better than it was before. Better, stronger, faster…

Jasper warily followed Barry into what in any normal

flat would be the lounge. But here it was mission control. Screens, PCs, cables, routers, printers, beeps, pings and clicks. The heat was immense, and so was the smell. Mucky Barry, just as the name suggests, was long overdue a visit from Aggie and Kim. The floor was festooned with a carpet of takeaway cartons and empty food packaging. If Barry had one mission in life, it certainly wasn't feng shui…

"So what can I do you for?" said Barry from behind his filthy optical double gazing.

"Do you still print the party invites and raffle tickets for the Legion?" inquired Jasper.

"On the odd occasion," Barry replied, still squinting like a mole that had just popped out of a freshly dug hole.

"In that case, Barry, you're just the man I need…"

Meanwhile, Annie was busy down at the local community centre. Her goal was to secure the participation of the local amateur dramatic society, The Oldbury Reprobates. They rehearsed on a Wednesday evening, so she was trying her hardest to work out what to tell them. It needed to be the perfect blend of fact and fiction. She wished now that Jasper had taken on this task, but the prospect of visiting Mucky Barry all alone was definitely not for her.

"Can I help you?" asked a rather flamboyant man wearing a bishop's mitre on his head.

"Er… Yes, I'm looking for Kenneth," replied Annie.

"I am he. And you are?" enquired Kenneth, holding out his hand.

"My name is Annie. I called you about doing a performance art piece in Birmingham."

"Oh yes, I remember," he said enthusiastically. "Tears for the Planet, I believe you called it."

"Yes, you were recommended to me by Wayne Sleep. He said that if I wanted a piece encompassing all that is great about contemporary dance, ballet and drama, then I should speak to you. Incidentally, he sends his regards."

Annie didn't look like someone who had Britain's most respected male ballet star on speed dial. However, Bernd's extensive internet research had turned up an old photo of him on stage with Kenneth and had correctly guessed that the merest mention of his name would see Kenneth open up like a lotus blossom.

"Oh, dear child, you are too kind. Those days with Wayne are long behind me, I fear. But I can still curve a toe if the opportunity presents, and for such a worthy cause I would be delighted to do so. Let's go into my office and you can tell me more about what you need my little troupe to create. Maureen! Refreshments for our guest and an Earl Grey with lemon and honey for me. I feel that great wisdom is about to tumble from the forgotten star that lurks deep within."

With that, Kenneth sashayed into his office, which was actually just 'the office'. It was his for three hours every Wednesday night and everybody else's for the rest of the week. Annie then explained to him exactly what she wanted him to do. Kenneth was delighted with the idea that someone needed him to create a performance with no limit on flamboyance. And no, he had no problem at all supplying the sound equipment.

Later, back at the Eagle's Nest, they all compared notes about their aspect of the sting. Bernd had spent the day researching the other materials they needed on the internet. After much deliberation, he had made his order for the necessary items and delivery was due on Monday. So they decided that D-Day would be set for the following Friday.

The morning of the sting was an unusually sunny one for early March in Oldbury. Jasper climbed out of bed and met the day with a big yawn and a stretch. He threw open the curtains and light spewed into the room. Would the day bring success or failure, he wondered? Their first-ever paid operation. It was still not clear what level of remuneration they would receive for their endeavours, but at least Melissa had transferred £100 to Bernd to cover their initial expenses, which were fairly minimal so far. Two Gregg's lunches, Bernd's long-awaited delivery and a Michael Jackson CD. So they still had ample funds for bus fare to Birmingham.

As Jasper threw open the curtains, Annie stirred on the other side of the bed. Stirred would be a generous description. It was more of a snuffling snore with a leg twitch.

"Time to get up, love, it's D-Day," enthused Jasper gently.

Annie honestly wasn't feeling it. But she moved the quilt off her head and rubbed her eyes. She had stayed over last night because of what she considered to be an early start. Unfortunately, Jasper had been rather enthusiastic with the resulting horizontal morris dancing, and now she felt like she'd run into a lamppost. She preferred to keep him on a very strict diet regarding such matters, but last night he'd gone 'off-plan', in her opinion.

"'Love', is it now? It was Hot Slutty Cougar last night." She propped herself up on the pillow to enjoy the full glow of Jasper's now obvious embarrassment at having his mid-coital utterances repeated to him.

"I didn't hear you complaining," he countered.

"That's because this bed makes so much noise that even if Brian Blessed himself was shouting 'Watch my fucking hip!' you would still keep going like an epileptic sea lion".

"While I agree that if he spoke he might be revealed as an impostor, I don't think the beard or belly would give him away." Jasper quickly left the bedroom to put the kettle on as Annie's pillow hit the wall above him. *At least she was awake now*, he thought. But then he had been a rather magnificent beast last night. Hopefully, today would go just as well.

Once again, the NFRS were assembled at the bus stop at 8 am. Bernd said very little at this time of the morning. In fact, he was generally a quiet man. Today he had made an effort to blend in with the crowd and was wearing a black hooded sweatshirt, jeans and an olive-green combat jacket.

"You look nice when you're not all punked-up," Annie said.

"Punked-up?!" Bernd bristled. Annie immediately regretted her flattery.

"Makes you look younger. Jasper, doesn't he look younger?" she said enthusiastically.

Bernd looked at Jasper. Annie looked at Jasper. Jasper looked hard at his phone. Conversation, in particular styling critique, ceased.

Although they still had Bernd's car, the cost of parking in the city centre plus the new congestion charge made the bus a cheaper option. And an expired MOT made public transport seem sensible from a law enforcement standpoint. The Oldbury Reprobates were going to meet them in the city. They had access to a minibus after 9 am, but not before, as it was needed for the school run. However, from 9.15 till 3, the driver was a gun for hire and purveyor of the shortest day trips in the land.

The meet-up point was outside Argos at 9.45. As the NFRS rounded the corner, they could see that Kenneth and his team were already there. It was hard to miss them, as even in Birmingham city centre, you rarely encounter a whole gang of people in fancy dress till nightfall.

"Everyone gather round," said Jasper. "Have we all got everything we need?"

"More than ample," said Kenneth with a wry smile.

"Right then. Let's do this thing..." barked Jasper 'Faceman' Skinner.

The first phase of Operation Golden Glow was down to Jasper. Admittedly, he'd never given leaflets out in the street before. Anyone who has knows it's all about attitude and eye contact. If your attitude is right and you manage to make eye contact, nine times out of ten your leaflet will be taken. Admittedly, Jasper was a quick learner, and after a few minutes, he began to hone his technique. The main thrust of the leafleting plan was to give them to people who fitted three main criteria:

1.   Looked like they would act on the information, as they had nothing better to do.

2.   Didn't resemble your usual tanning salon customers in any way at all.
3.   Looked like they'd twat you if you crossed them.

In half an hour, Jasper had given out most of his leaflets. Ignoring the young, the cool and the beautiful, he had gone for the large, the intoxicated and the odorous. This method had led to a stunted conversation with a rather large black lady about Jesus. A sort of party-political broadcast by a self-appointed messenger from God. Similar to church, but a fair bit more shouty. "You can go from the road of sin to godliness in one easy lesson…", etc., etc.

This approach largely worked brilliantly, as most busy people really don't want leaflets, and the people that Jasper was handing them out to were usually the ones that rarely got offered one. So they were massively flattered by the attention, and the speed-walking office types didn't have to bother fending him off. So everyone was happy. Well, not everyone. It's Birmingham. It's in the rules…

"Why didn't you offer us a leaflet?" said a rather indignant teenage girl while her friends looked on.

"Err… because I have to give them to certain demographic," Jasper replied, hoping to throw her off with a long word.

"What's that mean? Stacey, Google demmograffic on your phone," said the girl, addressing the sergeant in her posse.

"How do you spell it?" replied Stacey meekly.

Jasper waited to see if another member of the Intimidation Crew could spell, then said, "D-E-M-O-G-R-A-P-H-I-C."

Uncomfortable seconds passed before Stacey educated them by reading out "Targeting a particular sector of the population."

"That's racism," said the indignant teenage girl. "You can't give leaflets to one lot of people and not to others."

"No," replied Jasper "That's targeting a demographic. I am simply giving the leaflets to people that I consider are most likely to use them. Racism would be if I was purposely giving them to people of one race whilst excluding another. You could try me with elitist if you like?"

Again all eyes fell on Stacey, whose blank expression told Jasper he again needed to spell it.

"E-L-I-T-I-S-T."

More uncomfortable seconds passed before Stacey read out "Organised for the good of a few people who have special interests or abilities."

"So who made you the Leaflet King who decides who gets one and who doesn't?" said the first girl.

"My boss, the lady that owns the tanning salon…"

"Well, we want leaflets or we're gonna have a problem," she said, desperate to look like a violent Madonna and chewing her gum really hard six inches from Jasper's face.

"Tell you what, I'll ring her and you can speak to her. If she says it's OK, then that's fine with me," reasoned Jasper.

"Sensible man," said Violent Madonna, nodding her head slowly at the others in a 'watch this' kind of way.

Jasper took out his phone and rang Annie. He quickly relayed what had been said, addressing her as Della, hoping that Annie would guess what he wanted her to do. Then he passed the phone to Violent Madonna, who, judging by the 'innit' count and the hip-hop arm flings, didn't massively enjoy the conversation. When she huffily passed the phone back to Jasper, Annie told him to just give her a couple of leaflets and hung up. Jasper did as he was asked and Violent Madonna simply took them, sucked her teeth and stalked away, West Coast style. When she felt comfortable about the distance she'd covered, she turned, looked Jasper up and down and delivered her knockout insult.

"Paedo!"

"P-I-D-O," said Jasper, as Stacey looked to him for guidance.

"World-famous Filipino basketball coach," said Stacey, looking puzzled.

Chapter 6

The new Della loved Fridays. In her old life, she had hated them. Fridays back then were about collecting the money for the week's meals from the old folk. Most were proud and gave their money willingly in little envelopes or snap bags, meaning she was spared the awkwardness of having to ask. Some, however, would begrudgingly count it out to her from their purse or wallet. She hated that, because it made her feel guilty. Often she could see just how little money they had left after paying. It felt wrong to her that they should have to pay at all. But then, as she would soon find out, the world tends to be like that... massively unfair.

Her new Friday routine was all about what people were doing for the weekend. Nightclubbing, holidays, hen parties or weekends away. She heard about it all and she loved it. It was generally quiet till lunchtime, after which she often had people queuing for sunbeds in the little reception area. But little did Della know, this wasn't going to be a typical Friday...

The first thing she became aware of was the loud music. She walked to the window and looked out. Outside were around a dozen people dressed in what appeared to be flame costumes holding placards and standing in a semicircle in front of her shop. As she watched, the flames began to perform a synchronised dance routine to the music, which was Michael Jackson's 'Earth Song'. At first, she laughed, as it was ridiculous. But then in the strong sunlight, she began to see what the placards read backwards, and it dawned on her that this was a protest that was entirely directed at her business.

Life span, not sun tan! Sack the tubes, spare the boobs! Sunbed Redhead Deathbed! UV rays shorten your days! First you burn, then you learn!

Admittedly, some placards owed more to sloganism than to medical science. But either way, this wasn't going to help her business to flourish. Della rushed out of the shop to confront them. But the music was so loud and the 'flames' were so into their routine that her appearance wasn't noted, as quite a crowd of onlookers had gathered by then to enjoy the spectacle. She shouted, waved her arms and hollered, but, drowned out by the music and booed by the crowd, she soon retreated to the salon.

As she lifted the phone to call 999, an old woman carrying several bulging carrier bags entered the reception, and she reluctantly put the phone down.

"Hello. Welcome to the Bella Della Tanning Salon. How can I help?" said Della, quickly switching from panicked business owner to 'Hello, money' mode.

"I'd like to use the coupon I got this morning," said the woman, setting down her bags, which Della was now eyeing nervously.

"Coupon? What coupon might that be?" Della gently probed, sensing that this particular client may require delicate handling.

The woman thrust her hand into the pocket of the rather tired overcoat she was wearing and produced a card. Della took the card from her as the woman unbuttoned the overcoat to reveal that beneath it she had only her underwear on. As she read the card, she became aware of the 'intoxicating' new fragrance in the room…

Bella Della Tanning Salon INTRODUCTORY OFFER NOT TO BE MISSED!

Fifteen minutes of free sunbed time for new clients. See the new you in just a week!

"I think there has been some mistake…" stammered Della, the smell now affecting her ability to speak without retching.

"Have I got the wrong place then?" said the woman, who had now let the overcoat fall to the floor to reveal the full majesty of her grey, crusty smalls.

"You've got the right place, but that's not my leaflet," Della replied in a muffled voice from behind her hand.

"What do you mean it's not your leaflet? I got it from a bloke handing them out this morning. That's your logo, and this is the right address, isn't it? What you're really saying is because I'm not a dolly bird, I can't use the coupon?"

Della, for once, was lost for words. As she struggled to find an argument to defend herself, the shop door flew open once again. In walked Violent Madonna, looking less than happy, followed by Spelling Stacey. She wrinkled her nose at the smell but purposely ignored the obvious source.

"Is your name Della?" demanded Madonna.

"Err, yes," replied Della fearfully.

"Can you see any acne on this face?" Madonna got her snarly face right up close to Della's so she could get a really good look.

"Not at all…" Della smiled weakly.

"So why did you say I probably have a face like a pepperoni pizza?"

"But I've never met you before…"

"On your leaflet bloke's phone earlier. You said that if I had acne, a free sunbed session could help with that."

"I honestly haven't got a leaflet bloke, and I certainly didn't speak to you on his phone."

"Yes you have, that's where I got mine," said the old woman, still happily modelling her fragrant two-piece.

"I think you both need to leave right now or I will call the police. These leaflets are clearly some kind of scam. I don't offer free sunbed sessions to pensioners and I don't have a teenage skincare advice hotline," said Della, starting to find both her feet and her temper now.

"You calling me a liar?" said Madonna, now chewing her gum like a demented cement mixer with a pink brick in it.

"I'm not calling you anything. I'm asking you to leave."

"Make me! I'm not going anywhere until I get my free sunbed session."

Della had now had enough, and she was not about to give in to demands from a pock-marked princess. She couldn't understand why any of this was happening. Outside she had Pan's People dressed as flames waving libellous placards and dancing to Michael Jackson. Inside she had two freeloading morons with counterfeit vouchers and a smell that would knock a fly off a bucket of shit at 100 yards. At that moment, something snapped deep inside her. Della lunged at Madonna, grabbing her by the shoulders, intending to push her out of the shop. Madonna wasn't prepared for this sudden direct action and was understandably caught napping. She staggered back slightly and would probably have regained her balance had it not been for the old lady's discarded overcoat that tangled around her feet. Over she went, taking Della with her to the floor. Ordinarily, a hard landing would have awaited them, but the large collection of carrier bags acted as a convenient crash mat. That's when the smell went from really bad to absolutely sodding putrid.

The reason for that was the old lady liked cats, lots of cats! So that morning she had been to see a friendly fishmonger she'd got to know in the indoor market. He saved all the fish guts for her as he prepared the day's catch for sale. She would then take these home and boil them up for her many cats to eat. Unfortunately for Della and Madonna, their combined weight had caused this bag of free fishy fayre to explode like an organic dirty bomb.

"My fish!" screamed the old lady.

"Fuck your fish, look at the fucking state of me!" said Della, climbing off Madonna, dropping the posh act and going full Bartley Green.

"Shit…" exclaimed Madonna, who, because she had landed right on top of the carrier bags, had taken the full blast of the grisly gut grenade.

"S-H-I-T," replied Spelling Stacey confidently, while firmly holding her nose.

Just then, the door opened once again. In walked Bernd wearing a hi-vis council vest over his hoody and carrying a clipboard. He looked at the floor first, then at the two fishy wrestlers, and finally at the rather angry gut-splatted old lady. They all turned to face him as he spoke.

"Birmingham Council Environmental Health annual tanning salon compliance check…"

Della looked at him aghast, wondering how her favourite day of the week could get any worse. Resigned to her fate, she simply waved a stinky deeply tanned arm and said, "Knock yourself out…!"

Acknowledging that this probably wasn't the best moment to push his luck, Bernd began the process of pretending to inspect each of the five cubicles, leaving Della, Madonna and the cat fanatic to their own devices in reception. The row had now subsided as further argument seemed pointless, mainly due to the incredible stench. The old lady put her rancid coat back on and shuffled out with the remainder of the fish. Madonna hadn't got anything in her teenage indignation arsenal that applied to such situations. So she just sucked her teeth a lot and uttered a few random words before saying, "Let's bounce" to Stacey then storming out, looking more embarrassed than anything. Admittedly, it's difficult to be facety when you smell like you clean the toilets in a fish factory.

When Bernd had finished his 'inspection', Della was still on her hands and knees cleaning up. The tatty orange carpet was now a deep shade of 'ocean offal' and almost certainly a write-off. He passed her the clipboard to sign, assuring her that everything was OK. In the circumstances, it seemed cruel not to say something like this, as she had enough to worry about. He'd researched solarium inspections on the internet, so he knew enough tanning parlance to convince her that he was legit.

Outside, the Oldbury Reprobates had completed their lengthy performance and Kenneth was basking in the love from the crowd. Things had gone rather well, and he was fielding questions from interested parties about his glittering career in addition to several new group membership enquiries. Annie had filmed the whole thing with the exception of the internal drama, as, once again, events had taken a course that no one had anticipated. As they packed up and the crowd began to melt away Bernd saw a very miserable Della stick an A4-sized sign on the shop door that read:

Please note: We do not accept vouchers for free sunbed sessions. These are counterfeit and were not distributed by the Bella Della Tanning Salon.

Jasper had wisely kept his distance, as being recognised as 'leaflet bloke' at this stage in proceedings would not be beneficial to his health. So he was safely tucked away at the meet-up point in Sarnie Du Jour, enjoying an Avocado Sourdough Roll and drinking a fresh potato juice. Annie was not a fan of this particular food outlet as most of the sandwiches contained vegetables and it was a bit of a bind picking them all out. The only things she could really tolerate were the bacon and cheese bakes, which were basically flat sausage rolls for posh people. Exactly the same pastry, same grease, same calories, but with less social stigma. Bernd just bought a coffee. Annie had two bakes, a full-fat Coke and a bag of ethically sourced, hand-cooked salt and celery crisps, as, after all, it was Friday and yesterday was payday!

As they sat and ate, Bernd explained the rumpus in reception. Both Annie and Jasper were shocked at how, once again, fate had taken a hand in making a great plan even better. Then Annie showed them the footage on her phone from the world's most arty ever dance protest. They also checked social media, as a lot of the crowd had been recording the melee. Sure enough, videos and photos were popping up everywhere showing the Bella Della Tanning Salon and the dancing flames. This was all fantastic, but they knew there was yet more to come.

The next day, Della hastily replaced the carpet and thoroughly scrubbed everything in the reception. The smell eventually subsided with the help of three bottles of fabric freshener. The result of all the embarrassing publicity was that the salon wasn't as busy as usual on Saturday. Just some regulars and a little passing trade. So Della decided to mount an emergency marketing campaign, spending that afternoon on the phone to a few local celebrities offering them free sunbed sessions in exchange for some promotional photos. Famous or not, Brummies love a freebie, and she was delighted at the response she received.

So on Sunday morning she bought some sparkling wine and a boatload of canapés from Larks and Farts and got ready to schmooze the local glitterati. The day went well, and she returned home with the feeling that she had redressed the balance and that the Bella Della Tanning Salon was now back on top. That evening she sat with a glass of leftover wine and uploaded the photos she had taken to her Bella Della Facebook account, massively enjoying the buzz of excitement it caused amongst her friends and customers.

Monday was usually a quiet day for suntans, but the phone rang continually with lots of new clients and even some celebrity recommendations. Business really couldn't have been better, and the painful memory of Fish Gut Friday soon began to fade…

The first person to exhibit symptoms was Bryan Muggington, the leader of the Digbeth Symphony Orchestra. It was noted by members of the audience at a matinee performance of Stravinsky's 'The Rite of Spring' that he appeared to be a delicate shade of blue. This intensified as the recital progressed to the extent where he eventually resembled Papa Smurf, and the delicate heartfelt final notes were drowned out by sniggers from the audience, leading to him snapping his baton in half and kicking over a bassoon on the way out.

The expert on all things Birmingham, Professor Tim Twang, fared little better. Famed for his dramatic walking tours around the city, he experienced the indignation of hosting a 'Peaky Blinders' event while looking more than a little peaky himself. It's incredibly hard to inject a sense of serious drama into your work when you look like a badly cast stunt double for the Incredible Hulk.

Don Starman (the legendary Brum News anchorman) needed every trick in the book from the make-up department to present the news that Monday evening. He arrived at work in the afternoon sporting his usual antique pine hue. But by four o'clock he looked like a Tinky Winky tribute act at a kid's birthday party. He was purple in appearance and then purple with rage. It took Wes the weatherman's best gags and half a bottle of crème de menthe to calm him down enough to do the six o'clock bulletin.

On Wednesday, Kush Kool took to the stage with his band The Croaking Toads at the NEC, having spent most of the day having his liver unnecessarily cleansed of toxins by a shaman from Sheldon that his partner Indiana had recommended to him. It had been noted earlier in the day by the rest of the band that he was going a bit yellow around the edges. By the afternoon, he had a pipe up his jacksy and was being pumped full of dandelion water while he listened to Californian whale music. Singing their breakthrough hit 'Yellow Demon' that evening felt like karma. Later, when the cause of his skin-tone change was revealed, Kush gave a press conference, during which he just said 'awesome' a lot and used made-up words that Indiana had taught him in a big effort to appear cosmic.

All across Birmingham that week people were changing colour. Panic spread and the Birmingham Water Board experienced a massive surge in calls to their helpline. Checks were made and assurances were given. It was definitely nothing to do with the water. Accident and Emergency Departments saw a steady stream of brightly coloured people seeking help. This later became known as the Teletubby Epidemic. But what puzzled doctors was that it didn't appear to be contagious and all the victims were one of five colours. Then a switched-on medic realised that everyone she had seen with the condition was a sunbed user. Soon Della was having another really bad Friday...

The box that Bernd had received by mail order contained ultraviolet-activated chromatic ink, an entirely clear ink that is only activated by exposure to bright sunlight, or in this case the ultra-violet light from sunbeds. During his 'inspection', he had carefully dosed each of the large tubs of suntan lotion within the five cubicles with a different colour. By skilfully calculating the ink to lotion ratio' he had delayed the reaction, which allowed the victim time to go about their normal daily business and not immediately connect their new skin tone to their sunbed session. This was the final blow to the Bella Della Tanning Salon, which ceased trading that same week amidst a frenzy of colourful legal threats and a kaleidoscope of angry scenes. Soon Della's life returned to overcooked cabbage and congealed gravy, which was a very heavy price to pay for accidentally burning someone's arse.

Melissa, meanwhile, had seen news of the mission on social media, in the local press, on regional TV and in the tabloids. The case of the Technicolor Brummies struck a comedy chord right across the country – as if being from the West Midlands wasn't funny enough to start with. Initially, Melissa had been delighted with the little placard protest, but as it escalated to leading public figures imitating Teletubbies, she began to fear a knock at the door. Her life was now back in the fast lane as, following the disastrous holiday, she had managed to get Travis back into her web. The shy dental hygienist had proved to be, well, a bit too shy, even for Travis. Now they were reunited, and she was confident that he would soon propose. But if he didn't, there was always the new exotic underwear catalogue due out next month.

When early reports of the NFRS action against the Bella Della Tanning Salon had started to filter through, she gleefully told Travis what she had done. She felt empowered to get her revenge, and they had laughed together about the whole thing. However, when the second phase began to make the news, Travis changed his tune. Cavorting flame performances were one thing, but dip-dying local celebrities was quite another. As a solicitor and an upstanding member of the legal community, he felt he really couldn't risk any connection with a gang of 'liberty-taking' vigilantes. So when Bernd rang Melissa, impersonating a Cold War spy in order to conclude their business, he was more than a little surprised by the way the conversation went. On the other hand, Melissa was astonished that he was suddenly struggling with the letter W, since he'd lived in England for donkey's years!

"Hello, Melissa, it's Bernd. I vondered if you had been following our progress?"

"I have and so has Travis, as we have been reunited."

"Oh, that's great to hear. Are ve going to be invited to the vedding?"

"I think that is highly unlikely. Travis is more than a little worried about the whole thing."

"Vorried? In vot vay? He can always get you to sign a prenuptial agreement. You vud think he vud know that, vudn't you, given his line of verk?"

"Not the wedding! In case you are caught and the whole thing is connected to him via me. He's terrified of being struck off for being associated with the people that caused Kush Kool to experience a wildflower colonic irrigation."

"There is no danger of us ever been caught. I checked there was no CCTV in the salon, I vore gloves and, quite honestly, the police have better things to do."

"That's as maybe, but Travis is still worried. He would like us to conclude our business in cash, with a confidentiality bonus, if that is acceptable to you."

"Confidentiality bonus?"

"Yes, he would like to pay you £3,000 for the whole operation on the strict understanding that if you are apprehended you do not divulge who employed you under any circumstances."

"That vud be more than acceptable. Where vud you like to meet?"

"Anywhere you like as long as it's not Waynrose's in Blackheath. I got ketchup on the back of my coat last time and it cost me £20 to get it dry cleaned!"

"Vere vill ve vendez-vous ven?"

"Bernd, you pillock, stop putting it on! You sound like Inspector Clouseau. You just said where will we sell then!"

Bernd finally dropped the act, and a meeting was arranged. That evening, Jasper, Bernd and Annie sat round the small Formica dining table in Jasper's flat and stared at the pile of notes in a House of Major carrier bag in front of them. It was a long time since any of them had seen that sort of money, and they were discussing how they should proceed.

"Well, we can't bank it," said Jasper.

"Why not?" said Bernd.

"It might be a bit tricky to explain where we got it to the Department of Work and Pensions should they invite us in for a chat."

"Ahh, I see your point. Might we reinvest it in the business?"

"I can see the sense in that, but we're not really that sort of enterprise, are we? I don't think we're ever going to have an office, a bank account or a fax machine."

Annie had remained strangely silent. Then without any warning, she said: "Set meal for three from the Chinese with a mint Viennetta to follow. Bung Kenneth a ton fifty, get Bernd's car MOT'd and let's pay ourselves £50 a week."

As a course of action, it was a popular one, and as no one else had a better idea, the entire motion was carried unanimously.

Chapter 7

Bernd, the twenty-two-year-old East German punk, was now working full time in the Tost family bakery. Six days a week he rose bright and early with his father to prepare the day's bakes. It was a boring existence that he had just drifted into, the result of having no clear idea of career direction when he had finished college, in addition to the fairly limited opportunities for punk guitarists behind the Iron Curtain. But now he was trapped in a soulless routine that seemed to have his life set out before him as he watched his father grow older. The old man rarely complained and still worked as diligently as he had when he was much younger. But Bernd wondered if he had anything to look forward to in life, with the exception of the occasional cheeky leg-over and roast chicken on Sundays.

The clientele in the bakery was beginning to change, as was East Germany itself. Often on Saturdays, little cliques of students from the university came to drink coffee and talk endlessly about their political theories. Sabine and Deiter had softened with regard to their permitted customer conversation rules, as even they could see a new era of politics emerging. Bernd often wondered if he was listening to tomorrow's leaders from behind the counter. He had never considered himself to be political, because he was musical. Playing in a band got you girls, whereas politics often got you a kicking. From Bernd's point of view, it was no contest. He was happy to spend his evenings counting beats rather than counting his bruises.

There was one particular group that came in regularly which stood out from the rest. Unusually, the most vocal member amongst them was a girl rather than a fella. She had a severe bowl haircut and seemed to always dress in an oddly masculine way. However, when she came to the counter to order, she always took time to be sweet and polite. Bernd even suspected that she made an effort to lengthen their interaction past ordering coffee and asking if the strudel was fresh. He wasn't sure, but he thought that Renate the tomboy might like him.

Bernd was still playing gigs whenever he could. His band, Blitzkrieg Bullshit, had a strong local following, and this offered him a little local fame. Sometimes he would get recognised when he was behind the counter, even with his baker's whites on and the stupid hat that his dad insisted that he wore. It was a uniform that was impossible to customise to gain even a shred of street cred. He looked like a gynaecologist and he felt like the object of their labours. But three nights a week, he strutted and posed on stage, pulling faces like his Western heroes and thrashing his guitar till his fingers ached.

One Saturday night in October, he was playing a gig at Leipzig University. Blitzkrieg Bullshit was topping the bill and around halfway through their set, which mainly consisted of songs about the daily trials of living in the German Democratic Republic. The atmosphere was electric and the whole room seemed to pulse with the music. Gerhard, the lead singer, was belting out one of their most popular songs. Roughly translated, here's how it went:

My Baby Don't Queue for Tights

Darling, just don't bother,
Tights will only make you swelter,
Your skinned knees are fine,
Coz I just think you're a belter.

Baby, please don't queue for tights!

They'll only ladder when we fight!
Other lads say you're not right!
But four foot three's the perfect height!

I hate American Tan!
Prefer you pale and pasty,
Really don't want to feel no stubble,
Coz hairy thighs are really tasty!

Then, through the mass of pogoing, spitting kids, he
thought he saw Renate. Her brown helmet haircut
and her sexless clothes set her apart from the other
girls. Right at that second, he realised that she was
the girl for him. Then she was gone. He later found
out that an elbow to the face had taken her down like
an Easter Island statue and she'd suffered a fairly
severe trampling. But that night, that totally perfect
night, Renate became the apple of his eye.

A little later, backstage, he was putting away his
guitar when a familiar voice said, "Hello, Strudel Boy.
You were great tonight…" Bernd turned round to find
a dishevelled Renate standing behind him. Her
usually immaculate short fringe was damp and was
stuck to the sides of her head with gob and sweat,
giving her the appearance of a rather manky Max
Wall.

"Hello, Fraulein Black Coffee," he said, and from that
moment on they were an item.

They made an odd couple, the intensely political
Renate and the weedy baking punk. Over time,
Renate became plumper, as the cakes were now on
the house. In turn, Bernd got more political. When I
say more political, he just listened politely. He didn't
fully participate in discussions, as, in all honesty, they
were dreadfully boring and very intellectual. Frenzied
debate with lots of really enormous words, even for
German, which is long-winded at the best of times.

So now Bernd was pseudo-political. Put basically, really just pretending, as he had discovered that Renate could suck a beach ball through a drainpipe, and in all fairness that was worth being bored for.

Little did Bernd know that Renate was a bit of a dark horse, as she secretly led a double life. At weekends she spent her time with Bernd, who, conveniently, always went to bed early during the week due to his 4 am starts in the bakery. So on weekday nights, she hung around with a physics geek called Norbert. He was an intense sort of a chap who satisfied Renate's requirement for intellectual conversation and debate. They spent their time in student bars and political hangouts. Her double life caused her no guilt, as she was a modern East German woman, slave to no man, and she did exactly what she wanted. She did feel a bit guilty about the free cakes at times, though.

Eventually, one Saturday, Renate's two worlds collided. While holding court in the bakery, watched by Strudel Boy from the counter, she was caught bang to rights. Norbert had often heard about the little bakery debates from other students. And he had wondered why Renate had never invited him, because, after all, what could be better in life than coffee and a bun with a side order of political wrangling? So Norbert decided to invite himself! Striding in as Renate was in mid-flow about the bourgeois this and the establishment that, he marched straight over and kissed her, a manoeuvre that took Renate totally by surprise and Bernd right over to the Dark Side…

"Who the fuck are you?" demanded Bernd from the counter "And why are you kissing my bird?"

"Eh?" replied Norbert. "On the contrary, I'll think you will find she is my bird." He was not at all comfortable repeating Bernd's common vernacular, which was a little vulgar for a thinking man.

Bernd stared in shock at Norbert from behind the counter. Then he looked at Renate, who averted her eyes, which were now filling with tears. So it was true! Most weekdays, Bernd stirred custard in the bakery, but he wasn't happy with unwittingly stirring someone else's custard at the weekend. So summoning all his dignity and pride, he picked up a cream roll from the counter and threw it at Renate. He caught her full in the face and the delicate cream and sponge exploded on impact, instantly reminding him of happier times. With that he screamed, "Fuck off, you greedy bitch, and get your free cakes somewhere fucking else!" before mincing off into the bakery to cry his eyes out while being consoled by his sister Frieda. She was trying hard not to laugh, as by now she hated Renate and her stupid helmet haircut.

Renate stood in the shop and looked at Norbert, who swiftly weighed up his options. Renate was his first girlfriend, and he had been happy with the way things were going up until now. She'd given him the opportunity to do things to her that he'd only ever previously read about. He considered his chances of quickly finding another willing partner and the enormous effort that would take. Then, with all his thinking done, he took the best course of action open to him.

"Don't worry, sweetheart, we all make mistakes…"

Gathering Renate up in his arms, wiping the cream from her piggy eyes, he led her to the door and out into the street as Bernd wailed like a big tit from back in the bakery, and that was the last time he ever saw Renate Redlinger.

Chapter 8

Jasper was packing the day's eFlog orders when his doorbell played 'My Old Man's a Dustman'. Annie was sitting in the lounge watching 'Bickering Birds'. This was a programme she rarely missed as she always felt that she would make a great panellist should she ever manage to sufficiently raise her profile. The appearance of larger working class women on the show had empowered a whole generation of Annies. At last, having an acid tongue and looking like a Russian arm wrestler had come into vogue. So since their recent payday, she had been on a solid diet of Chocolate Hobnobs and Findus Crispy Pancakes, just in case they ever held open auditions…

Jasper put the 8-track tape he was packing down and walked up the hall to answer the door, as he knew Annie would just ignore it while her favourite show was on. He turned the Yale lock and immediately the door burst open, throwing him backwards. First Bernd came through the door, immediately followed by two rather large gentlemen, who in turn pushed him and Bernd even further down the hall. Jasper instinctively knew that this wasn't good. The old German had the look of a man who'd been invited to meet his maker. He had actually been hung upside down off his balcony until he had revealed the whereabouts of the other members of his team to the two gorillas now filling Jasper's hall. During that process, he had inadvertently wet himself, which had led to the further indignation of having his own urine seep down through his clothing, over his face and drip off his forehead. Pale, nervous and wet pretty much summed up his present status.

"Shall we go into the lounge?" said the nearest goon. Jasper didn't need asking twice. However, Bernd did, as he wasn't processing information at all well that day, so he was duly shoved in the general direction of the lounge.

Annie, while all this was going on, hadn't looked up from the television, as she liked it on loud. But when Jasper shuffled in, then Bernd stumbled in and two heavies followed, she broke off from her viewing and looked up.

"Who the fuck are you?" she inquired.

"Have you been the victim of medical malpractice?" inquired Talking Goon. "Did you go in for a gastric band but someone turned the trolley around and you got a personality bypass instead?"

Talking Goon laughed, his mate chuckled, Jasper smiled and Bernd just smelt.

"I see you were in the same hospital getting your arms shortened so your knuckles don't drag on the floor. We should both get a solicitor then," retorted Annie, making a mental note to twat Jasper later for smiling.

Talking Goon, outgunned by the female reincarnation of Bernard Manning, wisely decided to drop the comedy routine and get down to business.

"Sit down!" he barked.

"Bernd, have you wet yourself?" asked Annie.

Bernd nodded to confirm that he had, like a micro-bladdered three-year-old on a coach trip to the zoo.

"He's not sitting down, he's covered in piss!" said Annie, not thinking to spare Bernd's blushes.

"OK, you two sit down, the old German stands."

"So what is this all about?" said Jasper, attempting to soothe the situation.

"Are you responsible for this listing?" said Talking Goon, holding out his phone, which was displaying their Facebook advert.

"Erm, yes…" confirmed Jasper nervously.

"So then one could assume that you were the group responsible for the recent Tellytubby incident in Birmingham?"

Jasper felt his bladder freeze and instantly felt sorry that Bernd hadn't had the same far less odorous reaction to stress while under questioning.

"Why would you assume that?"

"CCTV from the vape shop opposite, plus Kenneth the Dancing Queen also sang like a canary. Admittedly, without the need for altitude inversion therapy…."

"Then your assumption…."

"Balls to his assumption. Cut to the chase! What do you want then, Knuckles?" interrupted Annie, who had quickly grown tired of the Columbo routine.

"My employer was one of the people recoloured by your antics," replied Knuckles. "At first he was more than a little annoyed, to say the least. But later he saw the funny side after a couple of days sat in the house with the curtains drawn. Now he would like to employ your obvious talents to settle a dispute that he has with a business rival."

"We don't do violence…" Annie stated quite emphatically.

"No, I'm quite sure that you don't. In this case, violence is not what's required. He merely needs you to put someone out of business. You will be well paid and all your expenses will be met."

"That sounds very interesting." Anne was keen on the idea of even more money for simply filming stuff on her phone. "But what if we say no?"

"That would displease my employer. His unhappiness aside, it would lead to the police being informed of your responsibility for the Teletubby attack. And that would no doubt result in civil legal action from around a dozen celebrities and business people for loss of earnings and personal distress, leading to sky-high legal costs, massive damages etc., etc."

"That all seems more than reasonable," said Jasper enthusiastically. He was keen to secure another job rather than a beating or time on remand in Winson Green.

"I thought that you might say that. So why doesn't your lady make us a nice cup of tea while your German friend here takes a shower and changes his clothes, as I've just had my Chelsea tractor valeted, and in the past, I've found that leather seats really hold the smell of wazz. Then I'll take you for a spot of lunch with my employer."

"Make your own fucking tea!" said Annie bravely before the idea of a free lunch registered. Then she cheerfully lumbered off to the kitchen without further protest.

The ride to meet Knuckles' boss was fairly uneventful. The manufacturer had thoughtfully provided his ride with ample seating for five. The large 4x4 always the vehicle of choice for gangsters worldwide, featuring ample boot space for dead bodies, drugs or weapons. Cars that will go anywhere, perfect for victim disposal in the sticks or looking good on the boulevard for collecting the boss's wife from the beauty salon. All mob requirements covered in one totally unreliable, gas-guzzling, posey package.

The now freshly showered Bernd sat in the front, Knuckles drove, and Chuckles, his mate, sat in the rear centre with Annie and Jasper on either side. Annie made ongoing efforts to flirt with Chuckles throughout the journey. Jasper rather optimistically believed this was clearly a clever effort to fake Stockholm syndrome in order to gain an advantage over whatever lay ahead. Annie knew it was actually a clever move to become Mrs Chuckles, as he had a great physique and a package like a snake smuggler at a swimming party.

As they cruised out of the Black Country over the border into Birmingham, they began to wonder exactly where they were going. Soon they were in the poshest part of Harborne. (The really posh parts of Birmingham are always easy to spot because they have enough off-road parking for the inhabitants of the property. The wannabees park on the road or rip the lawn up and park on that.) Finally, they turned up a long sweeping drive and stopped in front of a beautiful Georgian mansion with three floors and an enormous front door. Everyone clambered out, and the NFRS stood aghast, wondering who lived here that needed their help. Bernd was secretly relieved to see that there were no balconies, as he had no additional underpants available.

Knuckles walked to the door and Chuckles kept his eye on their reluctant guests. He pulled a knob to the side of the door and a bell rang deep within. After a minute or so, the big old door opened and a middle-aged lady in a maid's uniform politely ushered them in. All five dutifully followed her through the house until she led them into a large orangery with an enormous oval table set for lunch for four. The maid gestured to Annie, Bernd and Jasper to sit at the side settings. *Leaving the head of the table for the master of ceremonies*, thought Annie. Chuckles and Knuckles felt that their guests were suitably calm now and left the room to get a bite to eat with the kitchen staff.

After a couple of uncomfortable minutes, during which Annie and Jasper had a whispered disagreement over whether it was good etiquette to eat a bread roll to kill the time, the door opened again and in walked a man wearing a maroon shirt and a dog collar. As none of them were students of the clergy, they hadn't a clue who their host was. They were expecting a Russian gangster in all black, a psychotic Cockney with bottle-bottom glasses or even a bald megalomaniac with a white cat.

"Good afternoon, ladies and gentlemen. I am Richard Morris, the Bishop of Birmingham. I hope you will excuse the unorthodox methods of my security team, but you are rather difficult people to find," said the man now sitting down at the head of the table who was used to a slightly larger crowd but was still enjoying holding court.

"I expect you are wondering why I have gone to such trouble to make your acquaintance. The reason, as I'm sure Dorian told you, is that I am now a great admirer of your work…"

"What colour did you go?" inquired Annie, who was now suppressing the urge to laugh at the revelation of the head goon's real name.

"Green," replied the bishop. "More than a little awkward given that I am obliged to wear red in the course of my duties. It gave me the vague appearance of an upside-down set of traffic lights. I had to feign illness for a few days and wait for the effect to subside."

"What did you go with? I usually say diarrhoea, as no one questions you too closely about that. If they do, you just get into detail and they soon lay off."

"Ahh… Good advice, which I shall note for another occasion. I myself went with a bad back. Unfortunately, when I resumed my duties, I gave myself a bad back trying to feign that I had a bad back. Which was a little inconvenient, to say the least. Shall we eat? Then I shall present my proposal to you."

With that, the maid arrived with a soup tureen, out of which she ladled cock-a-leekie soup into each of their bowls. By the time she had served the bishop, last, Annie had finished hers. Jasper had tried to delay her from starting it by gently knocking her ankle with his foot, resulting in a revenge strike from Annie that nearly broke his leg and shook everything on the table. So he left her to eat as she wished, the last dregs going down with her clutching the bowl and slurping like Oliver Twist.

The main course was a smoked salmon salad with a Marie Rose sauce. Annie made a sandwich out of it with a bread roll. She only managed half of the salmon as she couldn't really stand the stuff, but slathered in the sauce and stuffed in the roll, it went down OK. The remainder she hid under her discarded salad. She felt confident that this went unnoticed, but it was actually as obvious as a soft-boiled egg in a golf ball factory.

During the meal, the bishop made polite conversation, discussing popular German culture with Bernd and talking about hospital visiting and music with Jasper. He didn't manage to find any common ground with Annie, but as Annie's style of eating didn't really allow for conversation, that was probably just as well. Imagine someone throwing food into a log shredder and you're not too far off.

Finally, they had a delicate lemon sorbet and coffee. Annie was disappointed about the lack of raspberry sauce and nuts, as the ice cream was a bit watery for her taste. But the coffee was OK, with three sugars in it and half a jug of cream, which resulted in a cream shortage and Bernd being forced to take his black.

When at last they had all finished eating, the conversation returned to the bishop's proposal, which, like his sermons, was long and exacting.

Around five years ago, the bishop had noted that attendances were falling off at the cathedral. There were always the usual spikes around Christmas, Easter, Remembrance Day, etc. But typically, numbers were well down and so, in turn, was the collection of revenue. Each time he submitted his quarterly returns to the Archbishop he would worry, waiting to see if this would be the time when he got 'the call'. Not the one from God, the one from the Archman himself, just in case he was 'skimming'. Eventually, one July, after a dismal second quarter, the call came. In the high church community, this was known as an 'Arch Bishing', or in any other profession, 'a shit sandwich'. Build you up, then break you down, only to build you back up again. The Archbishop was never a man to mince his words – he was the Alex Ferguson of the Anglican Church.

"Listen, Richard, you're a great bishop, everyone loves you. You keep the council on-side, the police think you're great and you're a godsend to the homeless. But that's not gonna keep slates on the roof. You need to be giving me some better numbers. Bums on pews equal cash on plates!

"Try to bear in mind I've got a whole shedload of little Ruperts hanging around who are just looking for a leg up the ladder. Bigger gaff, massive spire, huge listed palace to live in. So unless you get your shit together, I'm going to stick one of the over-enthusiastic feckers on the train and you're going out to grass in Lincolnshire. Your missus will love that. No more Botanical Garden tea parties, no more Brum News receptions, just a straight diet of sea wind and weirdos. So get busy. I won't ring again. If these numbers don't improve, you'll be blessing roller coasters in Skegness before you can say 'hold tight riders'!

"Oh, before I go. Loved the bit on YouTube you did about delivering a sermon in a Brummie accent. Very funny! But I'd watch what they put in your tea for a couple of weeks. They get a bit touchy about the Barry from 'Auf Wiedersehen Pet' references. Someone swapped Timothy Spall's Eucryl for Vim last time he was up there. The whiney feckers never forget."

Lincolnshire was well known as the Russian Front for bishops. If you got sent there, you were never coming back. So the Bishop of Birmingham, the Right Reverend Richard Morris, really needed a plan, and fast! He was well aware that increasing numbers at the cathedral was always going to be a struggle. You could rattle a few cages and attendance would increase for a couple of weeks. But realistically, the only invisible force that most Brummies truly believed in was electricity. So selling them eternal salvation was always going to be an uphill battle.

From reading trade publications, he noted that churches everywhere were getting trendier and changing the way that they 'did God' in order to survive. Some had cafés in the back, others offered guided tours, and a few even did ghost hunts in the crypt. But he needed something really different that would corner the market. Potentially having to tell his wife, Debbie, that she was moving to the Las Vegas of the Fens wasn't going to make her jam set. She came out in a rash if she got further than ten miles from Selfridges. Debbie was a former topless model who had met the then 'Ricky Rocket' in the mid-'80s when he was a champion disco dancer. For many years now she had been a lady who lunched and had understandably developed a liking for the finer things in life. He severely doubted that their marriage could survive the embarrassment of his drop in status to Roller Coaster Reverend.

He thought, he pondered and he racked his brains, but nothing came to him. So he decided that he would ask Numero Uno upstairs for advice. As he prepared to pray, he lit a candle to signify God's presence in the room. Then he had an epiphany. Of course! He dealt with candle suppliers every day, and it was something that he knew all about. Surely the people he dealt with didn't just make church candles? They must make all types. Fragranced ones, coloured ones, oddly shaped ones. So, quickly thanking God for his intervention, he got on the blower and Burn Again Candles was born.

Soon Richard the Bishop had commissioned a whole range of wholly holy candles that were shaped like biblical characters with fragrances to match. The Virgin Mary smelt of roses, Jesus smelt of frankincense and God himself smelt like Old Spice. However, the Christmas nativity scene was soon withdrawn as it "smelt like donkey shit and straw" according to one elderly parishioner. At first, the candles were sold from the cathedral. But increased demand soon led to Sunday-trading problems, and then it all got a bit messy, culminating in an unfortunate scene when a customer interrupted a christening to ask the bishop if Jesus was vegan-friendly.

Twelve months later, Burn Again Candles had six shops in Birmingham and the Black Country, plus outlets in a couple of department stores in the city centre. Business was booming and the bishop no longer feared submitting his quarterly figures to the big cheese. People really couldn't say no to a Christian candle or the charismatic disco-dancing bishop. They might not want to freeze their balls off on Sunday in a draughty church, but they'd happily buy a five-quid candle that might secure their place in heaven. 'Secure' was probably a strong word, but the hint was ever present in the promotional straplines the bishop used:

God is never happier than when you're blowing his candle.
Never doubt God's eternal flame.
Think of Jesus when you're straightening his wick.
Waxiness is indeed next to godliness.
Relight My Father (later withdrawn due to legal action from Take That)
Never take the Lord's flame in vain.

As the money rolled in, the bishop even began to watch the local news for events that may lead to a candlelit vigil. As a man of God, he didn't condone the actions of murderers or kidnappers; he merely ensured that candles poked through paper cups were available at the right times. Soon it was almost impossible to attend a vigil anywhere in the West Midlands that didn't have the Burn Again Candles logo all over it.

Across town, Bishop John Manzoni was watching the emerging Candle King with envy. Everywhere he went, it was 'Bishop Ricky' this and 'Burn Again Candles' that. He was even supplying scented candles to synagogues, for feck's sake! Bishop Manzoni had been a high roller on the spiritual scene in Birmingham until a few years back, always the 'go-to cleric' for local TV and radio for anything of a religious nature. Now he scarcely got a call, and when he did, it usually ended up on the cutting-room floor. Since that disco-dancing deviant had come on the scene, he'd barely got a look in. "Fuck it! I'm going into the candle business!" he exclaimed aloud, which quite startled the young priest standing in the urinal next to him...

Fast-forward three years and Roman Candles was now a force to be reckoned with. Their range of Vatican-approved candles had been a great success. Nothing sells like a Pope-shaped candle, and, along with a multitude of patron saints to collect it was a winner. Wary of opening shops because of their high overheads, Bishop Manzoni had hit upon the idea of setting up a network of nuns doing candle parties. It was genius! He just targeted a parish and spoke firmly to the local priest, who then read out a strongly worded party advert during Mass. The nuns did all the pressure selling with barmy product-based games, although 'candle musical chairs' led to an unfortunate health and safety breach that put someone face down in an ambulance. The deal was that the local priest took 20% commission, the nuns got 20% between them with Bishop Manzoni pocketed the rest!

Soon he was the Catholic Candle Party King, and, not content with the home crowd, he dispatched teams of hand-picked heavy nuns into the wider community. Soon a bitter sectarian wax war began and a wave of fear spread amongst religious candle fans of all faiths as stories circulated of intimidation, mass meltings and vicious wick stripping.

So now the gloves were off and Bishop Richard Morris needed to bring in some outside help to save his empire. Shop sales were down and he was being forced to take his personal security very seriously after an attempted drive-by melting had left him badly stuck to the pavement.

The NFRS listened closely throughout the bishop's story. Even Annie didn't interrupt. The whole thing sounded fairly serious.

"So what exactly do you need us to do?" said Jasper.

"I need Roman Candles completely out of the business," replied Bishop Richard. "I want him and his product thoroughly discredited so that Burn Again Candles can resume its total domination of the Christian candle market, or I've got a one-way ticket to Skeggy and a lot of lonely microwave meals to look forward to."

With that, he rose from the table, walked over to the sideboard and opened a drawer. He took out a large padded envelope, which he placed on the table in front of the three mischief makers.

"There's £2,500 in there and when it's done, there's the same again, plus expenses. All I ask is that the job in no way leads back to me."

Annie couldn't believe their luck. The only way things could get any better was if Chuckles popped round to do her housework in a wet mankini.

"Well then, we'll have to see what we can do," stammered Jasper, trying hard to look like he had the first clue how to put a Catholic Candle King out of business.

Chapter 9

Back at the Eagle's Nest, they tried to take in what had just happened. Bernd decided it was probably a good time to put a load of washing on while they were thinking, although he worried that going out on the balcony to peg it out might present a PTSD issue.

Once again they sat at the table staring at another pile of money trying to work out what to do next. Annie had still been a bit peckish despite having lunch, so she had got Knuckles to stop at the Quicky Mart for a packet of Tuc Cheese Sandwich biscuits on the way back. She was now devouring these as Bernd looked on, dismayed at the level of crummage being distributed by her munching.

Bernd had now pretty much recovered from his unexpected opportunity to check out the plants on the balcony below. He got the ball rolling by suggesting that they Googled Bishop Manzoni and checked out the Roman Candles website. The bishop, as you would expect from his name, was a man of obvious Italian heritage. He had a wide jawline, a strong Roman nose, slicked-back hair and a small pencil moustache. Had he not been a priest, he would have made a fantastic used-car salesman. Despite his religious connections, he didn't look like a man you should cross lightly.

Roman Candles had a strong internet presence. Merely the word 'candle' sparked a plethora of Google ads and price comparison site listings. The company was second only to Dagnabbit Candles from the USA, it would seem. They marvelled at the massive range of different items that you could get out of one simple wax product. It was difficult to believe that the Catholic Church had so many patron saints. There were candles for pretty much every biblical figure that they could think of, and a few more besides. In addition to this, there were gift candles aimed at particular crises of faith – for the times when your commitment to the Lord might be in question.

The Hip Replacement Candle promised to speed convalescence by stimulating your body's ability to form calcium around your new joint. Soon you would be waxing lyrical about God's gift of titanium to all that know you.

The Hair Loss Candle would focus God's power on your scalp. His soothing love would soon regenerate your follicles and you would amaze your friends with a new mane of strong glossy hair.

The Proposal Candle, when lit in the presence of your intended, would guarantee a holy union within a year, making betrothal the only sensible option for a reluctant bride or groom.

The more they read, the more they could see that the whole enterprise was based on exploiting the sad, the weak and the desperate, so taking it down in a hail of comic catastrophe was more of a public service than anything else. The £5K plus expenses was just a sweetener, and surely no one's God would begrudge them that.

It was decided that the only way forward was to get right inside the Roman Candles operation. To strike at the heart of the skulduggery and throw a massive spanner in the works. To accomplish that, they were going to need Mucky Barry and his computer-hacking skills. Annie bagsied not going to ask, so Jasper rang him and arranged to meet him for a cuppa in the caff with Bernd, which was obviously preferable to a trip to the technological health hazard that passed for his flat. Annie had another call to make elsewhere in the block: Elsie at number 47, the crafting queen of Derek Robinson House…

Jasper and Bernd were in good spirits. Bernd's inverted space walk aside, life was treating them very well indeed, so the short walk to the caff in unseasonal late March sunshine was a treat in itself. Mucky Barry was already there when they arrived. He was looking resplendent in two filthy halves of two different shell suits, set off beautifully by black slip-on shoes and crimson nylon socks, high-rise fashion for the 'on the go' ex-porn dealer. Barry already had a coffee, which he had generously complemented with two Tunnock's teacakes, and he announced they were on a tab that he had just opened on Jasper's behalf. Jasper and Bernd ordered coffee, waited for them at the counter, settled the tab, then sat opposite Barry in his booth.

"So what can I do for you today, gentlemen?" said Barry. His signature squint always got worse in any social situation that didn't involve a webcam.

"Today it's all about hacking, Barry. If we give you an email address, can you pull up all the traffic that has gone through there in, say, the last six months?" Bernd asked, being equally direct.

"What sort of email address? Government, police, armed forces?" Barry's squint went into overdrive with anxiety.

"Just clergy, nothing heavy. The SAS won't be kicking your door off at 3 am for looking at this," Jasper said, trying to soothe Barry's nerves.

"Fair enough. I just like to ask before I get started. I did a job for a Russian bloke a couple of years back. He was worried his missus was cheating on him. I thought it was funny for a Russian woman to be called Hilary. I had to go to my mom's in Tipton till it all calmed down."

Bernd thought it odd that a bloke who had the ability to hack a presidential candidate's personal email account would think he was safe from the CIA at his mom's house. But that's because Bernd had never been to Tipton, the Beirut of the Black Country. If a Black Hawk went down in Princes End, the US army would probably just leave it there and it would be every man for himself…

"What will it cost?" said Jasper, keen to get him focussed on the job in hand.

"Dunno… say a ton and if it's any more I'll bell you?" replied Barry, whose dandy attire spoke volumes of his lack of business acumen.

"Magic. I'll text you the email address. Here's fifty on account. Let me know when you have something." Bernd and Jasper necked their beverages in unison and happily left Mucky Barry to his coffee and confectionery.

In the lull between jobs, Jasper and Annie had decided to treat themselves to a midweek break while Bernd was preoccupied with planning their next outrage. They couldn't really do much until they had some inside information from Barry. So it made sense to kick back a little and enjoy some sea air while the weather was good. That evening, they packed their bags and made reservations online for a trip to Barmouth, on the north-western coast of Wales. It is an easy place to reach by train, being served by the Cambrian Coast railway, which dissects the town. Trains run direct from Birmingham, so there is no need to change at any point during the journey. They had booked two days of bed, breakfast and evening meals at a little place just off the promenade. The Windy Dunes hotel looked great on the website and had a sea view and a bar. Just what the doctor ordered…

The next morning at 8.15 am, they were waiting with two bags on the platform at Smethwick Galton Bridge railway station. Jasper's was a medium-sized sports holdall, Annie's was the size of an American's fridge. She always packed for every eventuality, including a blizzard, an earthquake or a typhoon. Naturally, she also had a large carrier bag of food for the trip.

For the outward journey, she had decided to dress in the style of Audrey Hepburn, so she was wearing a polka-dot headscarf, vintage style sunglasses and a raincoat with the belt tied in a knot. She hadn't seen any of her films, but she'd just found the raincoat in a charity shop and there was a framed poster of Miss Hepburn in the window, which had given her the idea. Jasper thought it was actually more of a tribute to Inspector Gadget, but as it was likely to be a three-and-a-half hour journey, he kept that to himself. Needlessly antagonising Annie in a confined space could lead to multiple dead arms.

There were only a couple of other passengers waiting, so when the train pulled in, there wasn't exactly a crush to get on. Jasper gave Annie his holdall while he struggled to get the 'fridge case' into the carriage. When he had eventually manoeuvred it into the luggage rack, Annie was already standing next to their reserved seats. The reason she hadn't sat down was that they already contained a couple of lycra-clad cyclists. Their bikes were part of the reason why Jasper had struggled so much with Annie's luggage. As he got within earshot, he could hear that all was not well…

"…. we reserved them online. Look, here are our tickets with the seat numbers on."

"I'm sorry, we got on at Wolverhampton. The seats were vacant. So they are ours!" argued Mrs Lycra.

"I'm sorry too," said Annie.

"Why are you sorry?"

"I'm sorry about your bikes getting damaged when I fuck them off the train and they get flattened by an Intercity going the other way!" expanded Annie.

Her words hung in the air for a couple of seconds. Jasper was understandably uncomfortable. Confrontation wasn't his strong suit, but to Annie, it was an art form. She effortlessly delivered put-downs faster than a lazy veterinary surgeon.

"How do you know they're our bikes?" said Mrs Lycra bravely.

"You being dressed like a burst Spiderman is a big clue." Annie retorted.

"Who have you come as then? Columbo's fat mom?" came the response.

Jasper winced, knowing that this last exchange was going to step it up a level. Annie turned, and without meeting his eye, she began to walk to the luggage rack. The train was already clanking out of the station, so she wobbled as she went, unaccustomed to the odd sideways motion. As she reached the rack, she held out her arms to grip the first bike. Mrs Lycra stood up just as the guard entered the carriage.

"Tickets please," he said cheerfully, then immediately sensed the Mexican stand-off.

Both male partners looked at the guard, praying that he was King Solomon of the railways. Both men knew that their partners wouldn't give an inch. Many previous conflicts bore witness to this.

"What appears to be the problem?" said the guard, already knowing what the problem was. But sometimes getting people to say it out loud could defuse the situation by making the issue seem ridiculous.

"They're sat in our reserved seats."

"She's been impolite and made threats against our property."

"OK. Firstly, can we all calm down? Madam, can I ask you to put the cycle down. Sir, can I see your tickets?"

Jasper handed the guard their tickets. The guard confirmed that the seats were reserved and that the cyclists would need to move. Mr Lycra rose gratefully and exchanged a secret look of relief with Jasper. The last thing he needed to mar his break was his missus locked in mortal combat on their first day.

Annie triumphantly took the window seat and set her carrier bag down on the table. She gleefully watched Mr & Mrs Lycra as they searched for seats elsewhere in the carriage, eventually finding space a few rows away on either side of the aisle, still facing Jasper and Annie. Annie was more than happy for them to watch her eat, as she could treat them to a big helping of shit eye as she did so.

The rest of the journey passed without further incident. By the time they reached Barmouth, Annie had devoured a wide range of highly processed snack foods, three bags of crisps and half a bottle of

Coke. Jasper, on the other hand, had enjoyed a thistle and quinoa salad, a bottle of water and a bag of beetroot and swede crisps. Annie most likely had a colon like a bombed church, he thought, whereas his was more like a vegan's pedal bin.

When they alighted at the fine old Victorian train station in the centre of Barmouth just after twelve, the sun was still shining brightly. They made their way out of the station, passed the fairground and walked over to the promenade, taking some time to enjoy the vista on a bench with some ice cream from a nearby kiosk. The silence was only perforated by Annie's eventual demolition of the cone. The walk to the Windy Dunes hotel was straight up the promenade with the sea on their left. Under normal circumstances it would have been a pleasant stroll, but with Annie's rather weighty luggage, it was a twenty-minute slog. Eventually, they arrived at their destination with Jasper sweating like a three-legged racehorse in a shotgun factory.

Jasper dealt with the check-in without a hitch. The receptionist gave them the room key and wisely decided to forgo the usual 'up to the room' tour, having already seen the size of Annie's case and Jasper's obvious distress at having to lug it there from the train station.

The room was nice and airy with a panoramic sea view and a neat little en suite bathroom. Annie was excited and so was Jasper, but sadly for different reasons, after she had instructed him that there was 'plenty of time for that tonight'. They walked into town for a mooch around the shops and yet another bite to eat, spending the rest of the afternoon enjoying a heady mix of coffee, cake and ice cream at various quayside establishments. Eventually, they retraced their steps back along the promenade just as the last rays of early spring sunshine were glinting off the sea. They gave way to a splendid red sunset, which completely filled the horizon, almost promising a final hiss from the hot sun as it wearily extinguished itself in the sea. They sat on the sea wall holding hands, enjoying the last moments of the spectacle before gently kissing and walking arm in arm over the road to the Windy Dunes hotel.

It's difficult to know which of the two Annie spotted first in reception, the Karaoke Night poster or the two rather familiar bicycles from earlier in the day. Either way, Jasper hoped you didn't have to reserve seats, owing to the obvious lack of armed security staff in this small, friendly Welsh seaside hotel.

Bernd had decided to use his 'down time' wisely back in Birmingham. As the weather was so agreeable, he decided to venture into the city on a reconnaissance mission. In order to successfully engage your enemy in combat, it was important to know his lair. So he took a short train ride to Snow Hill station, from where it was just a short walk to St Brad's Catholic Cathedral, the nerve centre of Roman Candles Ltd, managing director one Bishop John Manzoni.

The traffic was quite busy as Bernd threaded his way through the streets behind the train station. From the outside, the cathedral was stunning from any angle, in complete contrast to the modern buildings surrounding it. Once inside, he was immediately struck by the strong perfume on the air and the overabundance of candles that filled every available horizontal surface. As he walked further into the main body of the cathedral, he could see people standing close to an open door to the right of the pews. Continuing to pose as an eager tourist, he made his way down the aisle before settling within hearing distance of the small gathering. Now he could see that the person doing all the talking was the bishop and the people listening were clearly new recruits to his holy sister sales team.

".... Naturally you'll get all the support that you need in the field from either myself or Sister Bridget Brady here. However, all the information you will need is in the Roman Candles Sales Success folder: stock range, pricing, discounts, commission and even game ideas, right down to ordering sales literature or point-of-sale promotional posters to maximise your enterprise exposure. You'll find it's a flaming good read."

He paused for laughter, but none came. *Nuns are a tough crowd*, thought Bernd.

"Thank you all for coming. Please be sure to pick up a folder and a box of samples as you leave. May God light your way, and if he's not available, use a Roman Candle..."

Again, no laughter was forthcoming, and the nuns filed out with folders and boxes, leaving the bishop and Sister Brady standing by the open door. Continuing with his awestruck tourist act, Bernd gazed around again. Now, without the nuns blocking his view, he could see that the door was the entrance to a storage area, which had probably once been the Lady Chapel. Inside there were boxes upon boxes of what was, presumably, Roman Candles stock. After a short whispered conversation and a little giggling, Bishop Manzoni and Sister Bridget Brady disappeared into the stockroom, closing the door behind them. Bernd felt sure he then heard the sound of the door being locked from inside. Carefully checking that he was still the only other person present, he quietly moved over to the door to listen. From inside he could soon hear the familiar sounds of rhythmic grunting and gasping. Though Bernd hadn't had an active role in any form of lovemaking for a number of years, Candy, his neighbour, had a fairly successful 'companionship business' and her 'occupational opera' often made it difficult to hear his television when she was 'concluding a transaction'. So he knew what it sounded like, even though Sister Bridget was more of a baritone, if he was being truthful.

"Excuse me…"

Bernd turned. Lost in his thoughts, he hadn't noticed a lady wearing a tabard and carrying a large candle in the shape of Cardinal Newman walk up behind him.

"I hope you won't think me rude. But can I ask what you are doing?" hissed the woman.

Bernd was completely lost for words. Luckily, Valerie Bradford rarely waited for an answer before asking another question.

"Are you from the Vatican?"

"The Vatican?"

"Yes, have you come about my letter?"

"Your letter…? Yes, your letter. That's exactly why I am here…"

Valerie Bradford winked, put down the candle, then placed a finger to her lips and gestured for Bernd to follow her. She led him to the other side of the cathedral, through a door and down some steep stone steps. She continued along a short corridor, then went into a small room with a round bar table and two chairs that clearly formed an office of sorts. There were tea-making facilities surrounded by industrial cleaning equipment. Silently indicating for Bernd to sit down, she theatrically cupped her ear and tilted her head. Bernd in turn listened hard, then, as if by magic, he could just make out that the action in the Lady Chapel was now reaching its sinful conclusion, the actual substance of which was Sister Bridget openly stating to God that she had reached her intended destination. She didn't say this just once but several times, followed by the sort of noise an arthritic elephant makes when it lies down to die. Then it all went quiet.

"Heating ducts," said Valerie in a matter-of-fact way.

"Heating ducts?" repeated Bernd. Repeating everything Valerie said had worked really well up till now, he thought, so why change a winning formula?

"I've worked in the cathedral since 1974, long before Bishop Pantsdowni turned up and claimed it as his kingdom. When the present heating system was fitted in the 1980s, they didn't bother to block the hot air ducts used for the old one. This area was part of the old boiler room from where the hot air rose before being blown into the ducts and around the whole place. Of course, that's fairly inefficient by modern standards, but it was considered cutting edge when the cathedral was first erected in 1841. The result is that I can hear pretty much everything that happens throughout the whole building. You wouldn't be aware of that unless you spend as much time down here as I do, and I'm not going to tell anyone, am I? I hear it all through the ducts – from what horses he's backing to what he's getting for the Pope's birthday."

Bernd quickly reached the opinion that Valerie might be fairly knowledgeable about large-scale heating systems and bonking bishops. But she was unlikely to be an expert on European accents, so he decided he would continue to work the Vatican angle. Over a cuppa, he learned quite a lot from Valerie about the goings-on in the cathedral. Apparently, the bishop had got 'close' to a number of nuns down the years, leading to one or two leaving under a cloud with surprise postings to remote parishes. She also told him that a junior priest often composed his famed Sunday Masses, which he shamelessly passed off as his own work and naturally took all the credit. That the Roman Candles were actually manufactured in China from distilled red diesel and not organic soy wax, as proclaimed in the glossy sales literature. But most interesting of all, that the bishop had a forthcoming appearance on Shop Until You Drop Television presenting his wares to the 'devoted wax-buying' nation.

When it was time to go, Valerie let Bernd out through the old side door that had once been used for the heating oil delivery. That way, she said, the bishop would be unaware that anyone from the Vatican had even visited or indeed wonder how they came to be so well informed about matters at the Birmingham branch. After all, Valerie liked her job, it was just the boss she couldn't stand. The 'man from the Vatican' promised her faithfully that he would file a damning report at the next Bad Bishop Bitching Session. Obviously, he knew this was a lie, but what he now had in mind would have a far greater impact than even Valerie was hoping for.

Chapter 10

Annie was now wearing her improvised karaoke attire as they left their room and descended the stairs – a charming ensemble of a glittery pink catsuit and an orange miniskirt – and her greying hair had been backcombed till it threatened to snap clean off. Tonight, she fancied herself as Oldbury's answer to Toyah Wilcox. Jasper just really, really fancied her toying with his affections afterwards.

When they reached the entertainment lounge, which doubled as the restaurant depending on the hour, the party was in full swing. Music and disco lights filled the room, and the DJ was punctuating his sounds with inane chatter and name-checking the regulars in return for loud cheers.

"Nice to see Brenda Broderick's in the house... Glad to see she's got no sausages with her... Make some noise for Terry Cale... worst window cleaner in West Wales..."

Mr & Mrs Lycra were already seated on tall stools at the bar. Judging by the drinks they were holding, they were taking full advantage of the two-for-one cocktail happy hour. Jasper read the sign advertising this, then glanced at his watch and was relieved to see that it would be over in another five minutes. Annie looked at the clock behind the bar and formed the same opinion, except she decided she was on her holidays so she would order a double round to compensate. Mr & Mrs Lycra were clearly having a good time and had the familiar ease of a couple that enjoyed each other's company. Jasper followed with silent apologies as Annie bulldozed her way to the bar and invited the barman to serve her by whistling at him as if she had lost a deaf sheepdog. This not only gained the attention of the barman but that of Mrs & Mrs Lycra and pretty much everyone else in the room who wasn't sedated, even the DJ, who was now wearing headphones.

(Annie had perfected this whistling skill in a former job where she had helped crane kidney dialysis units into patients' back gardens. If the crane driver can't hear you, you get two tonnes of prefab on your head, so you learn to whistle loudly. Inevitably, with the relentless pace of progress, home dialysis machines were now the size of a large coffee maker, consigning Annie's whistle to the scrap heap along with her ability to carry four full crates of Davenport's Beer at Home across a dual carriageway in the snow.)

"What can I get you?" asked the barman.

"Two pina coladas and two woo woos," said Annie.

"Anything else?"

"Two packets of Scampi Fries and a Marathon."

"What's a Marathon? Is that a cocktail?" the barman was puzzled by the request and had every right to be, as he was only twenty-four years old.

"A Snickers, then…"

"That it?"

"Oh, and half a lager shandy for my bloke…"

The barman rolled his eyes and started to make the order. Jasper, who was quite used to being Annie's plus one, moved off to find a table that would allow them both a good view of proceedings and ample refreshment storage. Annie decided to spend her time waiting at the bar productively. So she fixed Mr & Mrs Lycra with the sort of stare that would make an arm wrestler blush. Soon the couple felt the full weight of her glare and shifted uncomfortably on their stools, trying hard to ignore her and continue with their convivial conversation.

As Annie made her way back from the bar, Jasper briefly waved to attract her attention. Sensing the opportunity for a comedy moment, the DJ waved back and everyone laughed. Even with her hands full, Annie was able to deal him a look that instantaneously informed him that further embarrassment-based hilarity would not be tolerated. He sheepishly took the hint and quickly switched the focus back to his cheesy patter.

"So, for the karaoke virgins in the room, here's what ya do. Get hold of the songbook from in front of the stage. Pick a song, pass me one of these little slips of paper with the title and your name, and I will call you out to sing. Don't be shy if you don't know all the words. Just look at the screen – the lyrics will be displayed in time with the music."

By this time, Annie had set the tray of drinks and snacks down on the table and had smartly headed off in the direction of the stage to grab the songbook and a slip before anyone else got there. Unfortunately for Annie, Mrs Lycra had the same idea. Now the race was on to see who would get there first. Embarrassingly for Toyah's tubby twin, it was Mrs Lycra, who gleefully grabbed the folder and with a triumphant flounce made her way back to her bar stool, leaving Annie to thread her way back through the tables to Jasper as people openly sniggered. Jasper wisely held an internal meeting and decided to cancel the duvet dancing he had scheduled for later, as he felt he would probably need a lasso and a large amount of ketamine to pull it off, judging from Annie's facial expression.

After what seemed like an eternity, Annie finally got

her hands on the songbook. Mrs Lycra had generously passed it the opposite way round the room in order to annoy her even further. As she intently studied the song choices, Mrs Lycra was taking to the stage to sing. Entirely devoid of tight nylon for the evening, she was fashionably dressed in a black casual top and jeans, which purposely complimented her figure. Even Annie had to admit that cycling clearly did more for your thighs than a pair of industrial Spanx off Blackheath Market could ever do.

As the first notes of her backing track rang out, Annie tightened her fist as Mrs Lycra began to sing her improvised version of a 1970s pop classic while fixing her with a smarmy smile…

Chew-chew train,
Chompin' down the track,
Big picnic hamper on it,
That's never comin' back,
Ooh Ooh got a one-way ticket to the scales…

By the second verse, Annie had demolished the first pina colada and was rounding off the second bag of Scampi Fries…

Got a one-way ticket to the scales,
Need take a trip to Weight-Loss Town,
Gonna need a long stay at Fat-Free Hotel.

As the music faded out, Mrs Lycra took a bow as the laughing crowd roared their obvious approval. Jasper mentally added nitrazepam to Annie's drug order, as her involuntary gurning told him she was battling to rule out extreme violence as a suitable response. Fortunately, good sense reigned, and she turned her attention back to the song choices. After a couple of minutes of further perusal, she filled in her slip and, without showing Jasper, handed it to the DJ.

During the next half hour, a selection of locals got up to sing. As you would expect, there was a lot of Tom Jones, Catatonia and Manic Street Preachers and, bizarrely, even 'The Snowman' by Aled Jones. Jasper quietly sipped his lager while Annie drained each remaining glass in turn before finally devouring her confectionery. She would need both courage and stamina for what she had planned.

At long last, it was Annie's turn. She walked confidently onto the stage like a Saturday afternoon wrestler with a killer hold. She then stood with her back dramatically to the audience, accepting the polite applause and waiting for the start of her track. As the music started, she rubbed her eyes hard and pulled her damp, sticky hair into two mental tufts, pushing these back over her ears like a pair of horns while moving her hips to the rhythm.

As the guitar loop faded to the distorted drumbeat, she turned to face the audience. Smudged mascara, eyeliner and eye shadow now filled her entire eye sockets, giving her the appearance of a dangerously disturbed hospital outpatient. Now swinging her hips wildly in time to the music, she opened her mouth wide and poked out her tongue, New Zealand Hakka style. With her red lipstick and her eyes bulging, she began to throw herself around the little stage like a demented sparkly gargoyle. The DJ prayed someone was filming this and bravely upped his Argos amplifier to its maximum setting. Moved by the climbing volume, Annie glared at Mr Lycra and began to fellate the microphone enthusiastically, to his obvious embarrassment. After giving the nylon-loving pedal ponce the show of a lifetime, she turned her attention to Mrs Lycra. Taking her cue from the pounding beat that was now shaking the stale ham baps off the covered plate behind the bar, she froze, her eyes boring deep into her adversary. Then she frantically screamed into the microphone…

Stitch the snitch up
Slap my witch up
Stitch the snitch up
Slap my witch up
Stitch the snitch up
Slap my witch up

The crowd went wild. They weren't entirely sure what
they were seeing, or even why, but they were swept
along on a tidal wave of crap cut-price cocktails and
cloudy Welsh lager and transported from a seaside
hotel to the late '90s glory days of electronic dance
music. The lyrics weren't too hard to alter, and hitting
the notes really wasn't the point. The Dragons were
roaring and Annie was their deranged, glittery leader.
Pretty soon, Mr & Mrs Lycra were the only ones not
singing.

Stitch the snitch up
Slap my witch up
Slap the witch up
Eaaaheeyheeaheyyyee
Aaahaaahaaaaaaaaaaahha
Eaaaheeyheeaheyyyee
Aaahhaaaaa
Aaahhaaaaaaaaaaaaaaaaaaaa…

As Annie wailed out the last notes, crowd-surfing on
her back past the bar, she saw the Lycras heading
for the stairs. The rest of the night was a blur. The
Windy Dunes hotel had never seen anything like it
before, and it's doubtful it has seen anything similar
since.

Breakfast the next morning was a fragile affair: coffee
and dry toast for the conquering crooner. Even the
waitress serving them winked as she brought their
pot of coffee. The bikes were gone from reception as

they walked through to take the air on the prom and for Annie to boke noisily into a wheelie bin. Oddly, they still weren't there later when they returned. Annie was utterly triumphant through the power of music without a single bike having been thrown.

The rest of their break passed without incident. Jasper quenched his excitement a couple of times. Annie did no further singing, and they returned to Smethwick Galton Bridge the next day completely refreshed and raring for more aggro.

When Bernd collected them from the station, there was a lot of catching up to do. He told them all about his trip to St Brad's Cathedral, the bonking bishop and his encounter with Valerie Bradley. In turn, Annie told him about smudging her make-up and driving Mr & Mrs Lycra off to bed with her singing. Bernd didn't seem massively impressed, and Annie sulked during the journey back to Derek Robinson House.

As Jasper was getting the fridge case out of the back of Bernd's estate, his phone rang. It was Mucky Barry with good news. He had managed to hack the Roman Candles email account, and he was forwarding everything he had found to Bernd's email address.

Gathered around the heavy wood table in the Eagle's Nest, they peered at the large amount of information that they now had at their disposal. A lot of it was fairly standard stuff – stock availability, quotations and complaints. But after about an hour of digging through a mountain of trivia, they found something of interest which confirmed what Bernd had been told by Valerie. In a week's time, Roman Candles had a Today's Special Value slot booked to present their wares on Shop Until You Drop Television. Bishop John Manzoni was going to be a TV star. There wasn't a lot of time to plan, but it was an opportunity they really couldn't miss...

Preparations were hectic, a plan was devised and props were sought. Kenneth from the Oldbury Reprobates was forgiven for his indiscretion under the threat of torture and brought back into the fold. His thespian skills were in great demand since the sunbed caper, and it took some very special flattery indeed to get him back on board. Soon the trap was set and all that remained was to spring it.

Once again, Annie and Jasper were standing on a train platform. This time, however, it was to say goodbye at New Street station. She was taking a train to London for a night in a hotel with Kenneth. Jasper and Bernd would be staying in Birmingham. Jasper made her promise to be on her best behaviour. Kenneth said that he would keep an eye on her. Annie threatened to shut both of his eyes permanently if he said that again. Kenneth wisely boarded the train and left them to canoodle. It was a kind thought, but as neither of them had a clue about canoodling, Jasper stupidly told her to be careful again. Annie reminded him that she wasn't a child and told him to fuck off before she twisted his nipple. She boarded the train and sat sulkily, peering out of the opposite-side window. As the train pulled out, Kenneth hung out of the window in a door, waving till he was just a dot in the distance. Jasper worried that he might have romantic designs on him, but Kenneth actually just enjoyed pretending he was Celia Johnson in Brief Encounter...

Candy, Bernd's vocal neighbour, was a matter-of-fact sort of girl. But then, of course, her choice of profession demanded a certain amount of emotional detachment. So when Bernd dropped round for a coffee following a cancelled appointment, she was quick to grasp how she was cast in the plot. Jasper was waiting nervously outside New Street station to be collected. When the old BMW rounded the corner, he was relieved to see that Candy was indeed on board and, by the look of her, entirely ready for action.

It was a short ride to St Brad's Cathedral, during which time Jasper ran through the plan one last time. Candy listened politely, but as she did this sort of thing for a living, she didn't learn much. They pulled into the multistorey car park over the road and Candy stepped out. She brushed herself down and carefully adjusted the transmitter in her bra. Jasper had wisely decided not to tell Annie about this part of the plan. Firstly, it didn't seem wise to worry her, and secondly, she might not appreciate him driving around Birmingham with an attractive sex worker. Death was a strong word and ruptured testicles were two more...

Candy strode into the cathedral and headed down the aisle to the steps of the altar. She was raised as a Catholic, so she was aware of the layout. She knelt down, took out her lace handkerchief and began to sob loudly. A few moments passed and then she became aware of a door opening to her right. Then soft air cushioned footsteps approached, whereupon a voice said:

"My child, what's the reason for those sad tears?"

She turned and, as expected, Bishop John Manzoni stood beside her in his best shirt and collar. Another man who had a train to catch today.

"Oh, bishop," she wailed. "I've made such a mess of things and I don't know what to do."

"Oh, come now, child, things are seldom as bad as they seem. A trouble shared is a trouble halved. Why not sit beside me here and tell me all about it? Then

God and I can help you find a solution," said the bishop in a soothing voice, gesturing towards the pews, then walking over to one and sitting down.

Candy tried hard to look as if she was thinking about telling him something, but in fact he had said exactly what she wanted him to say. Slowly she rose from her knees and allowed him his first full-length view of her. She was slim and in her mid-thirties, with shoulder-length blonde hair turned up at the ends. Her a red wrap-style dress had just a hint of a camisole top showing in her cleavage. Her dark stockings, patent high-heeled shoes and large round glasses accentuated her deep blue eyes and completed the Slutty Sunday-School Teacher look. Her make-up was flawless, her perfume intoxicating and her full red lips quivered when she spoke as she walked over to sit next to him.

"Bishop, I had a great job as a sales advisor at a car dealership and I worked very hard to hit my sales targets. However, I became close to my boss, who was an attractive, slightly older man like yourself. Recently I confessed my feelings to him, but he didn't feel the same way and I was so embarrassed that I left my job. Now I'm alone once again and out of work. I have no idea how I will find another job or how I will pay my rent…"

"Damn, she's good!" said Jasper, listening in on the receiver in the car outside. "You have no idea just how good," replied Bernd, who definitely seemed more laid back than usual to Jasper.

"What is your name, child?"

"Celine," replied Candy, running her tongue over her luscious lips.

"Well, Celine, I may be able to help you with more

than one of your problems."

"How would you be able to do that, bishop? Have you got a vacancy for a nun?"

"My child, it would be such a great pity to hide your beauty behind a nun's habit. No, I have a sales opportunity with a company that I run called Roman Candles. You might have heard of it?"

"That's your company!" exclaimed Candy, switching to full flattery mode. "They were my mother's favourite candles before she died. She collected every one of your Miniature Saint series."

The bishop really couldn't believe his luck. Celine was his dream girl.

1. Catholic
2. Gorgeous
3. Appeared to appreciate older men
4. Dressed in a way that appealed
5. Needed a job
6. Loved candles
7. Wasn't married to God, so hopefully not eternally wracked with guilt and obsessed with the irrational need to drop him in it by confessing all.

The bishop thought fast. His train was at 3 pm and it was 1 pm now. He gave himself an hour for the seduction, thirty minutes for the sex and thirty minutes to get to the station. It was a tall order, but if he could seduce a nun, he was certain he could charm a jobless bimbo.

"The storeroom is across there," he said, pointing to the door to the Lady Chapel. "Why don't we see how many of the Miniature Saint series candles you can remember? Then we can see about offering you a job as a senior sales coordinator."

Jasper laughed. "He's actually gone for it!" he said. He couldn't help thinking that Bernd looked slightly less happy about it than him. "Wunderbar" said Bernd glumly.

Candy and the bishop were now in the Lady Chapel, and the door had been locked from the inside. Candy was marvelling at everything and anything, relentlessly stroking the clergyman's ego. After around fifteen minutes of endless flattery, the bishop was ready to make his move and Candy knew it. She knew men like a good butcher knows bangers. Every man has different packaging, but underneath the wrapper, it's all about the sausage. Her brief was to keep him keen but at arm's length for as long as possible, and that's exactly what she intended to do.

Back in the car, Bernd couldn't stand it any longer. He had admired Candy from afar for quite some time. It was bad enough that he had to listen to her Pretty Woman routine through the wall. Now he was going to have to hear it all in glorious digital audio. Before picking Jasper up, he had confessed his feelings to Candy. She realised that he was a lonely old man far from home and had gifted him a 'mercy thrilling'. To her, it was a random act of kindness. To Bernd, it was definitely the start of a relationship. He opened the door of the car and got out. Standing outside a cathedral seemed a strange place to have your heart trampled on. He was right back in the bakery with Renate all those years ago, except here he had no cakes to throw. Then, over the road, he spotted a familiar figure in black and immediately knew exactly what to do.

"Sister Brady!" he called over. Sister Brady stopped, waved back, and waited for him to cross. She was on her way to wave Bishop Manzoni off from New Street station and was then meeting a friend for lunch in the

Grand Central shopping centre, above the station.

"Sister, have you seen Bishop Manzoni? I need to speak to him urgently regarding a personal matter, but I can't find him anywhere."

"Have you looked in the cathedral?" replied the nun, now looking puzzled.

"Yes, he's nowhere to be seen. I've looked everywhere..."

"Have you tried the Lady Chapel? He may be in there preparing for a big meeting he has tomorrow."

"No, Sister, I haven't. Could you show me where that is?"

"Of course. Follow me." She turned and walked purposefully across the paved frontage of the cathedral with Bernd following in her wake. Through the door and across the foyer, then along the right-hand side of the pews and over to the door to the Lady Chapel. Turning the handle, she found that, of course, it was locked. Taking a large bunch of keys from her habit, she unlocked the door and walked right in.

By now, Bishop Manzoni had progressed in his efforts to ensnare the rather delightful Celine. She was seated on an armchair entirely created from boxes of candles, legs akimbo, with the bishop enthusiastically nuzzling her neck. Bernd, on entering the room behind the nun, was relieved to see that things hadn't progressed any further, whereas Sister Bridget Brady immediately came to the realisation that she'd been a total fool and that the bishop was happy to share his candle with pretty much anyone.

"On our special candle chair? You dirty feckin'

bastard!" she roared.

The bishop was not expecting visitors. He was only expecting to make a delivery, so the hullabaloo that was breaking out behind him startled him. As he turned to face the door, his previous enjoyment of the situation was now plain for all to see. The front of his black trousers now resembled a horizontal Isis circus tent, but now his face was contorted by horror rather than ecstasy. His perilous situation quickly became apparent. Had he spent more time getting to know his ecclesiastical conquests, he would have known that Sister Brady had five elder brothers and until her late teens had been a gifted martial arts student. She hadn't hit anyone for over twenty years, mainly because she hadn't needed to. Admittedly, there's not much call for it when you're married to God and the Holy Ghost is your brother-in-law.

So if the bishop hadn't expected the rising punch to the head, he certainly wasn't anticipating the roundhouse kick to the cock. Furthermore, as the bishop fell to the floor, Sister Brady followed through with a close-quarter chop to the neck just for good measure. The bishop was now out cold, and Sister Bridget Brady had a lunch date to get to. With tears streaming down her face, she bowed like Bruce Lee and made for the door, vanishing as quickly as she'd arrived. Candy looked at Bernd, then they both gawped at the unconscious bishop. Bernd knew Sister Brady probably wasn't going to be too happy, but he didn't bargain on her being an undercover Shaolin nun either!

Candy was the first to act, putting the bishop into the recovery position and checking he was breathing. Bernd went through his pockets, removing both his keys and his mobile phone just as a familiar voice from the door said, "I hope you won't think me rude. But can I ask what you are doing?"

Then, true to form, without waiting for an answer, Valerie Bradley followed that with, "You're not really from the Vatican, are you?"

"Sorry, Valerie, no I'm not. But if you can make sure that he stops here till noon tomorrow, I guarantee that you will soon have a new boss and Bishop Pantsdowni will probably be the new priest on Anthrax Island."

Valerie took a couple of seconds to consider Bernd's proposition, then said, "No problem, you can count on me!" before unplugging the phone from the wall and taking the bishop's keys and phone from Bernd.

"That's the spirit. You won't regret it."

"I sincerely hope I won't," she said, locking the Lady Chapel door from the outside and going off to find some long cable ties and her 'Closed for Maintenance' sign from the cellar.

As Candy and Bernd walked back to the car, Candy gave Bernd's hand a little squeeze and said, "You didn't have to do that, I'm a big girl."

"I know, that's exactly why I did it…" replied Bernd, smiling bashfully.

Back in the car, Bernd and Candy tried to do justice to events in the cathedral. Jasper decided that fate had a way of improving their plans, or maybe today it was just God cleaning his house.

Chapter 11

If changing into costume in the toilets of a moving train wasn't an easy job, applying facial prosthetics had been nearly impossible. But after thirty minutes locked in the same tiny cubicle, they managed it. Kenneth had been transformed into Bishop John Manzoni and Annie had taken the role of his now-former friend with benefits, Sister Bridget Brady. When they eventually emerged like butterflies from a chrysalis, they raised a couple of eyebrows amongst the other passengers given the amount of time they had been in there and the amount of loud, filthy swearing that Annie did during the process. As their train finally pulled into Euston Station, they got a text from Jasper that told them phase one of their operations was now complete. It simply read 'Burn Again 1 – Roman Nil'.

The taxi ride to the hotel that would be their base for the second part of their outrage passed without incident. Shop Until You Drop Television had recommended it to the real bishop in their emails, as it was in easy walking distance of the studio. Annie was quite enjoying the respect that being dressed as a nun afforded her, plus the habit was rather flattering and comfortable. Perhaps she would look into black being her new colour? After all, it seemed to be quite popular in the Middle East. Obviously the women there were very liberated and the men clearly didn't get a say in what they wore.

Kenneth was living the dream. He was dressed as a bishop and entirely in character. He had decided on a slightly toned-down version of Marlon Brando, which came with an unintentional side order of Julian Clary. On the downside, he had stupidly forgotten the cotton wool balls to pad his cheeks out, but there was still time to find some before the curtain went up tomorrow. As Sister Annie lugged the heavy box of samples and their bags into reception, Bishop

Kenneth swanned out in front of her, bestowing blessings on guests and hotel employees as he passed. He was a vision in red and black with swishing sleeves, swinging chains, a false nose and far too much make-up for a serious clergyman.

The male receptionist viewed them with some interest as they crossed the foyer towards him. When Kenneth unexpectedly thrust out his hand, his interest quickly became bewilderment.

"Kiss the ring!" barked Annie like a giant penguin enforcer.

The receptionist did as he was told with an understandable degree of awkwardness while maintaining fearful eye contact with Annie.

"We have a room booked in the name of Bishop John Manzoni," drawled Kenneth, as if he was ordering a Godly Mafia hit.

"Err, yes, we've been expecting you, bishop. Everything is exactly as you requested. Will you be dining in the restaurant this evening?"

"No, I think we will order room service, as it's been a rather long day," replied Kenneth. Annie was secretly relieved, as in this light, he resembled a papal version of Widow Twanky. The make-up was a bit fierce, to say the least.

"As you wish, Your Excellency." Then the receptionist clicked his fingers and a bellboy appeared with a trolley to take their bags and the heavy box of samples.

When they got to their room, the bellboy opened the door, took in their bags and lingered expectantly by the door while they drank in the full ambience of their accommodation. It was large and luxurious by any standard. But when you're accustomed to a high-rise council flat in Oldbury, it was out of this world. Sumptuous deep-pile carpet, padded wall panels, a large chaise longue, an enormous flat-screen telly, fluffy robes plus a spectacular view. It was perfectly appointed in every way, had it not been for the enormous round double bed with champagne on ice and two glasses on the bedside table.

"Why is he waiting?" whispered Kenneth, as they took it all in.

"He's waiting for a tip," hissed Annie.

"Never date a hairdresser, unless you want your heart broken," said Kenneth wisely, forgetting for a second that he was supposed to be a bishop.

The bellboy looked at Annie, sighed in resignation and withdrew, closing the door behind him. She somehow got the feeling they might be carrying their own stuff in the morning. Kenneth walked over to the champagne, popped the cork and poured each of them a glass. Handing one to Annie, he proposed a toast.

"Here's to success tomorrow and God bless Bishop John Manzoni for his unashamedly decadent taste!"

Annie did her champagne in one gulp and poured herself another glass. She had never really understood the concept of sipping, especially in regard to free alcohol. Kenneth had now moved into the bathroom and was enjoying the excellent acoustics with a loud rendition of 'The Magic Flute'. *A Freudian slip*, thought Annie, smiling inwardly at how witty she was. Now she had two major concerns – one was the location of the minibar, the other was the room service menu. Because tonight Annie intended to give both of them a severe bending…

Leipzig 1978

Bernd Tost took some time to move on from the shock of losing Renate. He had a few casual encounters as he continued to play with Blitzkrieg Bullshit, but he didn't find anyone who made him feel the way that she had done. So he continued to work with his father in the family's bakery café while time rolled past aimlessly…

Whenever possible, the East German state had always liked to point out the failings of the West German state. So the rise of the Baader–Meinhof Gang became a big news item behind the Iron Curtain. Scarcely a week went by without news of a bank robbery, assassination attempt or bomb attack across the Berlin Wall. Bernd followed the news bulletins with some interest. For a twenty-four-year-old punk with nothing in his future except dough and hot ovens, it all seemed very exciting…

One afternoon, Bernd was serving behind the counter as usual in the little bakery. In between serving customers, he would watch the television that he had persuaded his father to install. His argument had been that they would sell more, as people wouldn't sit with an empty cup or plate if they were engrossed in a TV programme. What he didn't say was that it made his life more bearable. It provided a little window into the rest of the world, which provided a distraction from his otherwise mundane daily existence. Of course, Dieter knew this. He completely understood his son's restlessness, as every father does. He prayed it would pass when he met a nice girl, but hopefully not another greedy fucker with a comedy haircut who would attempt to eat them into the poorhouse.

When the customer entered the shop, Bernd barely noticed him at first. He wore an unremarkable brown suit, matching tie, glasses and a trilby hat. He came up to the counter, ordered cake and coffee and sat down. Bernd made his coffee and put the cake onto a little cardboard plate while watching the latest Baader–Meinhof news bulletin with one eye as he did so. When he took the food and drink over to the customer, he became aware that the customer was studying him closely…

"What do you think of all this Baader–Meinhof business?" enquired Mr Brown Suit.

Bernd wasn't used to being asked for his opinion. He tended to be a listener, an attribute which had been greatly enhanced during his time with Renate. She would instantly go off on one if anyone challenged her views. Bernd quickly realised that keeping his mouth shut made their relationship more harmonious and got his dolphin waxed with greater regularity. But he'd heard enough political ravings to write a book, so for once he didn't hold back…

"I think that they're showing all loyal East Germans that capitalism is to be despised and should be fought in all quarters. By exposing US imperialism and the coercive forces of a still-fascist society, they are simultaneously demonstrating the vulnerability of the West German state. I think they are heroes and should be lauded and not hunted like criminals." Bernd shocked himself with his seamless pseudo-political rant. His father would have been very proud had he not been snoozing in a chair in the bakery during his outburst.

Mr Brown Suit looked suitably impressed. Here was a loyal and intellectual East German youth who understood the fundamental reasoning for an insurgent armed struggle against the West German government. Not only that, but he looked the part of a weedy revolutionary, with his pipe-cleaner legs and pale complexion. Little did Bernd know, but he had just bought a ticket out of the bakery...

Six months later, Bernd was on a train from Rotterdam to Frankfurt. He'd never been outside East Germany in his life. Now he'd been in three countries in two days. He could scarcely believe his luck. He passed the selection process with flying colours. Every time he was asked an in-depth question regarding his political beliefs, he just gobbed out a load of guff that he remembered from Renate and her mates. The more complicated and nonsensical it was, the better they seemed to like it. How many ways could you say capitalism bad, communism good or West bad, East good, for fuck's sake? It really wasn't hard to work out what they wanted you to say. So he just said it, on the hour, every hour.

During his time at basic training camp, Bernd had received 'guerrilla-style' weapons and explosives instruction. He had no intention of killing anyone, or in any way putting into practice what he had learned. He just knew that in order to get out of East Germany, he had to look as if he was totally committed to the cause. His was a Black Ops mission, total deniability. Join Baader–Meinhof and cause chaos in the West. If he was captured then he was on his own. Yet, unbeknown to the Stasi, Bernd was a member of another radical organisation, The Bernd Tost Liberation Front. The primary objective: having a really good time!

Just being in Frankfurt was exciting in itself. He walked around the old town centre and marvelled at the open-fronted shops, full of goods and produce. He was amazed that there were no queues and if you had the money for something, you could just buy it. No rationing, no coupons required, even a choice of brands! Just how many people wore jeans surprised him. The East German government proclaimed that they were a symbol of the West, so they were frowned upon. If you had the chance, you bought them from sympathetic tourists, or those hard-nosed dealers in the flea markets if you were flush. If this was capitalism, he thought, no wonder it was so popular!

Bernd had to make contact with his handler at Frankfurt Zoo, which was a short walk from the old town. He had 100DM in his wallet and a further 50DM in each sock, as instructed by the course instructor. He didn't really understand the reason for that as everyone here seemed to be quite wealthy and 200DM wasn't a fortune by any means. It seemed unlikely to him that even a capitalist mugger would take the trouble to pull off both your socks while robbing you.

Bernd paid for his ticket and pushed through the heavy cast-iron turnstile. He had an hour to kill before his scheduled contact. He seriously thought about running away and making a new life for himself in the West. But he knew that this would lead to state reprisals against his family and their business, so he decided he would play along just long enough to make it look good. Then, when he spotted his chance to vanish, he would. After all, from what he had seen on the news, Baader–Meinhof was a tad chaotic, to say the least. For instance, in 1975 it was revealed that a quantity of mustard gas had gone missing from a US/British army storage facility. Baader–Meinhof immediately claimed to have stolen the gas to release in German cities, which, as you would expect, caused fairly widespread panic throughout the country. Using press releases, they stoked the population's fear by making veiled threats about where they may use it. However, when it was discovered that the gas had in fact been mislaid during a stocktake and not stolen as originally feared, they looked more than a little stupid. It took a couple of fairly disorganised shootings and a calamitous violent kidnapping before they were reinstalled at No. 1 in the Terrorist Hit Parade. They might be chaotic, but they were still fairly nasty with it...

After wandering around the zoo for forty-five minutes and enjoying a delicious capitalist ice cream, he thought it was probably time for him to make his way to the rendezvous at the monkey house. He sat down on the lone red bench as instructed, facing the mesh of the cage opposite, behind which half a dozen primates jumped, squawked and squabbled, making the time pass quite comically. At precisely 12 noon, Bernd felt the bench bump beside him. Casting a sideways glance, he could make out the female form now seated next to him. *Things*, he thought, *are definitely looking up...*

Chapter 12

It was now 3 am in Bishop Kenneth and Sister Annie's luxurious hotel suite, and the decimated contents of the minibar now lay scattered around the room. The only items to survive the onslaught were the bitter lemons and the pistachio nuts. Next to the dining table were two service trolleys that had previously groaned under the weight of the food on them. Annie had never had lobster before, but she'd had Scampi Fries, so she had a vague idea that she would like it. As a matter of fact, she liked it so much, she'd had two. Unable to decide on a choice of dessert, Kenneth had hit upon the idea of ordering one of everything, a decision that owed more to the contents of the minibar than any attempt at a gastronomic journey of discovery. Once again, the room service waiter had lingered for a tip. Anticipating this before his arrival, Annie had decided on "Don't wipe your arse on a broken bottle…" Given that this was slurred by an inebriated nun with garlic butter around her mouth, swigging from a half bottle of Campari, it seemed sensible to forgo a financial reward for simply pushing a trolley.

Following their main course and copious refreshments, it was only natural to be curious about what televisual treats they could enjoy on the rather large television. It didn't take long for them to discover that there were channels specifically aimed at 'lonely travellers'. As their tastes lay at different ends of the adult entertainment spectrum, they made use of the split-screen feature, which is perhaps another reason why the trolley dolly felt disinclined to linger for a tip. A nun and a bishop engrossed in 50 inches of flat-screen 'end-to-end' hardcore porn would trigger anyone's survival instinct.

At last the room was hushed, the silence only broken by the sounds of slumber. Kenneth now lay spread-eagled, face down, on the round double bed. Annie had realised despite her intoxication level that a night spent dodging Kenneth's snow-angel dreams might be less than restful, so she was lying on her back, snoring loudly in her bra and pants on the chaise longue. At this point in the proceedings, an orderly 10 am arrival at SUYD television still seemed entirely possible. That was until a loud knock at the door shattered the silence…

"Bishop Manzoni?" called a plummy voice.

Kenneth didn't stir. He was neither a bishop nor a Manzoni. Admittedly, he was an experienced thespian, but then even Robert De Niro doesn't method act in his sleep.

"Bishop Manzoni?" The knocking became louder and the voice more frantic.

Annie stirred and realised she needed two things. One was a wazz, and the other was for that twat to stop banging on the door. She rolled off her Dralon gurney onto all fours and decided which she needed most. The wazz soon won hands down.

"Just a minute!" she called on her way back from the bathroom. Still nothing from Kenneth, so she licked her finger and thrust it into his ear. This was 'rise and shine' improvisation at its very best. Kenneth immediately stirred and Annie told him to get the door while she put her habit back on. As he slowly peeled his face from the bed, his make-up left a Kenneth-inspired version of the Turin Shroud on the bedspread. Stumbling to the door and opening it a crack, he found the night manager standing there.

"I'm so sorry to bother you at this unearthly hour," he said, taking a backward step as Kenneth's triple-distilled breath burned his eyebrows off. "We have a guest who has been taken seriously ill at the hotel.

There's a doctor in attendance who has informed us that in his opinion the situation is terminal. Understandably, the guest's wife is distraught and wishes him to receive the Last Rites from a priest before his passing. The hotel wondered if you might be prepared to provide this service, as otherwise he might die before we are able to secure the services of our local priest?"

At 3 pm, this would have been a tricky situation. At 3 am, after demolishing a minibar and working his way through the entire dessert menu, this was a mighty tall order. Kenneth swayed a little and belched before Sister Annie ripped open the door and uttered the immortal words "Take us to the stiff…!"

Minutes later, the nun, the bishop and the manager entered the room of Ronald Brooks, an elderly American tourist from New York. His wife was seated at his bedside, and a rather young doctor wearing a stethoscope stood at the foot of the bed. To the trained spiritual professional, this was a delicate situation. To a half-cut bogus bishop with smudged make-up, this was a fucking calamity! Kenneth was neither Catholic nor a churchgoer. He'd heard of the Last Rites, but he'd never actually heard the Last Rites, so he had no clue about what was actually done or said. Sensing his utter bewilderment, Annie hit on the idea of providing comfort to Mrs Brooks, thus attempting to take a little of the focus off Kenneth while he got his 'priest' on. So she moved around the bed and held the hand of his soon-to-be-widowed wife, who was now gently sobbing as her husband's life ebbed away.

There was an awkward pause of several seconds before Kenneth's inner thespian eventually kicked in. He realised that it was fairly unlikely that anyone else present had actually heard the Last Rites either, largely based on the reasoning that they clearly weren't dead. So if he could utter something unintelligible with a decent flow, that would most likely keep the love in the room, thus preventing them from being exposed for the obvious charlatans that they were and entirely blowing tomorrow's mission. He stepped forward and placed his hand on the brow of the dying man. Bowing his head, he began to mutter in the style of a Benedictine monk on speed the only speech he knew by heart, the flamboyant closing monologue from the stage play he written about his own life, A Little Boy from Oldbury…

"They all laughed and said I could never do it. That someone born in rags from the backstreets of a town where the canals were filled with tears from a million broken dreams, could never be a star. But now here I am, proving them all wrong. A national treasure adored by millions and known the world over. And this is where it all began, St Mabel's Church Hall. This was my place, my stage, my beginning. So now I'm here to give something back and help you to dance your way into the world. That's my gift to you Oldbury, my love, my sweat, my talent! Amen."

As he finished, he made the sign of the cross on the forehead of the recipient, who was now fading fast, then crossed himself, and to his utter amazement Mrs Brooks did the same. She was closely followed by Annie, who did it backwards, which luckily no one appeared to notice. A few moments later, Ronald passed into the afterlife, where no doubt Saint Peter had serious reservations about his entry paperwork…

Five hours later, the Holy Duo were standing in reception at SUYD, now rather the worse for wear thanks to their overindulgence and unexpected lack of sleep. Annie had dutifully dragged the large box of samples over from the hotel on a 'commandeered' baggage trolley, which she'd quietly dumped in their car park. The effort required really hadn't done anything to improve her appearance. Kenneth was also a little green around the gills. He had been unable to track down any cotton wool, so he had stuffed his cheeks with some mini marshmallows he had found amongst the tea-making equipment in their suite. *It's going to take a miracle in make-up to make these two shine*, thought the receptionist as she passed them their lanyards.

"Hi, and a warm welcome to SUYD," said the female production assistant, breezing into the reception area. "My name is Bernie and I'll be helping you to find your way around. Our first stop, of course, will be meeting your presenter. From there we will go into hair and make-up to get you camera-ready and then onwards to the green room to allow you a little time to relax. Then finally into the studio for your live presentation, which I'm sure you'll find very easy. After all, you're obviously God's presenters, aren't you?" Annie didn't feel a great connection to God at this point, but for once she let it slide without comment. Kenneth was beginning to find his feet, but his Brando was far more Clary this morning. "Lead the way, Cupcake," he chortled. "I'm ready to meet my public." If Bernie was surprised to be called Cupcake by a bishop, she certainly didn't show it.

Bernie took them out of reception and down an entirely white corridor. The majority of the doors they passed had names on them. No Brians or Brendas here – it was all Kierans and Claudias. Bernie came to a door marked Cindy Miller and knocked quietly before entering and greeting the occupant in a rather theatrical manner. The dressing room was small and the lady in question was seated at a mirror while a younger woman was applying her make-up. Bernie indicated for them to stand on each side of the mirror so that their introduction could take place in the reflection.

"Cindy, I would like you to meet Bishop John Manzoni and Sister Bridget Brady," said Bernie enthusiastically, "who are representing Roman Candles on the show with you today."

Cindy's face lit up like a 6 am teasmade to reveal an unfeasibly white set of teeth that gave the impression her filler-enhanced lips struggled to close over them at night.

"How lovely to meet you. I've been a big fan of your products for many years. My grandmother loves them," she lied. She'd never previously heard of Roman Candles, and her grandmother hadn't spoken to her for twelve years. True to form, Annie instantly disliked her. She could smell bullshit from the next field, and Cindy was full of it. But she smiled meekly and bowed slightly in a humble nun fashion.

"Oh, and it's fantastic to meet you," cooed Kenneth. "You've been my favourite SUYD presenter for years." Cindy knew this was cobblers as she'd only been there six months. Prior to that, she'd been a singer and occasional quiz compère on a cruise ship. "There's only so many times you can sing 'Sailing' so I jumped ship" was her standard gag when discussing her previous entertainment background.

"How marvellous! A fan! I just know that we are going to sell a lot of candles together," smarmed Cindy. She then raised her open hand to her chest, which was a prearranged signal to Bernie to clear the room of plebs. She always insisted on a cup of lapsang souchong and ten minutes of Buddhist chanting before curtain-up.

"Well, time for us to go and see Marvin in hair and make-up," interjected Bernie, who had grown accustomed to Cindy and her pretentious superstar ways. She'd seen them all come and go over the years. The more grounded they were, the longer they lasted around their grumpy CEO. In her opinion, Cindy the Diva was well past her 'yell bye date'.

"Fantastic to touch base. Say hello to Marvin for me," gushed Cindy as Bernie ushered them out of the door.

In reality, Marvin Littleman and Cindy Miller disliked each other intensely due to a disagreement from that year's staff Christmas party that had been sparked by someone asking what they should do with the bone from their turkey leg. A tipsy Marvin had thought it amusing to suggest loudly that they should throw it under the table for Cindy. Cindy responded by likening Marvin's hair transplant to a saucer of cress growing on top of an under-inflated brown leather football. Since then, she had been allocated her own make-up artist and Marvin had both gained a collection of wacky hats and addressed his fake tan addiction. He believed the flamboyant headgear added to his larger-than-life persona, but in reality, it just covered his pathetic cranial salad bar.

When Bernie, Kenneth and Annie entered his room, Marvin was slumped in his make-up chair Facetiming his mum on his iPad. Today he was wearing a rather large luminous-green bowler hat similar to the ones worn by Ken Dodd's Diddy Men. This made him look as though he had an alien's spaceship on his head. On seeing them enter in the mirror, he ended the call and greeted them warmly.

"Good morning, Bernie! Who do you have for me here?" he chirped.

"This is Bishop John Manzoni and Sister Bridget Brady from Roman Candles, and they are going to be presenting Today's Special Value with Cindy."

"Oooh, how wonderful. I'm going to make you both look a million dollars. What lovely hair you have, bishop. The grey at the temples is so distinguished."

Kenneth always responded well to flattery. But when it was coming from his very own hair and make-up artist, who just happened to be just his type, his flirting went into overdrive.

"Oh, I bet you say that to all the boys!" He swooned once again, forgetting he was supposed to be Lothario-style Italian bishop rather than an ageing camp thespian with delusions of grandeur.

"Well, I'll leave you guys in Marvin's capable hands for the magic to happen. I have a couple of things to check on in the studio. Marvin, please ring me when you're all done…"

"Sure thing…" replied Marvin quizzically, staring hard at the bishop's nose (if you'll pardon the pun).

Bernie left the room, closing the door behind her. Marvin had worked in make-up for around twenty-five years, spending many years at Pinewood Studios, where he'd majored in special effects make-up. So, as you would expect, he knew a false nose when he saw one. A few more seconds passed before Marvin spoke…

"Right, my love, you are clearly one of Dorothy's friends, which I'm pretty sure rules you out as a Catholic bishop even in these enlightened times." Looking at Annie, he said, "And if you're a nun, I'm Mother Teresa." He laughed. "So do you want to tell me exactly what's going on, or do I have to call security?"

Annie totally understood straight talking, so while Kenneth stammered, she just spat the whole story out. Instead of being outraged, Marvin laughed. He really hated Cindy as she had made his life very unpleasant since Christmas. He had bitterly regretted his throwaway comment at the Christmas party and had tried to apologise several times since, but Cindy wouldn't allow him to, as she loved to hold a grudge and watch him squirm. He'd just had too many rainbow sangrias and had stupidly decided to make Cindy the butt of his gag. But as his mother had just told him when he was whining about it yet again, "People in thatched houses shouldn't throw bones". Now he could watch Cindy's new presenting career explode from the sidelines. Oh, what fun…

"Right, get in the chair, bishop. You're going to get a masterclass in facial prosthetics, and for pity's sake spit those marshmallows out. You're starting to drool."

Thirty-five minutes later, the bogus Bishop John Manzoni looked a great deal more authentic thanks to Marvin's talents and the excellent photos on the Roman Candles website they got up on his iPad. His nose was a perfect facsimile, and now his cheeks were padded with closed-cell foam from a make-up sponge. In addition, Annie now resembled Julie Andrews in her Sound of Music heyday. She was so pleased she took a selfie and sent it to Jasper. She wasn't so happy when he replied, "Who's this?"

Marvin wished them both good luck and said he would be watching the live feed with interest. Then he called Bernie to say that the Holy Duo were finished in make-up.

"Oh, don't you both look amazing!" gushed Bernie, sweeping in with her clipboard. "He is just so talented…"

Marvin winked at Kenneth as they left the room. Kenneth decided to add him on Facebook and really hoped he liked cats.

"Right, here's the green room. Make yourself comfortable and try to relax. Just ask the server for anything that you would like to drink. You're live in forty minutes. Your sample box is on set and someone will come in to mike you up just before you go on. Good luck!"

Annie scanned the room. There were a couple of other guests waiting to go on. One was a man with grey hair and a bald patch. He was talking to a blonde lady and seemed to gesticulate with his hands quite a lot.

"Bugger me, that's Austin Ripert!" exclaimed Kenneth a little too loudly.
Austin turned and smiled.

"Good morning, bishop," he said cheerfully.

Annie religiously watched all Austin's endlessly repeated fish cookery programmes despite only having a 'boil in the bag' and 'battered' relationship with fish.

"Where's Gurnard the cat?" she inquired.

"Still dead!" he replied icily, turning back to his conversation with Pamela Golden, who was boring him shitless about tit tape and Botox.

"Nice one!" hissed Kenneth, who had always had a soft spot for the Foxy Fish Fryer.

"What are you drinking, Austin?" said Kenneth, creeping.

"Sauvignon Blanc," came the reply.

"Two halves of sauvignon blanc," said Annie to the server, who laughed haughtily at her unintentional joke, as did Austin and Pamela, then quickly brought them two small glasses from the open bottle on the bar. Kenneth made a big show of taking a sip then swooshing it around his mouth like a proper wine ponce, while Annie did half the glass in one glug. She would have usually downed it in one, but she was on her 'best behaviour'.

"What do you think?" probed Austin.

"Rather fruity, crisp on the palate, quite a young wine if I'm not mistaken?" replied Kenneth, giving it the full Oz Clarke from 'Food and Drink'.

"Taste's a bit like Um Bongo to me," said Annie, giving it the full Oz Osbourne from 'Auf Wiedersehen Pet'.

Again Austin turned away and shrugged to Pamela. He was only here to plug his overpriced wine selection to bored middle-class housewives. Camp bishops and tubby nuns weren't really his market. As long as they didn't say it was shit, it was money in the bank.

Another production assistant wearing headphones entered the room and soon spirited the King of the Crustaceans off to his recording suite, leaving Pamela Golden looking like she was trying to join the convent amidst another painful lull in the conversation. She skilfully avoided their gaze and began to get busy on her phone.

Annie didn't really like Pamela Golden, mainly because she'd got more plastic in her face than

Action Man's mum. So she decided to have a little fun....

"I know why you enjoy talking to Austin."

"Why would that be?" replied Pamela, not looking up from her phone.

"Because he reminds you of your first fella?"

Pamela immediately stopped looking at her phone and fixed Annie with an icy glare. She didn't like being reminded of her ex-husband under any circumstances.

"If you weren't a nun, I'd tell you where to go..."

"Would that be Poundland, same place you get all that tit tape from?"

"Now, now, ladies, try to remember why we're here," said Kenneth, butting in, aware that Annie's temper could quickly escalate and saying this more for her benefit than Pamela's. He needn't have worried. Pamela flounced off to find her PA. She'd done enough Saturday night telly to know a GBH nun when she saw one.

Kenneth laughed. "Cleared the room. Quite the charmer, aren't we?" he said.

"I can't stand her, with all her pigeon-chest dresses. Poor bloke ended up back in the working men's clubs and living in his car. She just chewed him up and spat him out."

At that moment, the door opened and in came a sound technician with two radio mikes.

"Me first!" squealed Kenneth. Annie just rolled her

eyes.

Now on set, Cindy Miller was checking her angles in the monitor and doing her voice warm-up exercises. She was a confident woman with her eye on the top. This was her first Today's Special Value as the resident presenter was on holiday, so she had lobbied the producers relentlessly to get her big chance. Now she finally had it. An hour's prime-time, live TV carrying a couple of amateurs that would really allow her to shine. Her days on the cruise ships were now firmly behind her. No more standards around the piano with a comatose geriatric audience. She was finally going places!

Just as she concluded her tongue-twisting run through, Bernie brought 'Father John Manzoni' and 'Sister Bridget Brady' on to the set. Kenneth was in his oil tot, but Annie was beginning to have her doubts. Not wishing to be seen as a rookie, Kenneth began to engage with Cindy by throwing out a few industry buzzwords. Cindy saw this as the beginnings of a power struggle and decided to set out her stall to leave him in no doubt who was Morecambe and who was Wise.

"Listen, John. Can I call you John?" She didn't wait for an answer, she just ploughed on.

"This is feeding time at Seal World in the form of television. I hold the fishes up and you just jump up and eat them. You don't need to overthink anything. Just answer my questions and roll with the punches. That way we will make great television and get a lot of candles sold. I've read all your sales literature, so I know the answers to the questions before I even ask them. Therefore, we both know what's going to be said before you say it. You can just stand around and look holy." Cindy pointed at Annie. "John and I will do the talking, you can just pass us the samples and laugh at my quips when required."

Annie had anticipated that she might be relegated to a junior role from their previous encounter in Cindy's dressing room, so she had wisely enjoyed a little sparring with Austin and Pamela in the green room to get her up to operating temperature. She was going to enjoy taking Cindy apart because now it was personal. Nobody put Annie in the corner...

"OK, everyone... Countdown to live transmission... 5, 4, 3, 2, 1..." The director pointed at Cindy, who instantly started talking like the silicone-enhanced android she was.

"Hello, viewers and welcome to Today's Special Value with myself, Cindy Miller, and the lovely people from Roman Candles. Bishop John Manzoni and Sister Bridget Brady, who are here today to show us their fantastic range of ecclesiastical candles. Now, bishop, these are no ordinary fragranced candles, are they? Can you tell me a little bit about them?"

"Hello, viewers, and thank you for that lovely introduction, Cindy. You're quite right, these are special candles in every sense. In the Catholic Church, we light a candle to represent the presence of God when we pray. Quite often those prayers are offered up because of a specific problem that we have in our lives. We at Roman Candles realised that God may respond more favourably if we produced candles that were customised with respect to those reasons for prayer."

"Well, bishop, that's a very interesting concept. So you're saying that you produce candles with particular fragrances and shapes to make our prayers more effective?"

"Yes, that's exactly what I'm saying, Cindy. By

changing the atmosphere in the room when we pray, we can make our prayers more powerful, which I'm sure can positively affect the outcome."

"So have many of your customers had their prayers answered? Can you provide the viewers with some success stories?"

"I would be pleased to, Cindy. Well, in one instance, a lady in my flock found meeting people difficult. She longed for companionship, marriage and a family. But try as she might, she couldn't find the right person. In fact, she found it hard to make friends on any level. I offered her spiritual guidance and she found that the St Drogo candle from our Patron Saints range helped enormously. Within a few weeks, she had met a man and was beginning her matrimonial journey."

"Fantastic. So simply providing her with a candle entirely changed her life?"

"Absolutely. St Drogo is the patron saint of unattractive people, and trust me, she was an absolute fecking minger. She had a face like a baked potato that had been beaten with a barbed wire tennis racket. Without that candle, all she had to look forward to was a life of wrap around cardigans and soap operas."

Cindy was shocked, to say the least. There was no mention of any of this in the literature she had been given to read before the show. However, like the true professional she thought she was, she kept going.

"Wow, there's hope for us all then," she stammered, looking straight at the camera for the '*You'd be mad not to buy one*' shot.

"I also had a young gentleman who came to me with

a personal problem that he felt unable to speak to anyone else about. It was affecting his relationship with his girlfriend and causing him immense pain on a daily basis. Again I listened to his woes and told him of the power of prayer. He took home a St Fiacre candle and within days his pain has subsided and his relationship with his girlfriend was entirely restored."

"What a lovely heart-warming story, bishop. Is St Fiacre the patron saint of love?" inquired Cindy, feeling relieved that the bishop seemed to be back on message.

"No, the patron saint of sexually transmitted diseases. He was lousy with the clap, but God provided antibiotics and protection. So he was soon back down the youth club disco, putting it about behind her back."

Once again the bogus bishop had entirely wrong-footed Cindy. As she searched in vain for an adequate response, Kenneth ploughed on.

"A few months back, one of our parishioners was experiencing issues with his failing business. The fierce local competition was becoming a problem as other local enterprises sought to take his customers. Plus, he was experiencing increased difficulty with legal red tape and tough government legislation, the overall effect of which was an enormous reduction in his income stream. One Sunday he came to me after Mass and explained his problems in some detail. So I provided him with our St Jesus Malverde candle. When I saw him at Mass a couple of weeks later, he told me that his business was thriving again. He'd moved premises to avoid further legal problems and had taken a hard line with the competition, which had reduced their market share considerably. A total success story!"

"Marvellous. All his problems solved by simply buying a candle and lighting it whilst praying for guidance." Cindy felt reassured that this story couldn't possibly have a sting in its tail. "That's amazing! So tell me, what is St Jesus Malverde the patron saint of?"

"Drug dealers…" came the reply.

Annie, meanwhile, had opened the box of samples and passed one to Kenneth, who took it from her and placed it in front of Cindy. It was enormous, pale pink and in the shape of a clenched fist. Cindy welcomed the change in tack, although it was beginning to dawn on her that she was now Ernie Wise and Kenneth was most definitely Eric Morecambe.

"This one is from our brand new Aura range. Candles designed specifically to create the right ambience in the room for relaxation."

"Oh, that's lovely," whimpered Cindy weakly, "Now we all love a candle, don't we, ladies?"

"Not as much as you!" said Annie. But Cindy ignored her and kept digging.

"Does its shape signify that God is holding everyone in his hand?" she suggested, praying to God that it was.

"No, its fist shape actually signifies that it is a masturbation candle. The chosen fragrance of White Linen is designed to be relaxing and to cover any nasty little whiffs post hand shandy. Perfect for a teenager's room or maybe a gift for a bachelor uncle."

Cindy was now firmly on the rollercoaster to YouTube infamy. These people had seemed so easy to work with when she met them earlier. Now they seemed hell bent on not only bankrupting their business and getting themselves excommunicated, but also ending her TV career in the process...

"Oh!" stammered Cindy. "He's such a joker. He wasn't a bit like this earlier. Oh, what have they given you in the green room?"

"Austin Ripert's shite wine and Pamela Golden's nits," Annie piped up while passing Kenneth another enormous candle from the samples box. This one was in the shape of a woman wearing a crown and long flowing robes.

"Ahh, now, Cindy... this is our St Barbara candle. If we just light the wick, dim the studio lights and stand back, we can experience the full majesty of this beautifully crafted 100% red diesel masterpiece," said Kenneth, who whipped a lighter out of his cassock and did the honours with a flourish.

Cindy was now so traumatised she was just going through the motions. The director was screaming loudly in her earpiece as none of the bona fide special value offers had even gained a mention yet. "We have a warehouse groaning with Roman Candles products, and at this rate, none of it is going anywhere!" he bellowed. The whole thing was becoming a total nightmare and Cindy couldn't wait for it to be over. Little did she know that she would soon get her wish...

The floor manager took his cue from Kenneth and lowered the lights as he requested. The candle burned and flickered beautifully, and for just a few seconds order was restored. Sensing the sudden calm, Cindy rallied momentarily and decided that humour might be the way forward.

"So tell me, bishop, is St Barbara the patron saint of

Carry On films?" she joked weakly.

"No. Actually, she's the patron saint of fireworks," replied Kenneth, now visibly retreating.

The first bang was fairly tame as it served mainly as a cue for Kenneth and Annie to begin their escape. Then, as Cindy looked on completely aghast, the St Barbara candle began to erupt like Krakatoa, showering everyone present with fragments of flaming-hot wax. There were two single doors out of the studio, and now the entire production team was trying to get through them all at once. That is, except for Cindy, who now lay on her back in the darkness bawling bitterly as the Roman Candles continued to explode several more times before extinguishing with a sizzle, along with her precious TV career.

If Elsie the Derek Robinson House Crafting Queen had made a fine job of casting Annie's designs for their one-off sample candles, her son Dominic, the owner of a pyrotechnic display business, had made an even better one of installing an industrial firework right in the middle of St Barbara. Designed to thrill a crowd from fifty metres, it had absolutely terrified every fucker present from less than ten!

Twenty minutes later, Kenneth and Annie were dressed as civilians and aboard the 11.54 from London Euston to Birmingham New Street. As the first bang singed Cindy's fake eyelashes, they were already running down the corridor towards the reception area tearing off their holy disguises as they went. Now safely installed in a seat with a table in the buffet car, Annie got out her phone and composed a text to Jasper: 'Burn Again 2 – Roman Nil'. Then she sat back to enjoy the ride home as Kenneth queued for cheese and chutney sandwiches, three bags of Mini Cheddars, two bottles of Magners, plus anything he fancied himself, mainly because this bottle of

Austin Ripert's sauvignon blanc wasn't going to last till Milton Keynes, never mind Birmingham!

The fallout from the totally shambolic appearance of Romans Candles on SUYD was fairly instant. Despite not having SUYD on his papal cable package, the Pope was soon made aware of exactly what had taken place and so sent an envoy from the Vatican directly to Birmingham to gain further insight. He was massively annoyed for two reasons. One was that the Catholic Church had been made to look more than a little ridiculous in footage that was now trending worldwide on YouTube, Facebook and Twitter. The other was that the Vatican hadn't seen a penny of the money that this unsanctioned enterprise had generated. If making the church look stupid was unwise, not 'kicking up' a percentage of your ill-gotten gains to the capo dei capi was practically suicidal.

Bishop John Manzoni had rightfully protested his innocence and strenuously denied being the 'SUYD Cleric'. But that matter aside, the envoy and his audit team soon found a wealth of other matters that meant his cushy city cathedral days were now over. A month later he was cruising at 30,000 feet over Peru on his way to assist in the war on drugs. It was a country where even the priesthood feared the cocaine cartels, and his life expectancy would be linked to keeping his trousers on and writing exactly the right kind of Mass. All went well for a couple of years until another bitterly disappointed nun spoke frankly to her brother. Unluckily for the bishop, he had connections in all the right places and soon arranged for him to get bullets in all the wrong ones. In Birmingham, this would have been front-page news. In Peru, it barely got a mention and so the Catholic Candle Party King was quietly laid to rest alongside a multitude of other dodgy gringos.

A week later, once again, Jasper, Annie and Bernd travelled in large black 4x4 to meet their employer for lunch, the Right Reverend Richard Morris. But this time the venue was a swish coffee shop in Harborne called 2Posh 2Brew. Annie quite liked the sound of that, although she had never been there before. It didn't really sound like a smoked salmon salad sort of place. It spoke to her of tea and cake, which was far more to her liking than slices of greasy redfish.

Knuckles dropped them off in the back car park and they walked through the small courtyard past the alfresco benches to the back door. As instructed by Knuckles, they climbed the stairs to find the Bishop of Birmingham sitting in a booth in a quieter area of the establishment. Annie immediately noticed that he was wearing civvies and had the look of a man who was now enjoying life. He stood and greeted them all warmly with much handshaking and back-slapping.

"An absolutely fantastic job," he chuckled. "I must have watched it a thousand times on YouTube. It was probably the funniest thing I have ever seen. Apart from possibly the Archbishop of Canterbury's Mr Bean impression. He only does it at Christmas and he won't let you film it, but trust me, it's hilarious."

"How's the business now?" enquired Bernd.

"Couldn't be better! The shops are all thriving again. All the Roman Candles stock was immediately seized by Trading Standards, mainly due to the red diesel content, which effectively removed our competition. Now Burn Again Candles are once again the only holy candles on the market!"

"Can we order now?" said Annie boldly, who was utterly bored with candles and anything candle related. "I only had two chocolate Pop-Tarts for breakfast and I'm clammed." This interjection earned her a sideways glare from Jasper, which naturally she ignored and instead got him in a knee death hold under the table. This concluded in him madly shouting "Nasty bitch!" as if he had Tourette's, then smacking his head on the ornate lamp hanging over their table as Annie expertly sent his leg muscles into spasm.

"Oh, Annie, I'm sorry, of course. I particularly picked 2Posh 2Brew as I felt it would be more to your liking," said Reverend Richard, who was cool with the swearing as he had spent the morning at a primary school in West Bromwich.

It was a good call. Annie had seen the groaning counter of cake on the way in. As business meetings go, and she'd only ever been to a couple, this was straight in at number one. The next few minutes passed with everyone looking at the menu except Annie. Jasper chose smashed avocado on sourdough toast (trendy tosser!), Bernd had a croque-monsieur (due to the notable absence of anything German!) and the Right Reverend Richard Morris had poached eggs with smoked salmon on a muffin. Annie decided he was clearly a raw fish-obsessed weirdo and stomped off to make their order at the counter. When she returned, she had a chai latte and a tray of cakes. Only a couple of days previously, she'd asked Jasper what chai latte was. He described it as a frothy, hot-tea milkshake, which had intrigued her. So she thought she'd give it a go, as after all, the Church of England was paying. Sadly, Jasper's description was a bit wide of the mark as it tasted like liquid Shake n' Vac, so she spat it noisily into the vase of flowers on the table before going off to get a Coke and a cappuccino while making noises like a lurcher trying to puke up a particularly furry rabbit.

Eventually, when they had all eaten, the Right Reverend Richard Morris made good on his promise and passed another brown envelope across the table to Jasper.

"Neither God nor myself will forget what you have done for Burn Again Candles. He thanks you for restoring the coffers of the church. I personally thank you for saving me from Skegvegas and the North Sea wind. Therefore, I have also added a further £1,000 to the previously agreed £2,500 to ensure your out-of-pocket expenses are entirely met. Which I hope meets with your satisfaction."

"That is more than generous, bishop. It has been an absolute pleasure to do someone's business with you. Be rest assured that your name will never be linked to our actions in any way and we all hope that God's candle business will continue to prosper. If we can be any help at all in the future, then please don't hesitate to get in touch," said Jasper warmly, shaking his hand once again.

Back at the Eagle's Nest, it was carve-up time. Bernd had become a stickler for accounting and so he had a spreadsheet of their outgoings and money owed to 'suppliers' open on his laptop. Crafting Elsie and her son were awarded £200, Mucky Barry another £50, Kenneth got £500, the return train fare was £150, theatrical costume hire ran to £200, and Candy the Working Girl made £150. Fortunately, the Catholic Church had unwittingly paid for the hotel room, leaving them with a net profit of £4,750. Not bad money for simply knocking out a bishop, emptying a minibar, dispatching an old man to his maker, destroying a TV career, letting off a firework and meeting Pamela Golden and Austin Ripert. Orchestrated chaos was becoming a nice little earner...

When Kenneth had got home from their escapade in London, he found himself thinking about Marvin Littleman a lot. In fact, he had thought of little else during the train ride home. All the excitement of the planning and execution of the sting had given him a new lease of life. Now once again alone in his flat with just his cats for company, he realised how lonely his life had become and how he needed to share it with someone else again. Kenneth hadn't known the love of a good man for five long years. His previous partner, Sebastian, had been a wallpaper designer. They had lived together for fifteen years and had been very happy, or so he thought. Sadly, Sebastian's head was turned by a young plasterer that he met at a DIY store in Halesowen, and soon the 'writhing was on the wall', leaving Kenneth with an irrational dislike for wallpaper and anything spread with a trowel. He agonised about whether he should add Marvin on Facebook, as he seemed so glamorous, with his amazing hats and television work. He didn't know whether his kindness was just professional courtesy or whether he sensed a spark between them.

Meanwhile, one hundred and twenty-five miles away in London, Marvin had just experienced the bollocking to end all bollockings. Once the wax had finally settled at SUYD, the inquest had begun. The CEO simply didn't believe that Marvin, having spent so much time in make-up with the Holy Doppelgangers, hadn't realised that something dastardly was afoot. So when he looked at his browsing history on the SUYD server, his suspicions were confirmed. He was relieved to find that he'd merely spent a disproportionate amount of time on the Roman Candles website, looking at photos of Bishop John Manzoni. He was relieved because he had viewed Marvin's browsing history on a previous occasion during another disciplinary matter and had received extensive counselling afterwards.

Regrettably, there would be no more SUYD Christmas parties for Marvin.

Similarly, Cindy Miller was now on her way to join a ship sailing to the Norwegian fjords. Her complete loss of control on live television had enraged the channel's American owners, and so again the British CEO had no option but to sack her with immediate effect. Cindy was destined to be singing cruising's greatest hits until her bunions were finally too big to get into her wide-fitting stiletto heels.

Kenneth's finger hovered over the 'Send Friend Request' button on his phone. What's the worst thing that could happen? If Marvin rejected him, he would never know. Suddenly coming to the conclusion that he was tired of overthinking everything, he just pressed it and the deed was done. If it was meant to be, then Marvin would accept him. If he didn't, it was back to making eyes at that store assistant in Lush. He had bought so many bath bombs that if his cold water tank burst it would be like a remake of The Blob! As he envisaged the scene as involving a giant sea of fruity fizzing foam engulfing Derek Robinson House, his phone chimed. Marvin had accepted his Friend Request. Now Kenneth was almost certainly the happiest thespian in the whole of Oldbury!

Chapter 13

At first, Bernd found his new life with Baader–
Meinhof a little difficult. It was the exact opposite of
everything that he had known before. They operated
within a cell of seven people and moved around
frequently, as the life of the urban guerrilla was often
nomadic in order to evade capture. They ate
together, planned together and, happily for Bernd,
slept together. The only thing that truly mattered to
the Red Army Faction was fighting the establishment.
Therefore, anything else was considered to be
irrelevant. This was a war, and in war, anything goes.
So drugs and free love were frequently on offer and
Bernd had happily filled his boots for a short while!

But once again Bernd found himself in love. This time
the object of his desire was called Simone, who had
arrived a few weeks after him. She was sturdily built
with long blonde hair, which she often tied up with
traditional headscarves in an attempt to appear more
working class. Her family were wealthy, and she had
received an excellent private education, which
culminated in the opportunity to study politics at the
University of Hamburg. Nevertheless, great learning
can sometimes be problematic in a determined
young head. And within months of starting her
degree, Simone became heavily involved with the
Student Union. Soon she began to organise protests
and demonstrations about anything and everything,
from harsh toilet paper to poor-quality margarine in
the cafeteria. Many of her protests were quite
bizarre, and the university soon gave in to her petty
demands. At the end of the day, sending someone
round to the local supermarket for some soft toilet
paper or a better tub of margarine wasn't nearly as
tricky as negotiating the release of twenty Rhodesian
political prisoners or calling for a halt to the Sino-
Vietnamese War. But then it was hard work being an

ultra-left-wing political activist at the richest university in the country, as, quite honestly, there was very little to complain about.

As a consequence, Simone decided to look outside the campus gates for other opportunities to change the world. Soon she found what she was looking for in Baader–Meinhof and the Red Army Faction. Swapping margarine for a machine gun in order to rid the world of capitalist pigs seemed an easy step up for a privileged young lady herself born to capitalist pigs. Quickly her attendance at university ceased, and she went full time as a debutante terrorist. Regrettably for Simone, the armed revolution might have been in full swing, but the feminist cause wasn't quite so advanced. Her revolutionary efforts were therefore mainly limited to making coffee and cooking, neither of which she was particularly gifted at, as German socialites didn't tend to spend a lot of time in the kitchen. So fellow new recruit Bernd made it his business to help her, as, after all, it was second nature to Strudel Boy and he could see Simone didn't enjoy getting teased about her 'Scheisse Kaffee'.

During the day, their cell cooked, planned attacks, cleaned weapons and talked endlessly of their desire to wage war against anyone with power, status or money. Well, actually Bernd just mainly cooked and listened. He wasn't at all keen on guns and still found politics very tedious. In time he found that there was far more talking done than actual shooting or bombing. They didn't even practice, as gunfire of any sort had a tendency to attract a fair amount of police attention. They quickly arrived in vast numbers with far better guns and occasionally armoured cars or helicopters, so the cell members purposely kept a fairly low profile and did a lot of reconnaissance and loose planning, which thankfully no one ever seemed very keen to act on. This suited Bernd perfectly, as he then had more time to devote to the sexual revolution that he was frequently occupied with in Simone's sleeping bag.

One afternoon, when the leader of their cell arrived back from a meeting with more senior terrorists, he seemed quite agitated and immediately called a cell meeting. Bernd was halfway through preparing goulash and asked if it might be possible for the meeting to be postponed for half an hour. He didn't want to broil the meat and make it tough, so he needed to watch it carefully. The leader agreed that although tough beef in a goulash was more than a little disappointing, he'd just had a gun put to his head and been told he was a 'lazy shit terrorist'. So if Goulash Geek could try to remember why they were all actually here, he would consider it a great fucking favour. Bernd threw his apron down in fury. "You'll all be sorry when you're all picking your teeth like plover birds after dinner tonight!" he fumed.

The newly motivated 'lazy shit terrorist' leader explained that in order to leave the meeting at HQ without an additional nostril, he had been forced to agree to undertake an operation that had been planned by the more senior terrorists. As all junior terrorists know, senior terrorists tend to make plans for junior terrorists that are more dangerous than ones they'd plan for themselves. After all, if you're not going to be there, you don't give a monkey's if the people that are make the ultimate sacrifice for the cause. Taking into account that Bernd's cell had been about as busy as Gandhi's washing machine in recent months, you could see their point.

Now they all sat in a cross-legged circle. They listened as the newly motivated 'lazy shit terrorist' leader explained in detail (or as much as he could recall!) their mission. Until now, Baader–Meinhof had mainly confined their murderous activities to politicians, bankers and rich industrialists. Now, after years of audacious yet fabulously chaotic attacks, many of these people had immeasurably increased their security: bulletproof cars, armed guards, varied daily routes to work etc., etc. So head office had come up with a new breed of target… wait for it… confectioners. Nothing would provoke more outrage against the state than the death of the man responsible for West German children's favourite treat, the Kitz Happy egg – a chocolatey delight that not only tickled capitalist kids' taste buds but also provided the bourgeois recipient with a tiny toy encased in an easy-to-swallow plastic capsule. A product that was so ridiculously perilous that America had seen the need to ban it in all fifty-two states and entirely prohibit its import into their otherwise utterly fucking lethal country.

Bernd had sometimes seen the adverts on West German TV, but that's as far as it went. However, Simone had experienced the immense delight created by the foil-wrapped, tasty two-part treat countless times during her inconveniently luxurious childhood. Despite that, she wholeheartedly agreed that the owner of the factory was indeed a plutocratic pig dog who clearly deserved to die for his crime of selling millions of potential choking hazards. She was pretty sure that he was Italian and not German. Would that not be a problem?

"Ah, that's the really clever bit," said the newly motivated 'lazy shit terrorist' leader, who in fairness to him wasn't entirely convinced that it was clever at all. But he had been swayed in his thinking by the promise of a bullet placed next to his concerns if he felt moved to question the senior terrorist's reasoning. "His death has been sanctioned for crimes against the German language. Basically, 'Kitz' is our word for kids, not theirs. He didn't ask for our permission to use it. So Baader–Meinhof will send a message worldwide. German words are for German products only! Hands off, filthy capitalist foreigners."

"That's going to be a little worrying for the owners of Professor Siegfried's frozen pizzas if the Italian mafia decides on the same course of action," countered Simone.

"What the fuck is frozen pizza?" exclaimed Bernd, whose only experience of convenience food in East Germany was toast and instant coffee.

Three days later, all seven members of Bernd's 'lazy shit terrorist' cell lay in wait in two cars outside West Germany's leading importer of hazardous, German-sounding, plastic-stuffed Italian confectionery. They were in two stolen Citroën 2CVs, which gave them the look of a poorly attended classic car club. However, they were easy to nick and you could stand and fire out of the sunroof, removing the need to actually get out and shoot, which always ran the risk of getting left behind if it all went tits up.

They had been tipped off that the owner of the Kitz 'surprised it's not German' egg factory was planning a visit. The company was planning to launch an entirely new sugar-laden chocolate nut spread that was poised to set new standards in tasty tooth decay worldwide, so he was keen to let the German sales team have a taste so they could accurately describe the cavity-causing cocoa creation to their customers. Soon Germany's only amalgam-filling manufacturer would add a night shift based on a massive increase in demand for their product from dentists all across Germany.

"Why do I have to have the shit gun?" asked Simone, who had an old 9mm Luger with three bullets in it.

"Because you're new and a girl. Machine guns are complicated and require a man's strength to hold them on target. Think yourself lucky. Ingrid in the other car only has a hand grenade," replied the newly motivated 'lazy shit terrorist' leader from the front passenger seat. Bernd was driving, Simone was in the back and they had one seat spare in case things went really well and they decided to kidnap the owner of the Kitz 'surprised it's not German' egg factory instead.

"Has she used a grenade before?" inquired Bernd.

"No, but she's read the instructions a couple of times and she's pretty good at rounders,' replied the newly motivated 'lazy shit terrorist' leader.

"So your whole decision-making process for who gets what weapon is entirely based on outdated sexist stereotyping?" Simone asked, seething. She was really sick of having her coffee-making skills cruelly critiqued by ugly hairy men in flares.

"I hadn't really thought about it like that. But now you come to mention it, I suppose you're right…"

"You do realise that the Russians used women snipers in the Second World War that were far more deadly than some of the men?"

"Yes, but just for three weeks of the month. The other week they killed Nazis just by looking at them," joked the newly motivated 'lazy shit terrorist' leader, which was probably entirely the wrong thing to say to a premenstrual armed terrorist with a crap coffee complex and three bullets.

Utterly enraged for a nanosecond by his blatant chauvinism, Simone promptly shot him through the back of the head with her 9mm Luger. His cranium popped like a porridge-filled watermelon and the bullet exited the tin snail through the front windscreen. Ordinarily, that would have been fine, had it not been for the fact that they were parked immediately behind the other 2CV. The bullet entered the second car through the rear screen and promptly lodged itself behind Ingrid's forehead via her right ear. Again, that wouldn't have been a major problem if she hadn't been holding her grenade with the pin out, in direct contrast to the instructions that she had pretended to read but not entirely digested due to her undiagnosed dyslexia. As Ingrid's word-blind life unexpectedly ebbed away, the primed grenade rolled from her hand. Understandably, this took a couple of seconds to register with the other occupants of her vehicle, which was rather unfortunate, as that left only one second to grab it and chuck it out of the sunroof before it blew them to smithereens. This was a problem in itself as it had rolled under the passenger seat, making it a tad tricky to reach as they were four up and one of them was now a 'bit floppy'. So one further second later, the little 2CV completely disintegrated along with non-reader Ingrid and another three live members of the 'lazy shit terrorist' cell, who, moments later, all rained down in kit form on West Germany's leading importer of German-sounding hazardous plastic-stuffed Italian confectionery.

Bernd took a further moment to reflect on the mission's progress. Five members of the novelty chocolate egg hit squad were now dead, even though only one shot had actually been fired. Simone was clearly very touchy about monthly matters (which he duly noted for future reference) The police had almost certainly heard that bang and would soon arrive with a helicopter and armoured car (depending on traffic!). So he presumed that he was now in charge, as he had been a terrorist for a few weeks longer than Simone. From his understanding of such matters, that gave him automatic superiority, but it seemed wise not to inform her of his very recent self-appointed internal promotion, as she still had another two bullets and apparently no appetite for casual sexism or indeed any respect for authority.

He reached across the now totally demotivated 'lazy shit terrorist' leader and opened the passenger door. Giving him a firm shove in the least brain-spattered area of his shoulder, he rolled him out of the car onto the pavement. He gently removed the handkerchief from the hair of the newly dumbstruck Simone and used it to wipe the mess from the windscreen. He started the little French car's engine, threw the now grisly hair accessory out of the window and calmly drove away.

Chapter 14

Jasper and Annie were enjoying a breakfast treat at the instore coffee shop in the Oldbury branch of Green's hypermarket. Jasper, as ever the eager foodie trendsetter, was enjoying a Haloumi Breakfast, which, if you're not familiar with it, is a fairly industrial Greek cheese that has the texture of set silicone sealant and is entirely similar in taste. Easier to apply than silicone sealant, it is mould resistant, suitable for indoor and outdoor use but only available in mucky white at present. Annie, ever the traditionalist, was shovelling down a Big Breakfast, which was unofficially 50% bigger than advertised thanks to her cousin, who worked in the kitchen and to whom she had sent a text order on arrival. Jasper was also a reluctant party to this casual theft, as he had an extra hash brown and a vegetarian sausage. He would have preferred another slice of rubbery cheese, but sadly its distribution was closely monitored by the jobsworth catering supervisor.

As Jasper was pushing the last bit of wholemeal toast around his eggy plate, he became aware of a pair of eyes watching him. Annie had long since finished and gone to powder her nose, as was typically her habit immediately after her breakfast. Jasper prayed that store maintenance had finally fixed the extractor fan in the ladies, as the previous week, people had hastily moved tables after Annie had been absent for ten minutes or so. This embarrassing situation had not been eased by Annie's custom of making a noise like a foghorn and announcing a danger to vessels in a Radio 4 shipping forecaster's voice when flushing.

Finally, the eyes decided to make a move. Jasper instinctively moved his hand into his coat pocket and grabbed his bingo marker. Not the best weapon to fend off an attack, but if he could get a couple of good splodges in before he went down, it would make the job of identifying his assailant far easier for the police.

The old lady who owned the eyes now looked uncertain whether or not to continue. She wasn't sure why this young man had suddenly looked up at her and grabbed his crotch. Assuming that this was some kind of Michael Jackson-inspired greeting, she went with it and grabbed hers too. Annie, who was just leaving the ladies after announcing the arrival of the Queen Mary at Pier Three, was understandably bewildered by this spectacle and stood open-mouthed with the toilet door ajar.

"For fuck's sake shut the door!" bellowed a man with a breakfast baguette, who immediately regretted it as Annie shifted her focus like an overweight Terminator.

"Just say that again if you want your baguette rammed up your hole!" replied Annie, putting her wet wipes back in her bag like Arnie re-holstering his gun.

The man clearly didn't relish that prospect and made a great show of getting back to his paper while trying hard to pretend he hadn't heard her. The old lady waved with her crotch-free hand and Jasper just looked plain awkward in all respects.

"Are you the Negative Feedback Redistribution Squat?" she inquired.

"Err, sort of, but not really," replied Jasper.

"Who are you then?"

"Well, we might be the Negative Feedback Retribution Squad?"

"That's what I said."

"Well, actually it's not."

"It is, but I've just run out of Fixodent."

"Who sent you?"

"I did…!" shouted Annie's pilfering cousin loudly from the kitchen.

Now reseated at their table with three totally unsanctioned complimentary cappuccinos, Iris McKenzie began to 'thpell' out the exact nature of her problem. Until two years ago, her life had mainly been a happy one. She lived in a neat row of terraced houses that sat beside a small pub on the canal bank in nearby Langley. She had lived there all her married life, brought up two children and had lost her husband some ten years previously. Throughout those years, the pub had always formed the centre of their little world, a place to enjoy a sunny afternoon in the beer garden, hold a family celebration or enjoy an evening amongst old friends whenever she felt lonely. Various landlords had come and gone over time. Some good, some not so, until finally the pub had changed breweries. It was now run by the Hartwell Brewery chain, which had installed a publican called Alan Kelly. He swiftly applied for a late licence and, much to the residents' dismay, it was granted. Now it was a party pub in every sense of the word. Iris no longer enjoyed a quiet drink in the corner where she and her husband had sat for forty-five years. Cheap beer and loud music meant all her old friends now drank at home. But what customers most came in search of wasn't the ambience, it was drugs! From 11 am till two in the morning, the constant noise of cars arriving and leaving, doors slamming, loud voices and frequent fights made living by the New Inn a total nightmare. In the early days, Iris and her neighbours had tried to reason with Mr Kelly. But when his very sincere promises of change were followed by no action, they soon gave up. Now his enormous Rottweiler continually barked its authority from the pub's flat roof, and this only ceased when it was taken for a walk along the now turd-studded towpath.

In recent months, Iris had spoken to everyone from the council to the coppers. Everyone had promised action and used lots of clever words, but of course nothing had changed. Slowly but surely, Alan Kelly was totally killing their community and completely destroying their lives.

When she had finished 'thpeaking', she sat back and cried. They weren't tears of sorrow, they were tears of anger. What could she do? She was seventy-eight and had no one she could turn to. Annie and Jasper entirely agreed she had the right to enjoy a quiet life and decided there and then: Alan Kelly absolutely had to go…

Later that day, they relayed Iris's story to Bernd in Jasper's kitchen. He was in full agreement that this was a case that deserved their attention. Over tea and a packet of Jaffas, it was decided they would pop to the New Inn for a drink that evening. Annie wasn't sure what to wear for an evening out at a drug dealer's pub, so she settled on a pink tracksuit that she had worn for Zumba a couple of times a while back, but wisely decided the matching sweatband might be a bit much. Jasper considered that he might need something slightly more aggressive than a bingo marker as a weapon. So when everyone had left to get changed, he decided to make a knuckleduster by threading wooden beads onto elastic bands. It was all going quite well until a rogue bead twanged off and hit him straight in the eye.

When the NFRS met outside Derek Robinson House at 8 pm, they cast a strange shadow. Annie looked like a cross between Mad Lizzy from TV-am and a unicorn's mom. Jasper had a patch over one eye and was wearing a long raincoat, which he hoped might present the illusion that he had a sawn-off shotgun in his pocket, even though it was actually a further two bingo markers taped together. Bernd was sporting a black sweatshirt with the name of his favourite Scottish punk band, Jimmy's Bawlbag, on the front, a pair of zipped tartan trousers and a leather jacket.

The walk to the establishment in question took just over twenty minutes. Sure enough, Alan Kelly's massive dog signalled their arrival from the roof with a volley of loud barks as they crossed the litter-strewn car park to the door. Once inside, they were faced with the dilemma of which room to pick, the bar or the lounge. Jasper had always erred on the side of caution in such matters. When you're in a strange pub, treat it like a football match and use the visitor's end, the lounge. The bar is for home fans only, the regulars. Unfortunately, despite many years in England, Bernd hadn't mastered British hostelry etiquette and was already barging his way into the bar. Annie piled in after him, which left Jasper with little choice but to follow. The bar was dingy, with leaded windows, fake beams and a pathetic collection of horse brasses. The assembled clientele was the usual selection of barflies and sunken-eyed philosophers clutching pint glasses like babies' dummies and trying to remember the days when they had the option of something else to do. A man of around forty suddenly span round on a barstool and greeted them with "Bugger me, it's the Lost Boys!". His sycophantic bar-room audience laughed, cackled and wheezed, celebrating his lightning wit in the vain hope of getting a free drink. Annie felt Jasper's hand on her pink-nylon-clad arm. She let him off with it just this once…

From the description that had been provided with by Iris, they recognised the comedy genius on the stool to be none other than Alan Kelly. He was a tubby, unshaven mess of a man with arse-crack jeans and a taste for over-washed T-shirts that had maybe once possibly fitted him. He was everything they had been told he was – a loathsome scab of a man with all the sex appeal of a broken toilet seat who looked like his last proper job was probably giving the free milk out at school.

Bernd stepped towards the bar, gave Mr Kelly a sideways glance and ordered drinks from the barman. It seemed pointless to canvas tastes, so he just ordered three halves of lager. Annie could have moved a couple of bags of crisps, but she couldn't see them selling a lot, so wisely doubted their freshness. Jasper just stood and fondled the taped bingo markers in his pocket, fantasising that he could level his 'shotgun' at Alan Kelly and blow him off his stool without bothering to take it out of his pocket. He must have smiled weakly, as Alan Kelly took this as a cue to instigate some conversation…

"Anything else I can help you with?"

"Have you got any pickled onion Monster Munch?" asked Annie.

"Err, no…"

"What about Frazzles?" Annie liked her crisps puffy and highly seasoned, preferably without any natural ingredients if at all possible.

"Nope, we have ready salted, salt and vinegar and cheese and onion."

"What about dry roast nuts?" Annie considered nuts

to be dangerously close to health food. However, the dry roast flavouring had enough salt content to replenish the Dead Sea, so they were a useful fallback in any snack crisis.

"Nope, just the crisps…"

"OK, three bags of salt and vinegar." She didn't ask anyone else what they wanted, because they were all for her.

The barman duly added the three bags to the three halves of lager on the bar without comment. Annie lifted a bag and examined it closely.

"These are own-brand crisps from a multipack," she moaned.

"What's the difference, they're all crisps."

"Multipack bags only weigh 26 grams instead of 32.5 grams."

"But they're only 25p a bag…"

Annie, her freshness concerns now satisfied, indicated that this was also acceptable to her from a value for money standpoint. Taking her half of lager from the bar along with her three bags of underweight crisps, she went to sit down. Bernd paid for the refreshments and turned to face Kelly, still flanked by Jasper the Bingo Marker Gunslinger.

"Do you gentleman require anything else other than deep-fried potato snacks?"

"Depends what is on offer," replied Bernd, praying it wasn't a lap dance and a blow job.

"Recreational pharmaceuticals of the finest quality.

Why not step into my office and we can discuss your requirements and my terms… ?"

"Thanks, but I shall have to politely decline your offer and simply enjoy my lager with my friends," said Bernd, fixing Alan Kelly with his hardest stare. He was going for Clint Eastwood, but it was far closer to Captain Peacock.

"Well, if you change your mind, here's my card," said Kelly, hand outstretched. Bernd took it from it from him and peered at it in the gloom of the bar's mood lighting. The card had obviously been home printed on an inkjet printer with a partially blocked head, as the writing had thin stripes where the ink had missed. 'Party hard at the New Inn 07927 674312' was the only information it offered. Kelly was also clearly an expert in understatement. In a world full of flash business cards it was flimsy and cheap, but for those engaged in the business of pensioner crime fighting, solid gold!

Bernd thanked him for the card, relaxed his unintentionally comic stare and, with Jasper in tow, walked over to sit down next to Annie. Kelly the 'likely ex-milk monitor' shrugged, then turned and muttered something to the barman before climbing back onto his stool.

As Annie smashed her crisps in quick succession and they steadily drained their glasses of lager, a stream of pathetic souls and excited kids did business with Kelly in his 'office', which was, as you have probably guessed, the gents' toilet. The man clearly had no style as well as very little imagination. He was a poorly dressed plastic gangster with all the sales patter of a jaded double glazing salesman. However, if the footfall was anything to go by, he was a man on a massive earner!

When they stood up to leave, Kelly was busy with another client in his 'office'. The barman was washing glasses and gave them a flat smile, then chucked Annie another bag of salt and vinegar crisps and winked. Annie attempted to blow him a kiss in return, but instead just spat little bits of crisps everywhere and the moment passed.

During the walk home, they discussed what they had seen and how they might be able to bring about Alan Kelly's downfall. Jasper knew straight away that what they definitely needed was another chat with Mucky Barry…

Chapter 15

The next morning, Jasper put a call in to Barry at a reasonable time, allowing for the fact that he was a sloth and therefore no early riser. The phone rang twice and then a female voice answered, saying, "Good Morning, Bolan Communication and Technical Services."

"Err… hello," stammered Jasper. "Is that still Muck… I mean Barry's phone?"

"Yes, you have the right number, sir, I'll just see if Mr Bolan is free to speak to you."

The voice put Jasper on hold, where he spent a few pleasant moments listening to The Corrs.

"Good morning, Barry Dolan speaking. How can I help?" said a very businesslike voice.

"Hello, Barry, is that you?"

"Yes, it is. Good morning, Mr Skinner, and how are you today?"

"I'm very well. What's with the new corporate identity?"

"Well, to be truthful, I took a leaf out of your book. I do lots of little favours for people and decided I might as well turn it into a proper business."

"Nice one, good for you! Any chance Bernd and I can pop up to see you? We have a job we need you to look at."

"What time were you thinking of?"

"Dunno. To suit yourself."

"I have a couple of appointments this morning and I'm with someone now. But seeing as you are a long-standing client, I can move a few things around. How would 11.30 suit you?"

"That sounds perfect, see you then!" said Jasper, who always looked forward to being ankle-deep in rubbish with a man in a stained vest... not!

At 11.25 am, Bernd rode the unusually dry lift from the Eagle's Nest down to the ninth floor to collect Jasper, and then they continued down to the fourth floor for their appointment with Barry. When they arrived at his door, they were surprised to see it had been freshly painted in dark blue and a brass plaque confirmed it to be the business premises of Bolan Communication and Technical Services. They were used to hammering with the letterbox until Barry finally answered, but instead they pressed the button on the new intercom doorbell and waited. A couple of moments later, the same female voice that had spoken on the phone answered and buzzed them in. Once inside, they found that the voice belonged to Tricia, Barry's attractive new PA, who greeted them warmly and showed them into the lounge, whereupon two more things immediately became apparent. There was no smell, and the floor was entirely free of rubbish. Barry was on the phone, seated behind a glass desk on a chrome and leather office chair. He indicated that they should sit down and began to finish his call. Apart from a single Apple laptop, the phone, a notepad and an intercom, his desk was otherwise uncluttered.

"... stand on me. I'll be in there before the day's out, and if there's anything at all in there regarding rogue alpacas, you'll be the first to know. I've got to go as I have clients in front of me. Give my regards to the Big Cheese. Tell him I haven't forgotten I owe him a curry. Bye, bye, bye, bye..."

Jasper and Bernd looked at him quizzically. Barry thought it was because they wanted to know whom he was speaking to, when in fact it was his appearance that was the source of intrigue. Barry was dressed in a rather smart business suit, his hair had been cut and styled, he wasn't wearing filthy glasses and he had a golden glow about him. The room was clean and had seen a lick of paint. The multitude of computers and cables were nowhere to be seen, and the walls were hung with a collection of framed posters with inspirational business slogans on them: 'Dare to Soar', 'Think Bigger' and 'Commit to Success'. If you hadn't known better, you would have thought you were in an office on Canary Wharf, not the fourth floor of Derek Robinson House. Barry was Mucky no longer…

"Black Country News. They have a lead on a story about alpacas being stolen from Peru and smuggled into Wednesbury to keep the grass down in graveyards. They suspect a high-level conspiracy involving a local vet, so I'm having a little poke around on their behalf. Can I offer you a coffee, gentlemen? Latte, cappuccino, or maybe a mocha?"

Bernd asked for a black coffee, and Jasper, ever the foodie, wanted a mocha. Barry buzzed through to Tricia and gave her their order in a nasal voice that Jasper strongly suspected was modelled on Boycey from 'Only Fools and Horses'. A few seconds later, they heard a machine whirr and click and cups being filled, then Tricia appeared in the lounge with their coffees.

"So what can I do for you?" asked not-so-Mucky Barry.

Jasper explained their conversation with Iris McKenzie and her issue with the New Inn's toxic landlord. Barry listened intently without interruption while sympathetically nodding in agreement. Finally, Jasper passed him Kelly's card and Barry smiled.

"So what do you need me to do?"

"Can you get some spyware on his phone so we can see what he's up to? Then we can try to figure out a way to stop him".

"Shouldn't be a problem. Do you want to see everything or just the interesting bits?"

"Just the interesting bits should do it. We know he's a dealer, and no one seems particularly bothered by that, so we need something a bit bigger to use as leverage."

"OK, understood. So just the wheat and leave the chaff. Now, this is possibly the period during the conversation when we should discuss my fee."

"Fifty now and fifty when it's done?" guessed Bernd, hopefully.

"Err, no. Those were the terms of Mucky Barry. However, these are the terms of Bolan Communication and Technical Services Ltd. The consultation is free, as you are established customers. Then the first hour is £200, thereafter £75 per hour. When you reach £500, Tricia will send you a text asking if you wish me to continue. Any expenses incurred will naturally be in addition to this. You can pay by cash, card or bank transfer and you will, of course, receive an itemised invoice."

"Barry, for four cakes, it's us! What happened to a coffee in the caff and a couple of Tunnocks?" spluttered Jasper.

"That was the old Barry. The new Barry has decided to occupy his place in life rather than eternally sitting on the bottom rung of the career ladder. I have realised that my skills are in great demand and that I have a right to charge accordingly. Besides, how much did you pull from your last job?"

Jasper reddened and Bernd shifted awkwardly in his seat. They knew Barry had been the linchpin of their last operation and was fairly instrumental in the one before that. It was impossible to argue with his reasoning because they knew he had a point. The Y-front and filthy shell suit days were definitely behind him. Now Barry wore tanga briefs under a silk suit, and his upwardly revised pricing structure reflected the change. Reluctantly, Jasper and Bernd shook hands on the deal with Derek Robinson House's answer to The Apprentice, finished their coffees and rose to leave. They knew Barry's skills were something their enterprise needed in order to function, so they really had no other option but to agree. He had clearly found his inner entrepreneur, and they couldn't really blame him for that.

When they arrived back at Jasper's flat on the ninth floor, Annie was reclining on the settee enjoying 'Bickering Birds' with a tub of Ben and Jerry's Karamel Sutra. Evidence of extensive crisp use littered the floor. Though she might be a glutton, she had her standards. She always ate savoury before sweet.

As ever, Jasper and Bernd knew better than to disrupt Annie's daytime viewing. So they sat down quietly to listen to a woman explain how hot yoga had entirely transformed her life at sixty-eight, snaring her a twenty-four-year-old tantric boyfriend she had met while buying flavoured frozen yoghurt in a shopping centre.

Right after 'Bickering Birds' came the regional news roundup that carried the usual gloomy smorgasbord of violent crime, theft and job losses before ending on a rare light-hearted report. A local photographer was mounting an exhibition of shots she had taken through the years around the Black Country. They mainly showed how some districts had looked before redevelopment, and many of them centred on Oldbury and the areas immediately surrounding it. One photograph in particular from the late 1970s provided the main focus for the story. It was a grainy black-and-white shot of a young girl wearing boxing gloves, her arms held aloft in victory, leaning against the ropes of a boxing ring. Behind her was a boy of roughly the same age lying on the canvas with a man standing over him, clearly looking concerned. Around the ropes, a ragtag selection of scruffy kids in hideous knitwear were caught open-mouthed in shock. The look of absolute triumph on the young girl's face immortalised by the camera made this the stand-out centrepiece of the exhibition. Now the search was on to find her...

"... and now, over forty years later, in a time when women can box for their country at the Olympics, the question is, who was she? No records exist of the bout, and the wooden gym has long been demolished. Sadly, the trainer passed away some years ago, and as yet no former members can recall the event or the fighters involved. So if you are the 'Little Boxer Girl' or you know who she is, please get in touch..."

Annie put down the spoon and the carton and stared in disbelief at the screen. She barely remembered her short boxing career, let alone that knockout moment. But she knew that was her, right there on the screen. Annie was the 'Little Boxer Girl'!

Then, as she sat and reminisced about her days in

the ring, things finally made sense to Jasper. She had started when she was eight, as her schoolteacher had told her parents that it might tame her emerging aggressive streak. It didn't tame it, but it did channel it, and Annie was a natural in combat with the gloves on or off. Three nights a week she bobbed, jabbed and weaved her way around the little gym at the rear of a back street pub, an old wooden hut that was also home to the bowling team and the pigeon fanciers during the rest of the week. But to a little girl that had found her God-given talent, it was her church, and she worshipped hard. She skipped the fastest, punched the hardest and ran the longest. But for a girl boxer in 1978, being the best simply wasn't enough, and there was nowhere to fight except the playground. So at the tender age of eleven, Annie retired as the enthusiasm faded and the whispering started. Of course, she happily dealt with the whispering, because that was all the exercise her fists now got. They needn't have bothered, though, as she soon discovered boys weren't just for hitting. But then, let's face it, if the hardest kid in the school takes a shine to you, your life would be easier if you just went along with it…

As she rang the number for the Brum Television news desk, her heart was pounding. She had no idea why, but it felt like this was a big step. After all, it was only a local news item on a regional channel. What could possibly go wrong?

The journalist who answered the phone asked Annie a couple of simple questions based on her junior boxing career and whereabouts she lived now. She seemed pleased with Annie's straightforward answers and put her on hold. The next voice on the line she recognised. It was Don Starman, the veteran reporter and now anchorman of Brum News. It amused her that their paths should cross again so soon, and she wondered what colour he was today.

"Hello, Annie, I'm Don Starman. I understand from my colleague that you believe you are The Little Boxer Girl?"

"Hello, Don. I know I am, there's no believe about it. The gym was behind the Screaming Frog in Oldbury. My trainer was Jed Taylor, and I boxed until I was eleven. Unfortunately, it was frowned on for girls to box in those days, so I had no choice but to retire."

"Do you remember the photo being taken?"

"Not really. I remember there was a lady that was there a couple of times hanging around with a camera. But she never came back with any photos to show us, so I wasn't aware the photo even existed."

"Was it a staged shot just for the camera? Or had you really knocked the boy out?"

"No, it wasn't staged. I used to knock a lot of boys spark out. That's part of the reason I retired. None of them wanted to fight me any longer, and as I couldn't go on to any organised matches because I was a girl, there really didn't seem any point in carrying on."

"How would you like to come out of retirement for one last bout, Annie? Just a playful knock around on our programme with another local retired boxer? It would make an interesting news item as he has just written a book about his career, which he would like to publicise."

"I haven't boxed for over forty years and I'm a few pounds heavier than I was in those days, mainly because I'm no longer eleven. But if you think that people would be interested in watching a middle-aged woman make a fool of herself on TV, then I'm happy to come along."

"Great, thanks for being such a sport. I'll hand you back to my colleague and we will make arrangements to send a car for you tomorrow."

Arrangements were made and assurances given before Annie really had a chance to take in what she had signed up for. When she had finished on the phone, Jasper and Bernd sat looking at her in awe. Bernd now knew why a casual dead arm from Annie was like being hit with a press spanner. Jasper hoped that the wardrobe department had a sewing machine and some strong elastic in stock. Now, more than ever, he didn't feel the need to mention his costume concerns to Annie.

The next day, Annie woke early after a restless night's sleep. It had been so easy to agree to another TV appearance, but this time she wasn't undercover, so understandably she felt nervous and tried a little shadow boxing in the mirror on the back of the bedroom door in an effort to quell the fluttering in her stomach. Jasper watched from the bed and had to admit that she still had it. If Henry Cooper ever wore a Betty Boop nightie and knitted bed socks for training back in the day, that's probably how he would have looked.

As the day wore on, Annie became more and more doubtful about revealing herself on local TV as The Little Boxer Girl. But just as she was thinking of calling the whole thing off, the driver blew the horn for them at 1 pm as arranged. It was a black people carrier, which seemed silly for just the two of them as only Jasper was tagging along for moral support. The ride into the city took less than half an hour, as, unusually for Birmingham, the traffic was light. On reaching the studio, they walked into reception and were greeted by the journalist that Annie had spoken to the day before. She had an enlarged copy of the photo for her to see and they spent five minutes happily discussing the little boxing club and its characters, while the newswoman made notes. Annie even became a little emotional at one point when she mentioned Jed Taylor, her trainer. He had been a strong positive role model in her formative years, imparting wisdom such as how three things can influence your happiness: your head, your heart and your fists. And how a balance could be achieved by choosing the right one for each of life's challenges. Jasper tried hard to recall the last time he had seen Annie get emotional. Then he remembered her tears outside Woolworth's in Bearwood after its closure as the curtain came down on her weekly pick-and-mix harvest.

The journalist then went on to explain exactly how the follow-up to the search for The Little Boxer Girl was going to be featured. Recording would take place around a boxing ring in a nearby gym. The retired local boxer was a featherweight called Matt O'Dell who had recently written a book about his boxing career entitled 'Gloves, Rope and Canvas'. He was making a promotional appearance on the programme and it seemed a good opportunity to combine the two news items with a little gentle sparring. Don Starman would be posing as the referee and interviewing Annie beforehand. Initially, she would be hidden from view while Matt O'Dell was interviewed, with the focus then moving to the search for the girl in the photo. Annie would then be announced and climb into the ring like a returning champion. In order for the gym to gain a little gentle exposure, she would be fighting in a sweatshirt bearing its logo.

Everything seemed to be quite straightforward, so Annie relaxed into the role of the now 'Not So Little Boxer Girl' and happily allowed herself to be swept along with the nostalgia. She met the rest of the presenting team and was particularly taken with Wes the weatherman, who was very interested in her story when they were enjoying a frothy coffee and a chat in the canteen. But all too soon the time came for Jasper and Annie to go over to the gym, where an outside broadcast team had set up to transmit live into the region's living rooms. As they walked in, Annie was immediately struck by how professional everyone was and how much equipment it took to make one short segment of the show. However, she was far less impressed when the owner passed her a LARGE-sized sweatshirt to wear. The establishment specialised in training heavyweights and the journalist had assured her that her size wouldn't be an issue.

"Do I look like a large to you?"

"It's all I've got. I had some XLs and XXLs but they've all gone."

"Well, I can't wear that. It'll be miles too small! I'm not appearing on television looking like I'm wearing my little brother's sweatshirt!"

"No sweatshirt, no gym! If my business isn't gaining any publicity from this, then you can all unplug your gear and bugger off now!"

Don Starman, sensing the issue from his canvas director's chair, came over in his perfectly tailored referee's uniform to try and quell the fast-brewing disagreement.

"There's really no need for that," he smarmed. "This is a big opportunity for the viewers to see inside a real boxing gym. Just think, the next Frank Bruno or Chris Eubanks could be sat eating his dinner watching this, and without it might never discover boxing. The country could be denied a world champion, and that young man's life might spiral into crime…"

"Or woman," interjected Annie.

"Or indeed woman," said Don sheepishly, who now spent his whole life trying to say the right thing as opposed to just saying something, but still frequently failed miserably to be politically correct.

Annie finally folded and begrudgingly took the sweatshirt from the gym's owner, not because Don had persuaded her with his patriotic outburst, but for young girls everywhere. Young women who needed to know that if they wanted to be a boxer, then they could. Annie had never considered herself to be a feminist, but she realised this was her chance to be a trailblazer. If that meant wearing a sweatshirt that was too small, then so be it! The times were definitely a-changing, and Annie was going to be their Bob Dylan, or then again perhaps their Victoria Wood. The owner looked pleased with the outcome, Annie looked determined, and Don remained vaguely orange, which Annie thought probably suited him a lot better than purple.

Now it was getting close to transmission time and Annie was shown to the locker room, where she and Jasper persuaded the undersized sweatshirt to cover her ample curves. When they had finished, she looked like a fairly aggressive Michelin Woman. By this time, the real star of the show, Matt O'Dell, had arrived. He stood in the centre of the ring with Don as they ran through the questions for the interview about his book, after which he was shown The Little Boxer Girl photo and Annie was brought over from the locker to meet him. Unfortunately, old boxers tend to be less PC than old news presenters, and the sight of Annie struggling to get through the ropes in her straitjacket-cum-sweatshirt created some mild amusement. However, when she straightened up, and it became evident that the sweatshirt had 'TINY's GYM' emblazoned across the front, his mild amusement became roars of laughter. Annie stood her ground and eventually the guffaws subsided. The easy thing would have been to turn and run, flinging off the sweatshirt as she went. However, as she had needed help to put it on, she stood still, because flinging it off on the move was definitely a non-starter. Don just looked really awkward. In his head this had been a scoop, but now he regretted not palming it off on someone else when he had the chance. Don missed the 1970s and being a roving reporter covering wet T-shirt competitions and oddly shaped vulgar-looking vegetables. Now all he did was sit in the studio staring at an autocue or trying to look concerned about things he didn't give a monkey's about. This was meant to show the young producers exactly what he was made of and that he still had what it takes to make great TV. But now he was beginning to wish he'd never heard of the Little Boxer Girl.

Matt O'Dell wasn't really a bad man. He just belonged to a bygone era when you just laughed if something seemed funny. You didn't ask yourself whether it was appropriate to laugh or whether it might cause someone offence. You just simply laughed!

"So are we going to give 'em a good show, champ?" he enquired

"I reckon we might do, Mr O'Dell."

"Call me Matt."

"OK, I reckon we might do Mr Matt O'Dell."

"Funny! So when did you last step into a ring?"

"Oh not long ago. Around 1978, from memory."

"Don't worry, I won't hurt you. You just block and throw the odd punch back. I'll make sure nothing connects. We don't want your shirt splitting. Just bob and weave."

He turned back to Don, who was now seriously wondering what size Wes the weatherman was and if he knew anything about boxing. But given that they were now around five minutes to transmission, he knew he was going to have to steer this ship through choppy waters himself. Annie quietly ducked back under the ropes and passed Jasper, who had watched the meeting unfold from the safety of the locker room door. He followed her in, and they both sat down.

"Are you alright, love? We can walk now if you want. They're not paying us and we haven't signed anything. We could be on the bus home in ten minutes."

"I'm fine. Don't worry, I'm used to it. I used to get the same thing all those years ago. I'll just do it, get a free book and go home. You can eFlog the book if you like, as no doubt it'll be a signed copy. We can have a takeaway with the money. At least it's been a day out."

Annie's calm reply puzzled Jasper. In the ten years they had been together, he had learned to predict her response to most situations. Admittedly, sparring with an old boxing pro clearly wasn't amongst them, so he supposed he was on a learning curve.

Back in the gym, he heard the countdown to transmission and the request for quiet, and then Don began to weave his wordy magic...

"Well, here we are at a local boxing gym in Birmingham city centre, a stone's throw from the Brum News studio. We're joined by a boxing hero of mine, a man that you will doubtless all recognise, Mr Matt O'Dell."

"Hello. Don. It's a great pleasure to see you again and to be back in the ring on telly after all these years. I remember seeing you at a lot of my bouts back in the day."

"I was a great fan of boxing back then and sometimes covered the action when my colleague Harry Teflon was indisposed, so I had the privilege of being paid to see some of your best fights."

"If I'd known that, I'd have stopped sending you free tickets and putting a tab on the bar for you."

"Ha ha. Well, I'm led to believe that you've written a book about your boxing career called 'Gloves, Rope and Canvas'. I managed to find time to take a look at it over the weekend, and I can say that there are some great anecdotes in there, as well as some good advice for up-and-coming young boxers."

"Indeed there are, Don, right from my early amateur days boxing as a schoolboy to my Olympic career. Then, of course, turning professional and fighting in a World Championship. Loads of funny stories from this side of the ropes about people in the boxing game and the things that they get up to, and it's all been cleared by the lawyers. So if you love your boxing and you're old enough to remember the 1980s or you're a new buck feeling your way into the game, it's a cracking read!"

"I noticed that there's also a lot about your life in between fights. The training, self-denial, discipline and how that affects family life."

"Yes, Don, when you're a fighter the whole family is in the ring with you, watching your diet, the early mornings, endless hours in the gym. All for just one day off at Christmas."

"… and I believe that many of the photos have never been seen before. Is that true?"

"Absolutely. We've raided the archives of boxing photographers the world over, and of course our own family album. There are photos in there you won't believe existed until you see them."

"Well, I can thoroughly recommend it to any boxing fans watching, Matt. Talking of photos, have you been following our search for the Little Boxer Girl in this photo?" Don brandished the mystery photo causing all the bother, one last time.

"I have, Don, and I'm intrigued to know more about her…"

"Well, Matt, you're in luck, because she's here tonight. The power of Brum News has found her, and unbelievably she was totally unaware of her newfound fame. I can now reveal to you and the viewers at home that the Little Boxing Girl is, in fact, Annie Weeny, who to this day still lives in Oldbury."

Throughout her adult life, Annie had purposely kept her surname on a need-to-know basis due to its obvious comedy connotations given her size. As Annie bounced out to Rocky III's theme tune 'Eye of the Tiger' in her skin-tight Tiny's Gym sweatshirt, it was difficult for viewers not to spot that Matt O'Dell was now struggling to keep it together. But in spite of her size, this time Annie bounded through the ropes like she was still eleven years old, milking her entrance for all it was worth before eventually joining the two men in the middle of the ring. By this time, the seasoned pro was laughing so hard the sound engineer faded his microphone out and the cameraman zoomed in for a tight shot while Annie did her interview. Don simply asked the same questions he had the day before on the phone, to which Annie dutifully gave the same answers. As their chat drew to a close, he alluded to the reason they were in a gym.

"So we thought as we have two old boxers here, it might be fun to do a little boxing, with myself as the referee. How do you both feel about that?" said Don, whose supposedly spontaneous brainwave was largely betrayed by the fact that he was clearly dressed for the part.

"More than happy to oblige, although I might be a little rusty," warned Annie, pulling on her gloves.

Matt O'Dell had now partially recovered his composure, but only enough to nod his agreement and to glove up. Talking was still definitely going to be a problem! With that, Don pulled the mike down that had appeared over their heads and began to bring the 'fight' to order.

"When I say break, I want a clean break. In the event of a knockdown, you will be directed to go to a neutral corner. Protect yourself at all times. Touch gloves, go to your corner and come out at the bell."

A bell rang and the 'fight' was underway. Don moved to the far side of the ring to avoid blocking the camera and began to jig about as if he had underpants made from fibreglass matting. Annie happily rumbled across the ring to block O'Dell's first jab before lightly counter-punching to probe his defence. He took another shot, which Annie easily dodged but in doing so weaved a little too vigorously, causing her to momentarily lose her balance and stagger slightly. Amused by this, O'Dell inexplicably decided to goad her by sniggering her surname from behind his gloves, most likely in an effort to add a little fire to her boiler and further assert his superiority by easily sidestepping a couple of angry haymakers. That was definitely a shovel of coal too far for Annie Weeny, who was thoroughly tired of her comedy role in proceedings. She channelled forty years of missed opportunity and name-calling into one single powerful uppercut, which unexpectedly caught her tormentor squarely under the chin. O'Dell's lights gently flickered and his legs buckled as she followed up with a solid sledgehammer right. The room fell silent, the only sound being the snort from Annie's nostrils as the now dormant champion crumpled back onto the canvas with the word 'Weeny' still on his lips.

Annie retreated to a neutral corner as previously instructed. Don stood aghast as the local boxing legend, with a new book out, lay KO'd by a fifty-two-year-old woman who hadn't boxed for over forty years. Forgetting, in his panic, to count, the newsman referee finally came to his senses and rushed to crouch over O'Dell and remove his gumshield. In the dying seconds of the live outside broadcast, Annie once again posed at the ropes, perfectly recreating the scene from the old photo that had brought her there. The girl who misguided eight-year-old boys had once dared to call 'Teeny Weeny' stood utterly victorious once again!

Moments later, Jasper assisted Annie to remove her second skin in the locker room and together they quietly slipped out of the gym and into the street. Behind them, they left Don Starman grovelling to Matt O'Dell, who was now sitting up and had a radically revised view on over-fifty boxing for women and an unwelcome additional chapter for his book.

As they walked along Broad Street to the bus stop, Jasper's phone rang. The new Mucky Barry was just as efficient as the old version, and Tricia informed Jasper that 'Mr Bolan' had just emailed them the transcripts of some interesting text traffic from Alan Kelly's phone. He was tempted to enquire about the state of their account, but as Annie was probably still full of enough adrenaline to make a rhino tap dance, he thought better of it. Instead, he put in a call to a rather amused Bernd and they made arrangements to meet at the Eagle's Nest that evening for coffee.

Chapter 16

Bernd knew that it would only be a matter of time till the police had a description of their car. If they were challenged, the bullet hole in the windscreen and the remaining brain matter on the passenger seat would pretty much tell their own story. Plus the 2CV was not ideally suited to the role of a getaway car, so an urgent change of transport made sense if they were to evade capture. In 1979, the oddly shaped little Citroën was a popular choice for students and academics all over Europe. Cheap to buy and run. its frugal petrol consumption and environmentally friendly image appealed to anyone keen to save the planet. So Bernd deduced that if they dumped it in Goethe University car park, it might be some time before it was discovered, as pretty much every other car parked there would be a 2CV.

Driving swiftly but calmly, he made his way across the city and headed towards the university. As he was passing a seemingly endless stream of emergency vehicles heading in the opposite direction, he switched on the radio, which was already reporting on the mysterious roadside explosion, a semi-headless corpse on the pavement and a collection of body parts that had apparently rained down on a chocolate importer's warehouse roof. The reporter was speculating that this might be connected to Baader–Meinhof, or the Red Army Faction, but was struggling to identify who or what the target might have been. Bernd felt fairly sure that responsibility might continue to go unclaimed, on the basis that it almost certainly ran the risk of making the Banana Splits appear utterly deadly in comparison. Simone, who had been unusually subdued since her snap decision to force a change of management, chose this moment to begin back-seat driving.

"Where are we going? Shouldn't we go back to the safe house?"

"I don't think that's wise under the circumstances. I think the best thing we can do is to melt away quietly and hope the fuss soon dies down. You're new and so am I, so the police are unlikely to have any intelligence on us. The only thing linking us to the Kitz Chaos is this car. Once we get rid of it, I think we should split up."

"Split up? But you said last night…"

"I know what I said last night, but that was before you started working to rule. If we stick together, we'll be easier to spot. If we are lucky, they won't have any eyewitnesses yet who can identify us."

"But what about the revolution?"

"Stuff the revolution. I wasn't that keen on it to start with! Do you think you'll last a day once they work out you accidentally neutralised the other five members of the cell due to premenstrual tension?" Bernd immediately wished he'd taken the Luger from her before he'd said that.

"It was an accident! He was always being rude to me and making jokes about my coffee…"

"So you shot him in the head from point-blank range? Couldn't you have flicked his ear, maybe pulled his hair or something slightly less permanent like that?"

"I suppose on reflection I overreacted."

"…. and understatement of the year goes to…"

"I don't like sarcasm either."

"Well, I wonder if, due to these extenuating circumstances, you might see your way to making an exception and allow my brain to remain in my head. I will then attempt to use it to avoid spending a lifetime in prison or experiencing a rather unpleasant question-and-answer session with the Baader–Meinhof Human Resources Department."

"That sounded like more sarcasm to me."

"I apologise, but in my defence I have honestly never said anything about your coffee. Listen, why don't you return to Hamburg? Just ring your dad, say that you've been hanging around in a squat with some hippies. Do a bit of crying, look really sorry and go back to university. As long as you keep your mouth shut and your nose clean, it's unlikely anyone will work it out and you can get on with your life. The only person still alive who knows the truth is me, and I'm unlikely to say anything."

"I suppose I could do that, but why don't you come with me?"

"Because I'm an East German Stasi operative unofficially seconded to Baader–Meinhof, and if I don't get out of Germany altogether, I really don't fancy my chances either!"

With that, he pulled into the university car park and found a space well away from the main doors of the campus. He turned off the engine and the little Citroën gratefully whirred into silence. Turning to Simone, he gently relieved her of the Luger and tucked it into his jacket pocket. She knew what he had said made sense. Her terrorism gap year had come to an undeniably explosive conclusion. Perhaps she might be able to change the world with books and exams after all, rather than guns, bombs and really crap coffee.

They got out of the car and casually walked hand in hand across the car park. On reaching the road, they turned right down Reuterweg and past Rothschild Park, where they detoured slightly to allow Bernd to quietly slip the ancient Luger into a bin. Finally, they headed off into the pretty side streets, heading in the general direction of the central coach station. Bernd felt sure that the police would already have spotters at the train station, so the coach station was an altogether safer bet. You could buy a ticket, watch from the café and board the bus at the very last second. No barriers or queues meant less chance of being spotted if indeed the police had any idea at all who they were.

Bernd bent down and took his last hundred Deutsch Marks from his sock. He left Simone with a coffee and a cinnamon bagel in the first-floor café and went down to the ticket office to book her ticket to Hamburg. There were five windows, so he picked the one with a spotty youth who wore his uniform as if he hated it. Bernd remembered those days and sympathised entirely. Suddenly, thoughts of his family and the cosy yet boring life he had once known at the bakery filled his head. How had he got from baking buns and playing punk to being a wheelman for terrorism's answer to The Monkees? Bernd asked for a single to Hamburg and paid the youth. Neither of them made small talk or eye contact. For a terrorist on the run, it was the perfect transaction. Pleased with how well it had gone, he climbed the stairs to give Simone her ticket. But as he reached the swing door to the café, he stopped. Two men in suits were talking to Simone, and she didn't look like she was enjoying the conversation. Bernd had done his best, but he wasn't a hero. As far as he knew, no one at Baader–Meinhof owned a suit, so that almost certainly meant that they were police.

His assumption was that it wouldn't be long before someone told them that Simone had a man with her. He couldn't do anything to help her, now it was every revolutionary for themself. He knew he had to get out of there fast, but how, exactly? The ticket he had bought was now useless, as they would soon know he had it and the intended destination. As he calmly walked down the stairs, he could hear Simone screaming, "Get your hands off me, you fascist pigs!" behind him. At least he'd relieved her of the gun. No one else needed a permanent, deep centre parting today.

He walked out of the ticket office and instantly became aware of a large group of schoolchildren gathered around a coach. The noise they made was terrific, and his initial reaction was to move away until a voice shouted, "You're late!" The voice came from a prissy-looking man in a sports jacket and kipper tie who was also sporting a greasy comb-over. "You should have been here twenty minutes ago! Where's your bag?"

Bernd had no idea who the man was or where the coach was going. But he knew this was maybe his only chance to avoid spending the best years of his life in prison.

"Sorry. I went for a coffee," he stammered. "My bag is already on the bus."

"You young supply teachers are all the same. You're worse than the kids. What's your name?"

"Bernd Tost" said Bernd, who really hadn't time to think of an alias.

"Well, Bernd Tost, you'd better get on the bus, because it's a really long way to England!"

After a short time queuing, Bernd climbed onto the bus, which now contained a seething mass of noisy, hormonal fourteen and fifteen-year-old kids on probably their first trip away from their parents. The front rows were relatively calm, but as he walked further down the aisle, he felt the mood change and the noise level increase. Here sat the smokers, bullies and teacher baiters. Bernd found a vacant seat and sat down. Beside him sat a slightly built kid, with glasses and a moonscape complexion. At first, he eyed Bernd with some suspicion, then, realising he was a teacher, seemed to relax a little.

"Oh, look, Osterman has got a boyfriend!" said a voice, and half the coach laughed.

Bernd wasn't so long out of school that he didn't get the jibe. He turned to take a look at the resident smart arse. He was a small kid with piggy eyes and a front-room haircut. It looked like that particular Sunday night his mom couldn't find the good scissors or a bowl that correctly fitted his cranium. Bernd wasn't much of a bully fan, whether the bullying was physical or verbal. East German schools gave you hard lessons in looking after yourself, especially if your dad was the local baker. Bullies had tried to strong-arm their way to free buns on many occasions, but they had all failed.

"Did your mom cut your pubes to match your hair?" inquired Bernd loudly. "Or couldn't she find the really tiny scissors?"

The same audience roared this time, all except for Front Room Haircut, whose mouth just fell open like a car's glovebox. Even Osterman enjoyed the retort, giving a sly smile, but he was careful not to let his tormentor see him laughing. Bernd sat back in his chair and mused that he might actually enjoy being a teacher for a few days.

As his new follically challenged colleague did a headcount, the coach pulled out from its stop and an enormous cheer rang out from the kids on board. As the whoops and whistles died out, it pulled out into the road and he caught a glimpse of the still-ranting Simone being led away to a waiting police car. Her family was rich and her father very well connected, so Bernd consoled himself with the idea that it would be easy work for a good lawyer to persuade a court that she was really just a good girl lead astray by the wrong kind of people. He was still saddened, though, as he would miss their sleeping bag love-ins. She was a very naughty young lady indeed!

Now, with the coach wheels turning and the kilometres speeding by, his thoughts turned to more practical matters. Clearly he wasn't a teacher, but he did have extensive experience of being a pupil. So how hard could it be to simply just pretend? Then of course there was the more pressing problem that he didn't have a case, or indeed any other clothes at all. Still, at least he had his passport! Ever with one eye on his own agenda, he had suspected that their mission might not go entirely to plan. During the time he had spent with the cell, he had formed the conclusion that they were enthusiastic amateurs rather than deadly professionals. So against their leader's orders, he had tucked his passport into his jacket pocket before they left the safe house that morning. If he was killed, he at least wanted his parents to know what had happened to him and for the state to know that he had done his 'duty', sparing his family from any reprisals that might result from him just vanishing. On the contrary, they might receive a pension and a free state funeral for their hero son. Another scenario he had imagined was that he might somehow slip away in the resulting confusion, in which case the rest of the cell might believe he had been captured, as the media rarely reported the taking of terrorist prisoners. Either way, it made no sense for his passport to be in the safe house if that was later located. He decided, however, that the clothing issue would need to be addressed at the earliest opportunity. Speeding down the Autobahn towards the Dutch border, he felt that Plan B wasn't going too badly at all.

There were a couple of other teachers on the coach apart from Bernd and Mr Comb-Over. Each teacher was drawn from four different schools across Frankfurt with a corresponding group of kids from each school. So he found himself in charge of fifteen kids who had varying ideas of what extracurricular activities an exchange trip should offer. He sat back to listen to the excited teenage chatter as they began to forget that he was there. He soon noticed that Osterman didn't engage with the others. He just sat quietly, giving him occasional sideways glances and pushing his glasses back onto his nose at regular intervals. Finally, halfway across the Netherlands, he decided to speak. He didn't say a lot, but when he did, it was matter of fact and to the point.

"Do you speak English, Sir?"

Bernd felt himself redden. In his hurry to escape the scene at the coach station, he hadn't given much thought to what language skills might be expected of a teacher on an exchange trip to England. He did understand English to a degree, but he had rarely spoken it. East German schools didn't tend to put much stock in foreign languages. Even if they had, Russian might have been a more practical choice. Bernd's English came from punk records, West German radio and American Forces television. Not a classic education by any means, but possibly enough to get by in his new role as a representative of the West German teaching system.

Osterman still had his head turned, awaiting an answer. Now Bernd had first-hand experience of why the other kids might think his face worth punching. He knew that only an answer in English was going to satisfy this oddball kid, who would almost certainly be a tax inspector or a bank manager in later life. He continued to hold his gaze while he dug deep for something appropriate, and then at last Johnny Rotten handed him a suitable response.

"I'm not here for your amusement. You're here for mine."

Satisfied with this suitably witty comeback, Osterman smiled, pushed his glasses back up his nose and continued with the very important business of looking out of the window. Bernd silently thanked the Prince of Punk and settled back in his seat. It wasn't long before his eyes closed and the warm creep of sleep swept over him.

When at last he stirred, the Hook of Holland ferry terminal seemed incredibly busy to a man from a country where international travel was largely frowned upon. To comply with immigration regulations, everyone had to leave the coach and pass through passport control on foot, even large parties of unruly German schoolchildren. Bernd assembled his kids at the side of the coach and they impressed him by complying without the need for any further puberty-based insults or any querying of his non-existent teaching credentials. Following the lead of the bona fide teachers, he trailed over to the terminal building before fussing them through the door and into a single-file queue ready to present their documents. He cleverly ensured that he was the last in the queue so that he wouldn't face any awkward questions afterwards about his East German passport. All the children passed through without issue, and then it was Bernd's turn. If a DDR passport holder travelling with a group of West German children surprised the Dutch passport officer, he didn't show it and just glibly waved him through. Once the entire group was reassembled, Mr Comb-Over led them through the second half of the building to the foot passenger embarkation point, whereupon he instigated yet another pointless headcount before reading everyone the riot act with regard to their conduct once aboard the ferry.

"Remember at all times that you not only represent your school, but your country. No smoking, drinking, swearing, running, fighting or horseplay. You will ensure that you are courteous at all times to other passengers. Remember that you might be the first German child that they have ever met. Anyone who is seen to break these rules will be seated with myself for the remaining duration of the journey and will experience the shame of a phone call to their school and parents. Do I make myself clear?"

For once he didn't employ the teacher's usual trick of making them roar their agreement like a bored pantomime audience, most likely because this would have probably broken at least one of the directives that he had just laid out. Instead, he raised one arm and led them up the gangplank like the Pied Piper, his flared trousers flapping in the wind and the other hand keeping his cranial scrape over in place. Once aboard the ferry, the kids instantly dispersed into their tribal groups and vanished in seconds, leaving Bernd, Mr Comb-Over, the two other teachers and a few geeks fearing attack to form the world's most awkward travelling group. Bernd was in no doubt that in order to solve the clothing issue he would have to think of a way to free himself from this nerdy collective.

A while later, they sat in deathly silence following several tortuous games of I spy and charades. Using the time to think, Bernd had deduced that his best chance of some extended 'alone time' was feigning seasickness. Given that the sea was pretty much as calm a millpond, this was going to be a stretch of anyone's acting skills. He started gently, with a little stomach rubbing and quiet belching, which met with a raised eyebrow from Mr Comb-Over, who considered himself to be a good judge of imagined adolescent malaise. After around half an hour of constant gurning, he suddenly stood up and announced that it was 'time' before quickly scurrying in the opposite direction of the nearest toilet. This directional malfunction did not go unnoticed, but he steadfastly ignored the cries of "You're going the wrong way!" After all, being trapped in a toilet pretending to be sick wasn't going to help his outfit shortage. Soon the cries died out behind him as he burst through the door to the outer deck, supposedly to puke in peace over the handrail. But this actually allowed him to move around the outside of the ship and access other decks without being seen by the other teachers seated within.

Clearly, Bernd had never stolen clothing to order before, but he had formulated a plan in the time he had spent being bored to death with his new workmates. He would look for a man around the same build as himself whose style of dress he felt he could live with. He would then attempt to locate his luggage and steal it. He also thought that it might be prudent to select someone speaking a European language rather than English, in the hope that they were on their outward journey with clean clothes rather than on a return journey with dirty ones. After around twenty minutes of stalking men and dodging familiar schoolkids, he found a likely candidate crashed out on a settee near the bar. His slumped sleeping position betrayed him as someone who had overindulged in the alcoholic refreshments on offer in an attempt to gain some shut-eye during the crossing. To his right was a modern three-quarter-sized teal-blue suitcase with a chrome trim, which looked remarkably new and sported a German Anti-Nuclear sticker on it. Its owner in the Carlsberg Coma was dressed in a casual shirt and jacket, flared trousers and Chelsea boots. It wasn't quite Bernd's look, but definitely fitted well with his new occupation of trendy young teacher. He sat down opposite his prey, who was enjoying the fidgety sleep of someone with too much gassy lager in their system. Bernd felt sure that in time he would need to lessen his liquid load and that would give Bernd the opportunity to secure his 'lucky bag' wardrobe. Following some short-lived snoring and a couple of 'hero belches', the man suddenly rose to his feet and wobbled off in the direction of the gents. So it was now or never! Without pausing to check who was around, Bernd calmly walked over and picked up the suitcase. It was quite heavy, but that was far better than finding it empty. With his heart pounding out of his chest, he quickly marched down the corridor in the opposite direction to the one his garment donor had taken. Although he expected to be challenged by an irate bystander at any moment, with every desperate stride, he knew his chances of success were greater. Finally, he was descending the staircase to the lower deck and relief washed over him.

Now Bernd was faced with the second part of his mission: to locate his party's coach and safely stow the case in the luggage compartment before the theft was discovered. The first lower deck he entered contained only cars, with no coaches or lorries at all. The second lower deck was a mixture of cars, caravans, campers and smaller commercial vehicles, but again no coaches or lorries were to be seen. However, when he opened the heavy door to the third level, it looked far more promising. Now his challenge was to limbo round the tightly packed vehicles in order to find their coach. Ferrymen always like to pack them in tight. Consequently, this was no easy task as there was only just enough room to squeeze past with the stolen luggage held high over his head. By now Bernd was feeling fatigued by the day's events and his strength was fast ebbing away, but he knew that once the case was safely hidden in the coach, the crime would almost certainly go undetected, even once the drunk finally realised his luggage was gone. Plus, on arrival in England, he would look more like a teacher and less like a terrorist deserter. At last he spied the coach in the far corner of the deck. With one last heroic heave, he lifted the case over his head and wound his way between the massive vehicles, his puny arm muscles screaming. Finally, he reached his destination and sprang the luggage compartment catches open and the sizeable side door swung upwards with very little room to spare. Quickly he stacked the case alongside the others and tore off the luggage label that hung from the handle, crumpling it into his pocket and making a mental note to dispose of it later. Lastly, he pulled down the spring-loaded door and firmly slammed it shut. It made far more noise than he had expected, echoing loudly on the metallic walls. A few tense seconds were spent waiting for a challenge, and he was thankful when none came.

Mr Comb-Over was looking a little peeved when Bernd eventually rejoined the group on the foot passenger deck. He tried his hardest to look as contrite as possible while simultaneously reinforcing the notion that he had spent the last hour boking up his twin brother in the gents. He obviously created the right impression as he felt the atmosphere soften before he gratefully drifted off to sleep, sitting bolt upright. Casual theft was an exhausting business.

When he awoke for the second time that day, all hell was breaking loose. Mr Comb-Over was throwing a major wobbler and loudly demanding his input. Two lads from 'Bernd's school' had taken it upon themselves to collect as many toilet rolls as they could lay hands on. They had then smuggled these to the outside deck at the stern and had tied a free end of each roll to the handrail before bunging the roll off the back of the boat to create a massive hygienic streamer. One was funny and two might have been mildly amusing, but thirty-three caused a boat-wide bog roll famine, leading to embarrassing scenes of trouser penguins exiting cubicles in a futile search for available wipe fodder. The older teacher was urging extreme disciplinary action from Bernd while holding the prime suspects firmly by the earlobes, which was still seen as acceptable practice by educators for detaining children in the late 1970s. Looking on was an amused senior member of the crew who was trying his best to appear outraged when in reality it made a welcome change to the usual teenage shoplifting from the duty free shop.

The ex-terrorist bogus supply teacher looked at the two tiptoeing culprits and then back at the crimson-faced senior ear gripper. He knew the crime demanded a robust response, but he wasn't sure what form that should take. A smack of the legs seemed a bit pervy, a straight punch to the jaw massively over the top.

"Nipple twist or Chinese burn?"

"Eh?"

"Nipple twist or Chinese burn?"

"Chinese burn," replied Bog Roll Robber 1, who really wasn't sure he liked the sound of nipple twist.

Bernd dutifully lifted the boy's sleeve before administering a Chinese burn so extreme the kid nearly ripped his own ear off, screaming loudly as he bucked and wriggled in a futile attempt to break free from the searing pain being expertly administered to his wrist.

Bog Roll Robber 2 now had eyes as big as saucers. In the soft world of modern schooling, he had expected the often-employed 'You've let me down, you've let the school down, but most of all you've let yourself down' lecture. Sadly, Bernd wasn't at teacher training college that day, or any other day, for that matter.

"Nipple twist!" he finally blurted out, without any prompting as by now quite a crowd was gathering to add to his distress, doubtless in the firm belief that nothing could be more agonising than the pain they had just seen his co-defendant endure. This apparently sound basis for logic was swiftly found to be lacking as Bernd ramped up the anticipation by cracking his knuckles prior to taking a grip. This resulted in a twist so vicious that the kid suddenly kicked Mr Comb-Over in the balls as Bernd skilfully delivered a credible threat to his future chances of breastfeeding. The onlookers were aghast as the older teacher sat doubled up in pain while his two former captives furiously rubbed the affected areas, trying hard not to cry. Bernd felt that a helpful precedent had been established going forward. The supply teacher was clearly a fucking sadist, and it might be an idea to do exactly what he said in the future.

Chapter 17

Bernd was still smiling when he answered the door. He had watched the whole 'fight' live on TV, then several times again on social media a few minutes later. Annie had a habit of altering the course of events, however set in stone proceedings might appear to be.

As ever, Bernd was the perfect host. The strong German coffee was piping hot and the strudel was warm, and Annie realised just how hungry she was after her demolition of the piss-taking champion boxing author. She was becoming quite fond of the weird German food that she got at the Eagle's Nest, and Bernd clearly didn't seem to mind the vacuuming quite as much as he once did.

Eventually, their attention switched to the emails from Mucky Barry. Much of what they received was the usual text traffic between a drug dealer and his customers. However, one message clearly stood out from the rest. It was from someone called Cheryl, who they assumed was Kelly's cleaner, and it took the form of a resignation sentence, rather than a whole message: 'After the mess I came into on Sunday morning, you can stuff your job up your arse!'

"Somebody's clearly not happy. If you're a cleaner in a pub, I would guess that you're used to some grim sights. But whatever it was, it clearly tipped her over the edge," Jasper said, laughing.

"What date was that sent?" inquired Bernd.

"Day before yesterday."

"So Kelly has a vacancy for a cleaner then? That would be an excellent way to find out exactly how he runs his empire."

Jasper and Bernd turned to look at Annie, who had swapped her plate for Jasper's and was happily hoovering up the remnants of his strudel. It took a couple of seconds for her to realise that the attention in the room was now focussed on her. Then the penny dropped…

"What? You want me to apply for the cleaning job at the New Inn? Why? Because I'm a woman?"

"No," lied Jasper. "Because you are a fantastic undercover operative with an insatiable appetite for danger who just happens to be a woman."

"Why can't you or Bernd do it? Why do I have to get up early to clean toilets and clear up puke?"

"Because…."

"Because what?"

"Because the barman clearly fancies you and that will make it easy for you to get the job," interjected Bernd, who could sense that Jasper's train of thought was floundering badly.

Annie was used to a lot of things, but flattery and being the object of someone's desire weren't two of them. She tried hard to continue being indignant, but her face softened into a big grin. Maybe a job with an endless supply of free crisps might not be such a bad idea after all!

The next day at 8 am, Annie was walking to the New Inn for her trial as the new cleaner. It had been a simple matter of texting Kelly and pretending that she had heard of the cleaning vacancy on the local grapevine. This came as no surprise to the drug-dealing publican, as news often travels fast amongst the regulars of any pub. He was relieved to be solving his staffing shortage rather than suspicious of the applicant's source of information.

Annie had been a cleaner before, as well as a barmaid, childminder, shelf stacker, refuse collector, sandwich maker, dinner lady, fish fryer, sausage maker, lollipop lady, shop assistant and turkey plucker, but she had eventually decided that her future career path lay among the long-term unemployed. This was a non-occupation that she had excelled at, as doing nothing was her chosen speciality. Today she would dig deep, though, and would attempt to rekindle any remaining work ethic that had survived fifteen years of blissful feckless leisure.

As she dodged the massive dog turds on her approach to the back door of the pub, Kelly's dog howled at her from the roof. Whatever they fed him, it agreed with his digestive system. The rear yard looked like the 1970s episode of 'Dr Who' that had featured an invasion of giant maggots. Annie was relieved to find that the back doorstep had escaped the dog's attention and hammered on the door while praying that it didn't open outwards. She needn't have worried, as when it swung open, it was her barman admirer who beckoned her inside.

"So we meet again, Miss Salt and Vinegar."

"Indeed we do, Mr Multipack."

"So you're the new cleaner. Unless, of course, you're a new barmaid, in which case you're several hours early."

"Would that be a problem?"

"Oh no, not at all. I would be more than happy to take

my time showing you the ropes."

Annie smiled with the confidence of a woman who knew that she could snap him like a Walkers French Fry should he move past verbal chauvinism onto the more practical stuff. She felt the barman was going to be a useful source of information, but she had absolutely no intention of actually 'feeling' him in order to get it. Instead, she would just maintain the Benny Hill banter and hope that he didn't get bored.

"So, being as I am the new cleaner, rather than the new barmaid, can you show me what you need cleaning, how often and exactly where you keep your equipment?"

At this point, she thought the barman was going to burst with joy. He clearly thought he could see the runway lights, and by the look of him, it was a fair while since he'd landed. He possessed the delusional confidence of a man who didn't own bathroom scales or a tape measure and spent all his time with other similar men just talking about women. In short, an unshaven extra large wearing an overstretched medium, with an extremely fertile imagination.

For a second he considered a filthy retort, but instead, sensing that time was on his side, he led the way behind the bar. In the next few minutes, he conducted a tour of the pub's grime hotspots, occasionally pausing for an anecdote about 'one of those nights', which usually featured him as the star but which Annie strongly suspected wouldn't if someone else told it. Finally, he showed her where the ancient cleaning equipment was kept, under the stairs. Annie quickly came to the conclusion that Cheryl couldn't have been much of a cleaner as a cursory inspection told her the vacuum cleaner was partially blocked and that the mop was spreading more infection than it was removing. Neville (as she now knew him to be) seemed impressed with her apparatus appraisal and even more so with his own inspection while she was bent double examining it. After lingering longer than was strictly necessary, he eventually moved off as Annie pulled on Cheryl's little-used pink rubber gloves and got down to business.

After around two hours of solid graft, the toilets smelt fresher than they had in a long time; the bar had been thoroughly vacuumed and dusted; the kitchen floor smelt of bleach rather than grease; and the backyard was no longer an organic canine minefield. As Annie put the last bag of giant cacks into the dumpster, she sensed a pair of eyes watching her from the back door. When she turned, it was Alan Kelly, and she could see that clearly he shopped for clothes at the same store as Neville the barman.

"Nice work!" he yawned lazily, stretching and rubbing his belly as his shirt rose up like the 'before' photo on a Bullworker advert. "Can't remember the last time this place was so clean…" Now in the bright light of day, she could see he had teeth like an old fence someone had painted yellow, set alight, then kicked the fuck out of to extinguish the flames.

"Was Cheryl a bit of a looker then?"

"Not bad at all. Very easy on the eye."

"Thought so. When you're good-looking men tend to put up with you not doing your job properly. Sadly, I've never had that advantage, so I just do the work instead." Annie smiled. But she meant it. He smiled too, knowing that she did.

"So the job's yours if you want it. 8.30 till 12, five days to suit yourself, £120 a week, cash in hand."

"£150 a week sounds more like it!"

"£120 is what Cheryl always got."

"Well, Cheryl didn't clean properly."

"OK, call it £140?"

"£140 and free crisps."

Kelly laughingly pretended to study Annie's figure.

"OK, £150. I reckon the free crisps clause would put me out of business!"

Annie smiled. She liked winning, and putting this mouldy prick out of business at a later date was going to be her pleasure. She crossed the yard, took off her right glove and offered her hand. Kelly took it and they shook.

"Welcome to the firm," he said, with a smile that would make a dental hygienist reach for a hammer and chisel.

Annie spent the next hour and a half sweeping, tidying and generally nosing while closely noting the comings and goings. A countertop cleaning session in the kitchen yielded no further clues. Even the freezer (the film favourite for drug storage) just contained a few hazardous-looking microwave burgers and mucky ice cubes. Nor could she see evidence of drug usage anywhere, not even an ashtray full of broken cigarettes, folded cardboard or roaches.

From 11 am, when the doors opened and the music went on, the pub attracted a regular flow of chemically challenged patrons. Some lingered for a pint, others that looked more strung out just paid and left. Absolutely everyone visited the gents with Kelly, even the female clients.

Inside the men's toilets was just as you would expect, despite doubling as Kelly's busy 'office'. There was no sign of drug paraphernalia of any type, so she reasoned that the stash was kept elsewhere and this was just the handover room where money changed hands. Presumably, Kelly had advance warning of what his customers wished to purchase and had it on his person when they arrived. Clearly, this was a tighter operation than they had at first imagined. Kelly really did seem to know what he was doing after all. The only thing that Annie did eventually notice was a faint 'whooshing' noise that seemed to occur whenever Kelly did 'business'. Other than that, she saw nothing at all of any consequence apart from Neville's habit of having one hand in his pocket whenever she was close by. She hoped this was an anxious reaction to once losing his wallet, but in all probability, she knew it probably wasn't. The extension of his jaw that accompanied it put her in mind of another dirty old man, Albert Steptoe.

It was half twelve when she arrived back at Jasper's flat, and she was surprised to find Bernd there too. The two men in her life were seated at the little Formica kitchen table with three fresh coffees. An unopened packet of Fox's Chocolatey Milk Chocolate Rounds sat before them, always one of Annie's more decadent favourites.

"We thought that the worker amongst us might require nourishment after a heavy shift."

Annie wasn't used to such treatment, but she wasn't going to look a gift horse in the mouth. She threw off her coat, dropped her bag and sat down for a calorie-laden debrief.

"So how did you get on?" probed Jasper.

"Fine. The barman is a bit of a perv, but I can handle that if I need to."

Jasper ignored the obvious dick gag as, since the boxing debacle, he'd been more respectful of her punching power. He liked his nose with a bone in it.

"… and Kelly?" prompted Bernd.

"He's got really bad teeth and all the panache of a flatulent warthog. But I got £150 a week out of him." She smiled, recalling her victory.

"What about drugs?"

"Didn't take any."

Annie was really enjoying the slow drip-feed of information. Usually, the two men chattered between themselves and she just listened. Now she was the sole source of intrigue. The biscuits were a nice touch and Fox's were always a nice melty confection with a cuppa. She could see that Jasper was becoming impatient, a bit like Tuesday nights. The begging might be a bit embarrassing with Bernd here, though.

"But did you see any?"

"I saw the people that came to buy them. I saw Kelly take them into the gents to do the deal, but I didn't actually see any drugs, or any money either, for that matter."

"Did you have a nose around to see if there was anything lying about?"

"No, I just pushed the fucking Hoover round with my eyes closed. Of course I had a poke around, but there was nothing there."

"Did you check the freezer?" said Bernd, the big film fan trying to be helpful.

"Yes, Tarantino! It was full of shitty microwave burgers and ice cubes that looked like they would add an unexpected depth of flavour to any drink they graced."

"So nothing incriminating at all?"

"It was my first day! I'm not Miss Marple! Give us a chance!"

And with that, Annie rose from the table, taking her cup and the now half-depleted packet of biscuits to go and watch 'Bickering Birds' on catch-up. She lingered momentarily to extract the Chinese takeaway menu from the kitchen drawer.

Jasper knew that further interrogation was futile and ran the risk of Annie turning the alarm off tomorrow and not bothering to go. She ran on a knife edge of compliance at the best of times. It was much like being a demolition expert. Chip away for too long and you get a block of flats on your head. So, for now, they would have to be content that they had managed to infiltrate Kelly's operation.

By the time Bernd left, Annie was fast asleep on the settee. Coming out of retirement had clearly been a shock to her system. Jasper picked up the menu and decided to order the set meal for two people. He wasn't that hungry, but he guessed that Annie might be when she eventually stirred. He dialled the takeaway and gave them his order then settled down to watch the six o'clock news while Annie did her very best to drown it out by snoring.

When Annie awoke early the next day, it was raining heavily. She reluctantly climbed from her bed to peer out of the window at the gloom. Below her, she could see the massive puddle forming in the car park by the main door. Already there was a muddy path across the grass as people took an alternative route to avoid it. She really wasn't feeling the idea of mopping floors and cleaning toilets with a twenty-minute trudge in the rain to get there. Annie's rainy days were usually about the three Ts – tea, toast and telly! But she knew that the sweet little old lady was relying on them to bring about Alan Kelly's downfall. So with a heavy heart, she made a cuppa, got dressed, put on her coat and left the flat.

Last night she had woken up on the settee to a set meal for two from Yung Lung that Jasper had paid for without requiring a contribution from her. She had particularly enjoyed her sweet and sour prawn balls but always found it a waste that they always gave you so much sauce that got thrown away, so she'd stuck it in the fridge to dip crisps in later. Pulling her coat tight around her, she stepped out into the early morning gloom with her bag on her shoulder, fighting hard to keep her balance as she skated on the muddy path around the now giant puddle. Although her new cleaning career was only in its early days, she already knew there weren't going to be any long-service medals.

As she crossed the pub yard to reach the back door, she winced at the sight of the new turd crop she'd have to harvest. She was just thinking how grateful she was that the pub only had one dog, as, right on cue, it began to bark from the flat roof above before stopping abruptly as a young female voice called it to heel. Annie looked up and saw a girl of about seventeen peering down at her. She had a pinched little face and wore her hair in an untidy ponytail. She smiled warmly and the girl hesitantly smiled back. Then she quickly retreated back across the roof and in through the patio window. Annie watched her go before loudly banging the back door to get Neville to let her in out of the rain. She didn't have to wait long before the door opened and the beaming barman ushered her in.

"Filthy weather! Bet you're soaked to the skin."

Annie immediately spotted that his face had seen a blade dragged across it, which clearly explained the pungent aroma of Brut mixed with stale beer that was now launching a noxious assault on her sense of smell. Yesterday's all-too-small Jägermeister T-shirt had given way to today's less ill-fitting Strongbow polo shirt, which she strongly suspected had still been in the packet half an hour ago, judging by the deep square creases across his upper belly. Neville didn't have a chest, just an upper and lower belly.

"Ach, I'll soon dry out once I get going."

"The doctor can give you cream for that. And patches."

Annie understood the joke but felt it was high time that Neville understood the balance of power between them. So she gave him the sort of hard stare that a cat gives a sparrow before ripping its head clean off and gutting it. He stood awkwardly, still fully expecting a playful retort to his painful menopause-based gag, which had landed like a lead Frisbee in Annie's ears. As the long seconds passed, he felt the wind from the Grim Reaper's scythe and finally realised that no retort was coming. Neville blushed, a line was drawn, and it was silently acknowledged by both parties that Annie was definitely the one holding the pencil.

"How about a cuppa?" offered the now crimson Neville, his cheeks blazing.

"That would be lovely. Milk and three sugars," said Annie, dropping her stare down a few notches. "I noticed a young girl on the roof with the dog just now. Who's that?"

"That's Alan's… err… niece, Vasara."

Annie knew that this slight hesitation in his answer meant the chances of the girl being Alan's niece were minimal. Given her name was clearly Eastern European made it even less likely and possibly explained why she looked so fearful that Annie had seen her.

"Vasara. That's an unusual name. Where's that from?"

"Search me." Neville realised that he had possibly said more than was wise and ended the stilted exchange by disappearing into the kitchen to put the kettle on.

Chapter 18

Jasper wasn't used to waking up alone. Most days he was the first to wake and he always took Annie a cuppa in bed. Admittedly, a good percentage of those days it got poured down the sink stone cold when she finally rose at eleven. Today, he eventually sprang to life at 9.15. Unaccustomed to the solitude, he made the decision to treat himself to breakfast in the caff. He quickly showered, shaved and dressed, leaving the house around twenty-five minutes later. The rain had eased to an annoying drizzle by then, and as it was only a short walk, he rode his luck by sporting just a light jacket.

The caff was busy with the usual mid-morning clientele of pensioners, loafers and hiding council employees. The latter cunningly left their vans parked outside the nearby tower blocks to give their gaffers and local busybodies the impression that they were working inside them. Jasper ordered the 'Health Breakfast' of two poached eggs, bacon, tomatoes, mushrooms, brown toast and coffee. He paid, then took his coffee, the wooden spoon with his number on and cutlery wrapped in a paper serviette to a vacant table and sat down. Once seated, he realised that someone was already reading the caff's copy of the paper, so he popped next door to the newsagent's to buy his own copy.

It took him longer than expected due to a row that was taking place between the shop owner and his assistant, most of which was in Punjabi, apart from the odd word such as 'fuck', 'lazy bastard', 'special offer' and, bizarrely, 'sherry trifle'. Jasper stood politely and waited with the paper in his hand and the correct change until eventually the assistant stormed off into the back and the owner rewarded him with the finger during his retreat. Jasper then listened while the exasperated retailer explained that the prices on his till were automatically set by head office. When special offers ceased, his underling had the job of removing the promotional tickets from the shelves. Inconveniently for the owner, the assistant found this to be a less than stimulating application of his talents, and instead (to quote his boss) preferred watching "wank videos on his phone" or "talking to schoolgirls". This failure, he explained, led to customer confrontation when their till overcharged for items that were no longer on special offer but still had the reduced price displayed on the shelf. This resulted in refunds, lost profit and, last but not least, serious workplace tension. During this monologue, the assistant reappeared wearing his coat and stormed past Jasper, lingering for a split second at the till to deliver a further line of abuse in his mother tongue, which Jasper assumed to be an expletive-peppered farewell.

On his return to the caff, Jasper unexpectedly found two men in suits seated opposite him at his table. One was older than the other and had a world-weary demeanour; he was wearing a cheap man-made suit and a well-worn raincoat. His thread-veined complexion betrayed the fact that he routinely looked for answers at the bottom of a bottle. His younger cohort, who had a much trendier outfit and an obvious exercise habit, looked directly at Jasper as he approached. Jasper wasn't someone who routinely sought confrontation, and as there were other spare tables, he merely sought to retrieve his cutlery and the wooden spoon.

"Sit down, Mr Skinner," ordered the older man abruptly.

"It's fine. I'll just move to another table," replied Jasper weakly before realising that the man knew his name.

"We'd rather you sat down," said his oppo, more politely but just as firmly. "We know who you are and what you do."

Jasper considered the chances of defending himself with a cheap wooden spoon and a newspaper before wisely choosing to sit down instead.

"Is this anything to do with sunbeds?"

"Why would it be?"

"I just wondered. Candles?"

The older man shook his head.

"Cassette tapes?"

He shook it again. "The New Inn…" he replied.

Jasper gulped nervously.

"I see that has got your attention. Allow me to explain. I am Detective Inspector Jim McClean. This is Detective Sergeant Dean Dodds. We are interested in your partner's new job at the New Inn and, in particular, one Mr Alan Kelly."

Suddenly Jasper didn't feel that hungry. That urge had now been replaced by a strong desire for a pee. He just looked at the two policemen, partly relieved that they weren't from a really formal drugs cartel, but now beginning to worry about what they actually did want. The lady behind the counter called out 'sixteen' and Jasper gingerly held his wooden spoon up as she trundled over with his meal. As she placed the plate in front of him, she looked directly at Jasper's uninvited breakfast guests.

"Are you going to share this? Or are you going to

order something, being as how you are taking up two seats for paying customers?"

Dodds attempted to reply, but McClean touched his arm in order to quieten him. Dodds instantly fell silent and the older man began to speak.

"Madam, would I be correct in assuming that you were on holiday when they did the customer service course?"

"What customer service course?"

"Ah, apologies. Please forgive my understandable mistake. You were clearly excused from formal training due to your entirely natural gift for public relations. Allow me to put before you an attractive proposal before we waste any more of the joyful repartee with which you ply your trade. If you wind your neck in and go and fetch us two teas, I won't radio the station and have a marked squad car placed on permanent patrol outside your establishment, which, judging by the nature of your clientele, might spark a serious downturn in the price of your shares on the London Stock Exchange. In fact, a crash that might be so serious that it could see your CEO loading the freezer with a large amount of unsold pig meat that might then be deemed entirely surplus to requirements."

He accompanied this with a flash of his warrant card and the well-practised smile of a man who delivered threats like golden syrup delivers diabetes. Left in no doubt that this was a tussle that she really didn't want to take part in, she smiled weakly and retreated to fetch two teas. The inspector watched her go and then turned his attention back to Jasper.

"Now, where were we?" he pondered for effect.

"The New Inns," the sergeant reminded him, which instantly earned him a pained look of disdain.

"We have been trying to get an undercover officer into Kelly's operation for some time. But given that there are only three of them, we have found it challenging to say the very least. So when word reached us that Cheryl the cleaner had decided to vacate her position, we thought we were 'game on'. That is until your partner, Miss Weeny, beat us to it and applied before we could manage to field a suitable candidate. Do you follow me so far?"

Jasper nodded. The puddle of now tepid fat was starting to congeal around his bacon, making it appear less healthy by the second. He thought about eating a slice of toast, but as there was now a noticeable absence of saliva in his mouth, he couldn't see it being an enjoyable experience. So he just lifted the coffee cup to his lips with the slight tremble of a cornered man.

"So in short, we would like to speak to Miss Weeny to see if she would be willing to provide us with inside information that might help us to bring about the closure of Alan Kelly's operation. In return for your joint cooperation, we will overlook your previous hilarious escapades, working while claiming benefits and obviously the undeclared cohabitation. How does that sound?"

Jasper nodded again. His coffee tasted like milky Bovril. It was an excellent example of cheap catering coffee. Sadly, the Crud Coffee Company forgot that people actually had to drink it, even if it was only two quid for a tin the size of a dustbin. The lady returned with two teas and again McClean smiled at her. She didn't return it this time. Instead, she went back to the counter where the other members of staff were making a very poor job of not staring.

"So do you need her to wear a wire or a miniature body camera?"

"No, nothing like that. Think less 'Miami Vice' and more 'Happy Valley'. We haven't got the budget to sanction an operation like that these days. He's just a small-time drug dealer with an unusually tight operation that just happens to operate from a pub in the same road as the chief constable's cousin, who apparently has shaken the family tree to the point where it's getting a bit embarrassing at family parties. We also believe that he is the local source of a new drug that's come to the market from Japan. It's a new breed of amphetamine that has been developed in laboratories over there that's starting to cause us major problems."

"We call it Japanese whizz, or jizz for short." The sergeant laughed, once again earning him the older man's displeasure for the unwarranted interruption and a weak smile from Jasper.

"Consequently, Dodds and myself have been given a little wiggle room in order to get the job done. All we need is solid intelligence regarding his delivery system, the location of his stash and what resistance we are likely to encounter when we blow his back doors off, so to speak."

The sergeant took another breath with the obvious intention of delivering a witty jizz/back door-related double entendre, but read McClean's pained expression and wisely decided against it.

"So I have your word that if we provide you with this information, you won't report us for anything else?" said Jasper tentatively.

"Why would I? You've been a useful source of

information that I might rely on again in the future."

Jasper didn't like the sound of an ongoing relationship with someone who had just casually threatened him. But then he'd been threatened by a lot of people over the years. 'I'm gonna smash your head in, you weedy twat!' was common or garden and really didn't bother him these days. Whereas 'I'm going to cut off your source of revenue, ruin your relationship and attempt to put you in prison' had definitely got his attention. So just like the lady behind the counter, who was now two complementary teas down, he begrudgingly nodded his agreement.

Satisfied that he had adequately demonstrated his considerable leverage, McClean raised the cup to his lips and gulped down the last of his gratis brew. Dodds, sensing the conversation was drawing to a close, attempted to do the same, but coughed, as the nerves in his throat hadn't been dulled by the smoke of a million fags. As they rose to depart, the older detective deliberately leaned forward to quietly deliver his final parting shot.

"Speak to you soon, Jasper. Don't be a stranger. By the way, the chief constable plays golf with Don Starman. Says he's still looking a bit plum coloured around the edges." He laughed at his own joke while his sergeant quite literally choked his agreement.

The now crestfallen Jasper watched them leave the premises, as did pretty much every other person in the caff. Then he looked down at his breakfast. The grease was now fully set and looked about as healthy as a tarantula smoothie. He pushed it away. The unexpected meeting with his new employers had been the ultimate appetite suppressant and was more effective than any holiday swimwear photo taken from the 'wrong angle' and stuck to the fridge by a well-meaning spouse.

"You finished with that?"

Once again, Jasper was entertaining at his table like a drunken lottery winner in a lap-dancing club. On this occasion, however, his honoured guest was Clive the Claw, who had now occupied the still-warm seat left by Oldbury's answer to Jack Regan.

"All yours if you want it." Jasper grimaced, pushing the deep vein thrombosis pick-and-mix towards the opportunistic amputee.

Clive could scarcely disguise his delight at a free plate. Jasper watched as he expertly jammed the previously unused knife into a slot in his prosthetic right hand before securing it with a strong elastic band he'd taken from his pocket. Jasper stared as he set about torturing the plate with the cutlery. The scraping as he sawed through the bacon jagged through Jasper's teeth like an errant sliver of foil on an old-school Kit Kat. Jasper rose from the table in order to escape the din, picking up his unread paper as he did so. Clive gave him his well-practised 'puppy eyes' and he reluctantly replaced it. The mono-handed freeloader rewarded him with an egg-stained smile as he reached over for the remainder of his coffee without any hint of embarrassment.

"This means a lot," lied Clive, who habitually uttered those words on an hourly basis to obtain free stuff from those he considered more fortunate than himself. "You're a legend, mate!"

Jasper, sensing this to be a milestone moment in their previously casual association, felt that he should gain something special in return for his outstanding generosity. There was no better time to seek the answer to a question that had troubled him for quite a long time.

"You're welcome, Clive. Any chance that you could settle an argument for me before I go? Might I be so bold as to ask exactly how you lost your hand?"

Without looking up, the one-armed breakfast bandit killed a thousand rumours with a single sentence.

"I was high on magic mushrooms and cut it off with a plastering trowel because I thought Yoffy from Fingerbobs was controlling my hand."

"Why a plastering trowel? Why not a knife or an axe?" wondered Jasper aloud.

"Because I was a fucking plasterer!" replied the now slightly irritated Clive, beautifully missing the point.

Chapter 19

Annie really wasn't enjoying her second day as the New Inn's cleaner. The sparklingly clean toilets that she had left yesterday had been transformed into a cesspit overnight. Now she was tasked with clearing up someone's puked up chippy tea that was blocking a urinal. Sadly for her, whoever had parked it there had carried on pissing, so mopping up second-hand beer was to be her second glamorous job. It was during the first seconds of her second task that she noticed that her right hand was beginning to feel moist. She stopped for a moment and withdrew it from her rubber glove. Sure enough, it was leaking and her hand was tainted with angel water. She stood for a second, struggling to control her temper. She'd got up early for a job she didn't want. Battled through the rain and cold. Now she had someone else's body fluid on her right hand and it wasn't even Tuesday night! Why was she doing this? What was the point?

Annie thoroughly washed her hands in the sink using a generous amount of the pink soap from the dispenser. Exploding from the gents, she tore over to the cupboard under the stairs and virtually ripped the door off its hinges. She searched in vain for a replacement pair of gloves, but there was none to be found. Ancient Brillo pads, remnants of liquids and gels for long-forgotten floor cleaners, filthy tea towels, but absolutely no other rubber gloves. She slammed the door loudly and went to find Neville. When she found him, he was bottling up behind the bar.

"Can I have some petty cash to go to Green's and get some Marigold gloves and a few other bits of cleaning stuff?"

"How much do you need?" Neville was happy to

comply if it made amends for his earlier attempt at humour.

"Twenty quid should do it. I'll get a receipt…"

"Can't see why not." Neville turned to the till, opened it and withdrew £20 from the float. He passed it to Annie then he wrote a chit, which he pushed back into the note clip.

"At least it's stopped raining," he said enthusiastically. "Bring a packet of biscuits and I'll make us a cuppa when you get back."

Annie nodded in agreement, pulled on her coat and stepped out of the back door. Neville was correct. The rain had at last abated, but it was still a landscape better seen from a cosy high-rise window. Green's Hypermarket was just a short walk up onto the Wolverhampton Road, then a few hundred yards down. As the familiar green neon sign drew closer, she saw it reflected in the large dark puddles that covered big areas of the uneven car park hastily built on the site of an old tractor factory. At this time of the morning, the store was fairly quiet, with just a few staff busy restocking the shelves ready for the day's rush. In the café there were three workmen in hi-vis jackets noisily enjoying a cheap breakfast, a harassed mom in a business suit looking for last-minute school cooking ingredients in the baking aisle and a woman shopping in pink unicorn pyjamas pretending to herself that doing so was entirely normal.

Annie considered herself a connoisseur of supermarkets. She didn't need the sign over the door to know which one she was in. Green's always liked to make you walk past the stuff you knew you shouldn't buy right by the door: trays of iced ring doughnuts, fresh pizza and the takeaway curry bar were all carefully arranged to tempt away your dietary resolve. Undaunted, she strode straight past, along the centre aisle that crossed the store and into the cleaning section. In a few minutes, her basket was filled with her favourite cleaning materials, plus two pairs of standard rubber gloves and a further pair that had much longer arms for cleaning the urinals. From there she passed round to the biscuit row to make her selection. She tried to think about what Neville might like. After much thought, she decided to play it safe with chocolate digestives. She dropped them into her basket and made for the checkout. There was only one open and there were a couple of people queuing. Annie reasoned that time spent queuing was more fun than time spent cleaning, so she happily stood in line rather than using the self-service area. While she was waiting, a supervisor came over to the till and stood behind the young lad operating it as he completed the transaction with the customer before Annie. When he had finished, the supervisor opened the till and drew out all the notes from the clip, which she fastened into a plastic pod and then pushed sideways into a tube that ran up into the ceiling.

Whoosh…!

For a moment it didn't register, then suddenly Annie recognised this as the same noise she heard in the pub every time Kelly was in his 'office' dealing with a customer. That must be why there were no drugs or cash to be found anywhere downstairs. The customers clearly made their order by phone and the 'buy' was prepared in advance. Kelly would take the cash in the gents and shoot it upstairs in a pod, and the drugs were delivered to him by the same method once the money was safe. Genius! Annie quickly paid for her purchases and packed them into a brand new bag for life. After all, she wasn't paying! Hurrying out of the store, she immediately pulled out her mobile to ring Jasper, and stood under the canopy by the entrance that kept the trolleys dry. It rang a few times before he picked up.

"Hello… You took your time. Everything all right?"

"On a scale of one to ten, one being ulcerated tonsillitis, ten being a 100 to 1 Derby winner, zero!"

"Why? What's happened?"

"I have had the misfortune to make the acquaintance of Oldbury's premier crime-fighting duo, who are aware of your new job and urgently wish to recruit us as informants."

"I ain't no copper's grass," replied Annie, who instantly settled on a code of ethics regarding such matters.

"They said that if you don't tell them anything you find out, they'll report us to the Department of Work and Pensions for cohabitation and undeclared income. They will also investigate our previous operations to see if any crime has been committed, which, from the negative tone of the conversation, is most likely a foregone conclusion."

"F-U-C-K," said Annie slowly. She was revising her original manifesto and thinking that now that she fully understood the situation, giving them a few helpful clues didn't seem so bad on reflection.

"Also, they suspect that Kelly is behind a new Japanese drug that has started turning up locally. It's a kind of speed, apparently…"

"What, Japanese whizz? That would make it jizz, wouldn't it?" Annie was pleased with her gag but was annoyed that Jasper wasn't laughing.

"That was a good gag for me," she said indignantly.

"Sorry, I'd already heard it from one of the coppers, so forgive me if I'm not booking you a slot at The Glee Club. What's your news?"

"I've just worked out how he does it."

"How he does what?"

"How he moves the drugs and money around without anyone seeing. It's a system with a pod in a pipe. They must have one in the gents."

"The only pods that go down pipes in any gents that I'm aware of definitely don't contain money or drugs."

"Very funny! I've just been in Green's and I recognised a sound that I hear every time he has a punter in. It's the thing they put the cash in at the till that goes up into the ceiling."

"Hang on, I'm in front of my laptop. I'll Google it."

As Annie waited, she watched with amusement as people repeatedly chose and discarded the same trolley that appeared to have a parcelled-up nappy and half a sausage roll in it. Annie wondered if the nappy contained the other half. Then decided that it obviously wouldn't be possible for a toddler to instantly digest half a sausage roll during a shopping trip unless it had unexpectedly contracted explosive gastroenteritis.

"It's called a pneumatic tube system according to this, and it's switchable. So you can send as well as receive pods. So where do you reckon it goes?"

"That's the other thing I've found out today. There's a

young girl upstairs in the flat with the dog… called…. umm… Viagra."

"Viagra? She must be amazing to look at, then," said Jasper, laughing.

"Oh, I dunno… some foreign name. Anyway, I better go. I only came out to get rubber gloves and some biscuits. "

"Oh, I see, one of those parties, is it?"

They said their farewells and Annie began to walk back to the pub. The clouds were lifting a little and the merest speck of sunshine was peeking around them. Which was ironic, as a storm seemed to be brewing for Jasper and Annie…

When she arrived back at the New Inn, Neville was in high spirits. He had made an effort to atone for his earlier comedy faux pas by having the kettle ready boiled, with two matching mugs out for her return, complete with tea bags and a dainty plate for the biscuits. He had put the plate on a table in what he considered was a more intimate area of the lounge. He met her at the door with a bar cloth draped over his arm and ushered her to the table like a waiter, then vanished into the kitchen to make two teas, as if this was a tricky culinary manoeuvre. Annie sat waiting while staring blankly at the plate. She usually ate biscuits quickly from the packet, just like a skeet machine fires shotgun clays. The plate felt a bit formal, like she was at her posh aunties or… shit… on a date! This realisation hit just as the jukebox began to softly play 'My Cherie Amour' in the background.

Neville returned from the kitchen with two teas and set them down on the table. He had hoped that Annie might pat the seat beside her, but quickly gathered from her expression (as he paused awkwardly, dripping tea from mugs that were now beginning to burn his hands!) that there was more chance of Trump converting to Islam. So he settled for a chair on the opposite side of the table and reluctantly plonked himself down, hurriedly setting the mugs on the table and flapping his hands around like a model drying her nail varnish before stuffing them under his armpits while sucking in air like a whale to quell the pain.

Annie had waited long enough and expertly negotiated the red rip tape around the top of the packet of biscuits before dumping some out on the plate and taking three to set beside her mug. Neville hesitated, then just took one, as he worried the flow of conversation might be impeded if he overindulged.

The jukebox had now moved on to 'Je T'aime'. Neville had clearly forgotten the gasping climax midway through the song. Once again he coloured up as he tried to make small talk while a breathless French lady blew the harbour gates off in the background.

"Green's busy?" he inquired.

"Not really. Only a few folks about, but now the rain's knocked off it will get busier…"

"Do you usually shop at Green's?"

"Sometimes. I usually go to Balzi, as it's a bit cheaper, there's not so much choice, if I'm honest."

"I like the cooked meats in there and the Frickerdellers."

"What are Frickerdellers?"

"Little ready-cooked beefburger-type things. They look a bit like… err… testicles."

Annie laughed. Neville laughed. They were sort of pals again…

"Would you do me a favour?" said Neville, looking slightly more serious.

"Anything you like as long as you don't want me to touch your Frickerdellers!"

"Please don't mention to Alan that I told you about Vasara. He's a bit weird about people knowing she's up there."

"Why's that? There's nothing weird about a middle-aged man keeping a teenage girl under lock and key in the upstairs of a crummy pub."

Neville laughed nervously, which suggested to her that he was afraid of Kelly.

"He doesn't like people to know too much about what goes on here."

"No problem. I won't say anything."

Neville looked relieved and spent the next fifteen minutes telling her his life story, while Annie drank her tea and ate more than her fair share of the biscuits. The rest of his playlist was quite varied, but with a common theme: Abba, 'Take a Chance on Me', Percy Sledge, 'When a Man Loves a Woman', and finally Minnie Riperton, 'Loving You'. Meanwhile, Neville rambled on about ex-wives, absent grown-up children and where it all went wrong. Annie tried hard to look interested, though she really wasn't but made the effort all the same. In fact, it was difficult for her to decide whether he was more unattractive than boring or vice versa. Finally she felt her brain stem starting to melt as Minnie Riperton sang far too many la, la, la's in 'Loving You' and Neville was in mid-flow about his internet dating exploits, which mainly consisted of bitter disappointments on rendezvous with women who felt his profile photo wasn't an up-to-date representation of the romance on offer. She really couldn't take any more and suddenly stood up in the middle of his recollection of Paula from Preston, who had a facial tick and an unhealthy obsession with ferrets.

"Anyway, we better sup up. I have those toilets to finish," Annie said.

With that, she stripped her mug like a builder, jammed another whole biscuit in her mouth and made for the men's toilets, pausing only momentarily to pull on her brand new rubber gauntlets like a rectal surgeon preparing to remove a 'misplaced' cucumber. Neville was left with half a cup of lukewarm tea and the depleted packet of biscuits to regret his total domination of the conversation.

With the toilet door closed behind her, Annie ignored the pressing matter of the fish supper puke and instead turned her attention to finding the location of the pneumatic tube system. She remembered that the tube in Green's came from above and that it was quite wide. She looked up at the ceiling. There was only one pipe coming from it, and that seemed to terminate in the condom machine, which, now she thought of it, did seem a bit odd. She smiled to herself, as the irony of jizz travelling down a pipe and terminating its journey in a Durex vending machine wasn't lost on her. She tried the front door to see if it was open, but of course it was locked. Kelly wasn't that stupid. No one could resist free condoms in three fruit flavours, male performance boosters or a battery-powered tickler, which might lead to awkward questions about the lack of stuff to nick and exactly why there was a big fuck-off tube in there.

Satisfied that she was now making progress, she set about the job of cleaning up with her new leak-free gauntlets. As timing went, that was a great move, as around a minute or so later the door opened and Alan Kelly surveyed her labours from the door.

"You always seem to catch me at the most glamorous part of my working day."

"You'd only be bored at a country club. I like to think that we offer a wider range of cleaning opportunities at the New Inn with our diverse and eclectic customer base."

"I'd be happy to give it a try if there's one on the phone."

"Alas, no. I see that you had a little tea party with Neville. You want to keep an eye on him. He'll have his oven gloves and the paper doilies out next."

"I'll keep that in mind. You're welcome to join us next time."

"Thanks, but I'll pass. I've heard it all before. Some people are just unlucky in love."

"What about you? Is there a Mrs Kelly?"

The banter abruptly stopped and Kelly gave her a look which told her the conversation was almost over.

"Never felt the need. I like to keep it simple."

With that, he gave her his usual wide yellow smile and left her to it.

Chapter 20

Bernd had experienced no further unruly behaviour from 'his pupils' during the remainder of the ferry crossing. In fact, the long coach journey from Harwich to Oldbury had been a fairly subdued affair, mainly due to a lack of sleep. So apart from an unsavoury insult-swapping session regarding a rather swollen male breast, he felt that being a teacher was money for old rope so far.

When they had got back into the coach after the ferry crossing, Bernd had successfully secured himself the window seat. Osterman had made no objection to the swap, as he now felt protected by the psycho supply teacher for the remainder of the journey, during which Bernd had quietly marvelled at how well capitalism seemed to work as they travelled along England's motorway network. Lots of smart modern cars, bright clean service stations with shops and restaurants and seemingly the freedom to fill up with fuel without the need for any lengthy queues or rationing coupons.

At last, the coach turned off the M5 at junction 2 and a loud cheer rang out from its excited young passengers. They were looking forward to seeing the England they knew from the television. Men in bowler hats and striped trousers, cricket on the village green followed by cucumber sandwiches and scones with jam and cream, and quaint little whitewashed cottages with thatched roofs and tiny leaded windows. So it was no surprise that they were more than a little dismayed by their first glimpses of the heart of the industrial West Midlands. An enormous electrical substation set in the centre of a busy traffic island, a large black-and-white pub that had seen better days, and a car dealership opposite selling cars made in the country they had just come from.

Masses of grey concrete fencing hiding tired, decaying factories, overgrown polluted canals and a grim working-class town stained black by the soot of a thousand chimneys. This was the reality of living in Oldbury in the late 1970s. On the upside, though, Bernd instantly felt right at home.

As the coach swung right from Joinings Bank into Moat Road, their long journey neared its conclusion. They passed the poplar trees and St Michael's vicarage before drawing to a halt with a final hiss of air brakes outside Oldbury High School. Another cheer went up, but this time it was far weaker and entirely orchestrated for their waiting hosts by Mr Comb-Over. On the pavement stood a welcoming committee of children and parents, all eager to see which one of the German adolescents would be their houseguest for the next week. As they disembarked, bags were claimed and kids eyeballed each other with disgust as painful introductions were made. Faltering pleasantries were stammered in both languages by those forced to try out what they had hopefully learned in the past couple of years.

Bernd stood amidst all this frantic activity, nervously clutching his stolen suitcase. His confidence was understandably draining away. He barely spoke the language, had no teaching experience whatsoever and was by now possibly a wanted terrorist on the run. After what seemed like an eternity, during which he passed the time by endlessly grinning at everyone like a village idiot, Mr Comb-Over walked up to him with a man that he rightfully assumed was one of the English teachers.

"Bernd, this is Mr Gappy. He will be your host for this week," explained the older teacher before walking away to initiate another Anglo-German introduction. Mr Gappy held out his hand and Bernd shook it firmly and smiled. The Englishman wore a tight claret and blue tracksuit and had a whistle around his neck, which suggested an athletic ability that wasn't altogether supported by his obvious paunch. His angular face was topped by a rather comical haircut, which appeared to have been designed solely with the intention of highlighting his enormous forehead. Their handshake went on far too long, and Gappy's grip was more about determining superiority than conveying friendship. Bernd instinctively felt that his host might just be a tosser.

"Welcome to Oldbury High," said Gappy enthusiastically in heavily accented German. "Did you have a pleasant excursion?"

"Not bad," replied Bernd, slightly amused by his choice of phrase but relieved that Gappy was happy to take the intellectual high ground by speaking German. "A couple of kids decided to bung toilet rolls off the back of the ferry, but apart from that it was fine."

Bernd quickly deduced from Gappy's blank expression that his German was more at the level of 'Where is the railway station?' rather than discussing amusing teenage escapades. He wasn't looking quite so intellectual now, and his face began to match the colour of his tracksuit as silent seconds slowly ticked by. Finally, he just smiled and nodded, employing the international code of embarrassment for anyone who has linguistically bitten off more than they can chew. Bernd realised it might be counterproductive to further dent his confidence in his language skills, as a switch to English ran the risk of revealing his own shortcomings, so he decided to throw him a fish to spare his blushes.

"I am happy that the sun is shining today, but I am a little tired from the journey."

Gappy instantly rallied, as he'd understood 80% of that.

"I also adore the sunshine! Would you like a bottle of coffee in the staff room once the children have been minced."

Bernd once again resisted the urge to smile at Gappy's obvious issues with vocabulary and instead smiled warmly, as if mincing children was all in a day's work for a teacher in Germany.

"I would like that very much. You are very kind."

Gappy obviously got all of that, as he simply nodded rather than risk further conversation that he couldn't decipher before lolloping off to deal with an emerging accommodation crisis sparked by musical differences between an indignant mod and a spotty German heavy metal fan.

Once again Bernd stood alone. Many of the children and their luggage had already been loaded into cars for the short journey to their new home for the next seven days. Others had been shocked by the news that they would have to walk, lugging their case with them, as not every household in Oldbury owned a car in 1979.

"I bet you could murder a coffee," said a soft female voice in excellent German.

Bernd turned to face the source of the enquiry. It came from another teacher he hadn't previously noticed during the havoc of their arrival. She was smiling broadly and her hazel eyes twinkled as she spoke. Long dark hair cascaded past her shoulders in a spiral perm, and Bernd tried hard to keep his eyes from going lower in order to study her further.

"That would be great! Mr Gappy mentioned there might be some in the staffroom."

"That'll be instant coffee. That's what most English people drink. It usually tastes similar to water that slugs have died in. I have German coffee, a kettle and a coffee pot in my classroom, if you'd rather?"

"Thank you for the kind offer. Lead the way!" said Bernd, totally delighted by how things were turning out for him.

As they began to walk across the school car park towards the main building, Bernd heard Gappy shout something in English, which he didn't understand. His new friend turned and shouted something back. Judging from his crestfallen expression, it wasn't altogether welcome in Gappy's ears. Bernd just smiled like a village idiot again and decided to play the dumb German, which was working remarkably well for him so far, as he'd copped a quick look at his companion while her attention was taken and was more than happy with what he saw.

During the next half an hour, Hanna Klein attempted to explain her life in England to Bernd. She had been in Oldbury for the last three years. During the previous two, she had taught at a school in Liverpool but had struggled to settle there so decided that she would try a post in the Midlands before she gave up altogether and returned to Germany. She had found the English education system to be a little lacking compared to the one back home. The pupils weren't so disciplined and she often found herself struggling to be heard, particularly with the fourth and fifth years. On the upside, the pay was good and England was a far cheaper place to live than Germany. She had therefore done a lot of sightseeing and made the most of the longer school holidays. The food had taken some getting used to, but she confessed to becoming a big fan of fish and chips.

As per usual, Bernd really didn't do a lot of the talking, he just listened. That suited him fine, as until now his only experience of teaching was shouting and handing out playground torture. If the conversation turned to his own educational history, it was going to be a struggle to instantly invent something plausible. The coffee was good and the company was even better, but like all good things, it had to end. Just as it seemed as if he might have to start spinning tales, Gappy stuck his head around the door.

"It's the moment to go my address. My car is not slow. We will eat soon, food."

Hanna looked at Bernd and rolled her eyes. This was the same bad grammar that Gappy had been killing her with for the last three years. He meant well, but he had designs on her and she knew it, so her main defence had been pretending not to understand when he continually attempted to ask her out in German, hoping that no one else in the staff room had understood. They didn't need to; it was blindingly obvious, and even the kids laughed about it.

Bernd thanked her for the coffee and, lifting his stolen suitcase, obediently followed Gappy to his car. He had changed into black Farah slacks and a matching polo-necked jumper, topped off by a black wet-look blouson-style nylon jacket with gold GT stripes down the arms. Bernd guessed that the intended aim of the outfit was to give him the appearance of a part-time racing driver or secret agent, but it actually made him look like a squashed packet of cigarettes.

Given Gappy's sporting attire, a small French hatchback wasn't what Bernd had expected to see, but then he wasn't an expert on small Western European cars and therefore hadn't spotted the Gordini badge on the tailgate when he lifted it to deposit his case in the back. The moment the engine sprang to life and settled into a deep rumbling throb, he correctly guessed that this was no Saturday shopper. Gappy grinned maniacally as he pulled on his driving gloves, theatrically smoothing the perforated chequered vinyl over his knuckles and carefully fastening the press-stud under each wrist. Then he stretched out both arms and flexed his fingers, like a maestro before his grand piano. He placed them on the wheel, strummed the accelerator and whacked the gearbox into reverse. The little car shot backwards, weaving across the car park before Gappy span the wheel and simultaneously pulled on the handbrake, performing the well-practised J-turn that the headmaster had spoken to him about several times. As the front shot round, he rammed the car into first, and with just a cursory glance both ways at the gate, they flew up Moat Road far faster than was legally advisable.

"Very fast, yes?" bawled Gappy over the din of the screaming engine.

Bernd nodded grimly and held on for dear life. He hoped it wasn't far to Gappy's house. If it was, he really couldn't see himself requiring any food when he got there. After around seven torturous minutes, both Bernd and the little Renault were relieved when the pilot announced their imminent arrival.

"This is my lovely address. I like that you hope it!"

"It's very nice. You must be very proud," lied Bernd. It was a small terraced house on a steep hill with rubbish in the garden. Gappy parked outside in the same style that he drove, with much revving and unnecessary arm flinging. Finally, he blipped the throttle and turned the ignition off in the mistaken belief that this would make it easier to start. The instant odour of petrol that accompanied this action told Bernd that most likely wasn't the case.

Gappy sprang from the driver's seat and walked round to the rear of the car to retrieve Bernd's case. His passenger felt the blood flow back into his fingers as he released his desperate grip on life, and he gratefully climbed from the car. His obviously pallid complexion prompted his still-grinning driver to ask if he was unwell. Bernd shook his head, as even if he told Gappy he drove like a fucking lunatic, he wouldn't understand unless he phrased it like a three-year-old would, so he really didn't see the point in passing comment.

Once past the front door, Bernd could see that Gappy's house was a shrine to all things manly. The living area boasted a large silver Marantz hi-fi system that dominated the room and had floor speakers about a metre tall. A white sheepskin rug sat dead centre, with an oval coffee table placed on it. Spread across this, in a carefully arranged fan shape, was a selection of pristine magazines about 'manly' pursuits, which had clearly been placed there in an attempt to create the illusion of a successful playboy rather than a deluded comprehensive school teacher. On the wall over the fireplace was the famous poster of a female tennis player scratching her bottom. Bernd decided that Gappy was clearly a cliché but that it would probably be a good idea to keep it to himself unless he wanted to spend half an hour miming it.

"Sit down, please, and snooze. I will make us eating in the kitchen," said Gappy enthusiastically. He looked pleased with this utterance and had clearly been brewing the sentence for a while.

"Might I be able to see my room, please? I would like to unpack my things," countered Bernd, who was understandably anxious to see what his stolen case actually contained.

Gappy looked puzzled for a moment, then led the way through the kitchen and opened a door at its rear. Bernd stepped in expecting to see a bedroom, but instead, he found a bathroom. His host closed the door behind him, but Bernd quickly opened it again, which was obviously a surprise. This time he made the question far simpler. Just one word.

"Bedroom," he said quietly, and placed two hands at the side of his head in a sleeping mime.

"Ach so!" replied Gappy, like a Colditz guard watching his first pantomime.

This time, he led him back through the kitchen and through a door off the lounge which hid a steep flight of stairs with a sharp turn in it at the bottom. Once at the top, he opened a door to the left and then withdrew to allow his guest past. Bernd nodded his thanks and stepped in as Gappy retreated back down the stairs to the kitchen. It was quite a small room, and the window looked out onto the road. The only items of furniture were a single bed covered by a tired floral duvet, a wood-effect wardrobe with a hanging rail and three drawers, and a matching bedside table with a distinctly medical-looking adjustable lamp. There was a large poster on the wall. This time it showed a character from 'Star Wars', which had been one of the big films from two years previously. It had been clumsily Sellotaped to the emulsioned woodchip wallpaper, which had gone brown and lifted in places, taking the paint with it and leaving a bare patch on the wall.

Bernd threw the case onto the bed and made short

work of defeating the locking mechanism with a cheap screwdriver he found in the drawer of the bedside table. When the catches sprang open, he was relieved to find that it did actually contain just clothes and some personal items. Over the last twenty-four hours, he had imagined many scenarios regarding its contents – everything from a ventriloquist's dummy to a large quantity of illegal drugs. But as he slowly unpacked its contents, he started to form the opinion that its rightful owner might just have been a John Travolta fan. First out was a white suit with matching waistcoat and a black shirt with flared collars. Luckily, this was followed by two pairs of Sta-Prest trousers, one grey, one black, a pair of Levi jeans and five pairs of brand new Y-fronts. For his top half, there was a Village People sweatshirt, a cream Aran-knit polo neck, a bottle-green V-neck sweater, a yellow Simon shirt and two plain white ribbed T-shirts. Footwise, there was a selection of nylon socks in garish colours, a pair of white Adidas pumps with blue stripes, and some shiny black brogues, both a size too big. He also found a bag of toiletries, containing shaving gear, Denim aftershave, a brand new toothbrush, toothpaste and an Old Spice deodorant stick. He breathed a sigh of relief. He knew it could have been far worse.

He opened the wardrobe and loaded in his new outfits using the wire hangers that he found on the rail. As he closed the last drawer, which now housed his swiped smalls, Gappy yelled from downstairs to announce that the meal was ready. Bernd really had no idea what to expect, as he knew very little about English cuisine, so when he walked through to the little kitchen, he was surprised to see a plate of spaghetti bolognese waiting for him on the table. He only knew what it was because he had seen it in films on American Forces television back in East Germany. The chef was glowing with pride at his culinary endeavours and had even placed a glass of breadsticks in the middle of the table.

"Please down sit. I like you hope it" Gappy said enthusiastically, passing him a small green and red cardboard pot with a perforated plastic top as he did so.

Bernd peered at the label. Although his English was limited, he recognised the word 'cheese' and so obediently shook the container over his meal. A cloud of fine yellow dust settled across his plate, reminding him of the foot scraper his mother used after her bath. Midway through his first mouthful, he really wished he hadn't bothered. The long-life ready-grated Parmesan of the late 1970s smelt like baby sick and definitely tasted no better. He quietly stirred it in and added an excess of salt and pepper to drown out the taste. It took him a few tries to copy Gappy's obvious prowess with fork twirling, but bar a few hiccups he managed admirably for his first spaghetti experience. When they had finished, Gappy sat back expectantly and Bernd quickly took the hint.

"I liked it very much. You are a great chef."

Gappy beamed his appreciation of the praise and quickly cleared away their plates. Just as Bernd was wondering what the spoon was for, the chef placed a small dessert glass in front of him which contained a thick, brown, glutinous substance that resembled something you would punish your dog for doing on the carpet, rather than a pudding.

"I gift to you chocolate mint pudding instant."

Bernd picked up his cutlery and tentatively took a spoonful. It tasted the way it looked, like the by-product of an effluent leak at the elephant hospital.

He swivelled his eyes and saw that Gappy was studying him closely. His childlike enthusiasm for absolutely everything was beginning to exhaust him.

"Very nice. I like it very much. We should have this in Germany," he lied shamelessly, for the second time that day.

It was a longer sentence than his host was used to, but he seemed to gather the sentiment. Bernd forced another three spoonfuls down before declaring himself full with a level of theatre that Marcel Marceau would have been proud of. Hanna Klein was absolutely right. English food was really going to take some getting used to.

Chapter 21

That afternoon, an NFRS general meeting was held at the Eagle's Nest. There was both a slew of new information and a great deal of added complications that needed to be fully discussed. As always, there was good coffee and warm strudel, so Bernd and Jasper had to wait while Annie ate two slices of strudel; being a lady, she refused to talk with her mouth full.

When at last she had finished, her two male cohorts listened intently as she described in detail the cash and drug delivery system that Kelly had installed at the New Inn and filled them in with what she knew regarding his 'niece' in the upstairs flat. In doing so, she also enjoyed the added bonus of making Jasper jealous by slightly 'bigging up' her tea and biscuit interlude with Neville. This misrepresentation took the form of a little footsie under the table and some minor hand brushing. If she played her cards right, she might get a Domino's and cookies tonight!

Then a rightfully jaded Jasper explained in detail his one-sided conversation with Oldbury's premier law enforcement team and their veiled threat to tear their playhouse down. Annie was amused by the Paul Young reference, but Bernd didn't understand what she was laughing at, so Annie sang it for him, but he still didn't get it and shoved his fingers in his ears, laughing. In retaliation, she blew all the strudel crumbs off the table, and suddenly he wasn't laughing any more.

Bernd had no news, really, apart from the fact that Candy was still giving him a heavily discounted 'sympathy special' whenever she had a cancelled appointment. She didn't get many, so he reasoned that was going a long way to keeping the spark in their 'relationship'.

When they had finished talking, Bernd sat back and smacked his lips, as he knew that got on Annie's nerves. If his time with the Stasi, Baader–Meinhof and the NFRS had taught him anything, it was that plans seldom go to plan. However, he accepted that, despite this, what they needed most of all was a plan. Since that was definitely his department, he felt it wise to look as if he might be coming up with one. During the last week or so, his involvement in their enterprise had been, at best, rather limited. He worried that this might be pointed out to him and his benefits package adjusted accordingly, as even half an hour with Candy on mates rates cost more than an entire week's shopping. It wasn't a problem to lower his sausage and strudel intake, but life without oompah time would definitely be much harder to bear. After they had gone, he drifted off in his armchair and thought back over his life.

"Think, Strudel Boy, think…"

Suddenly, he was wide awake and waiting for his laptop to boot up. The floaty, warm stage when the brain relaxes just before sleep takes over had brought him the answer. Now all he had to do was make it happen…

Annie was surprised when she arrived at the New Inn the next morning and Alan Kelly answered the door. She hadn't previously known him to be up and about before eleven when they opened.

"Where's Neville today?" she inquired.

"Don't tell me you're missing him?" smirked Kelly, without looking up from his phone.

"Missing might be too strong a word, but he does make a very good cup of tea."

"His mother has suddenly been taken ill, so he's at the hospital. Hopefully, he'll be back in a couple of days. You know where the kettle is. Make me one while you're at it."

Annie decided to ignore the casual sexism for the sake of the bigger picture. As she walked through to the kitchen, Kelly put his phone into his pocket and followed her. Annie filled the ancient stainless steel kettle and put it on to boil. She noticed two mugs on the side, one of which was still half full of tea, which was odd. She emptied it into the sink and then ran the hot tap to wash them along with a couple of used teaspoons lying on the drainer. Kelly eyed her from a distance as usual, but not in the way that Neville did, like a toddler in a dummy factory. She suspected he was gauging her body language before launching an inquisition. Being an old boxer, Annie knew a thing or two about the art of delivering a surprise attack. So she was ready when Kelly began to gently probe her.

"So, how are you getting on here so far? Do you like it?"

"One floor is much the same to mop as another. It's the people that make the job good or bad."

"That's not really answering the question."

"So far, so good then." The kettle clicked off and Kelly waited as she poured the water. Annie was aware he was waiting. Hot water is a good weapon, but unbeknown to Kelly, her fists were a far better one.

"When did Neville hear about his mom?"

"His sister rang around 8 pm last night. He went straight away. She's in a bad way, apparently."

"I'm sorry to hear that. I hope she pulls through."

Annie squeezed the tea bags with the back of a spoon and threw them into the bin.

"Milk and sugar?"

"Milk and one sugar."

Annie finished making Kelly's tea and passed it to him. He maintained eye contact as he grasped the handle of the mug, but Annie stared him out and he looked down as he set it on the unit before taking a slurp.

"You see, the thing is, none of the regulars seem to know you, and I just wondered how you got to know about the vacancy. Who did you say told you?" Eye contact was back on. Kelly was looking for a tell.

Annie knew this was the haymaker. She'd seen it coming a mile off. During her text conversation with Kelly about the job, she had been careful not to reveal any specifics regarding her source. Something had clearly rattled Kelly's antennae and now he was checking her out. Kelly was good, but Annie was better…

"I saw it on Cheryl's Facebook feed. She'd posted a status that a friend of mine saw and they messaged me to say there was a job going here."

"What sort of status?"

"You don't want to know."

"I wouldn't ask unless I did."

"Something along the lines of 'I told my wanky boss to shove his job up his arse'!" Annie knew this was a lie that Kelly could easily disprove by ringing Cheryl, but who would admit to it when asked? It was a gamble, but one she had no option but to take.

"That does sound like Cheryl. Never one to mince her words."

Annie could immediately see that Kelly had relaxed his stance slightly. Her explanation was plausible and awkward enough for him to believe. The eye contact had gone from total to minimal, so she was confident that he had swallowed it. Taking a swig of tea, she moved towards Kelly, who was still standing in the doorway, effectively blocking her exit.

"Anyway, better get on. Any puke in the bogs today?"

"None that I've seen. Maybe it's your lucky day?"

They both knew that wasn't what he meant, but she tried hard to look like it was. Kelly moved enough to let her past but not enough to look polite. Annie felt like the ice was cracking beneath her, but as Kelly had locked the back door when she arrived and Jasper was relying on her to keep them both out of court, she couldn't twat him and make a run for it. Instead, she calmly collected the mop and bucket from the cupboard under the stairs before returning to the kitchen and filling it with the remainder of the hot water from the kettle. Pulling on her rubber gloves, she strode purposely towards the gents, kicking open the swing door as she entered. Then she stopped dead in her tracks. If the sight of a severely beaten Neville tied to a chair wasn't a total shock, then Vasara stepping out of a cubicle holding a handgun definitely was. Annie, for once, was lost for words, and by the look of it, Neville was lost for teeth.

"How's your mom?" enquired Annie brightly.

"Never knew her. I grew up in care," moaned a very messy Neville. At last shedding light on his obvious relationship issues.

"I really wasn't sure until you mentioned Cheryl's Facebook feed. She doesn't do Facebook. Considers it to be full of braggers, moaners and piss takers, apparently." Kelly blocked her exit from the room once more, having followed her from the kitchen.

"Was that really necessary?" Annie nodded her head towards Neville.

"Nothing to do with me," said Kelly.

Annie noticed that Vasara had splashes of blood on her top and that her white trainers made her look as if she had a part-time job in a very sloppy abattoir.

"I kickbox a little," she explained, smiling. Annie briefly thought about smashing her smug face in for her, but concluded that her knowledge of guns wasn't really sufficient to know a real one from a replica. So she put her hands up slowly instead.

"Did I tell you to put your hands up?"

"Sorry, I thought it was pretty traditional in these types of situations."

"Maybe in cowboy films, but not in real life. Put them together behind your back."

Annie did as she was told and felt Kelly tie them together with what she strongly suspected was a cable tie, judging from the sound it made. Admittedly, the fact that Neville had a matching pair lashing him to his throne was also a big clue. Kelly checked her pockets and removed her mobile phone, which he duly turned off and dropped down the toilet.

"Get her a chair from the bar," ordered Vasara. This surprised Annie, as she had wrongly assumed that Kelly was the master of ceremonies. Her own inbuilt sexism astounded her. If the situation had featured a slightly different dynamic, she would have been delighted that there was a strong woman was in charge. Kelly dutifully returned with a chair and set it behind Annie, then forcefully pushed her down onto it.

"OK, so now we play Find Out Who the Cleaner Really Is," announced Vasara. Annie guessed that she had hosted violence-based game shows before, judging from her obvious ease in the role of compère.

"That's not a very catchy title." Annie smirked.

Vasara span around on one foot and delivered a kick to the side of Annie's head with what looked like a reissued Reebok aerobic trainer from the mid-1980s. After a couple of minutes, when Annie could finally see just one Vasara, she decided that she would simply focus on the questions for the remainder of the game.

"Not so funny now, eh Mrs Mop? First question. Who knows you are here?"

"No one," lied Annie.

"Mmmmm," mused their host, putting the muzzle of the handgun against Neville's kneecap. "I think the wrong answer and too quick. Think again or Big Mouth Neville gets a plastic knee after two years in a wheelchair on a waiting list."

"My boyfriend." Annie was quickly picking up the rules of the game. Wrong answers meant a permanent dole pole for Neville and a possible ricocheting bullet hazard for everyone else present.

"Who else?"

Annie considered her answer. She didn't see the point in mentioning Bernd, but she knew another answer that might throw a spanner in the works.

"The police!"

"You lie!" Vasara tightened her grip on the trigger and the gun's hammer moved slightly. The only thing that eased the tension was the sound of Neville's urine splashing on the tiled floor.

"No, honestly. The police!"

Vasara shook her head and squeezed the trigger a little harder. The hammer moved a fraction more. This time there was no sound at all from Neville. His tank was clearly empty.

"The fucking police! The rozzers, the filth, the Polizei, the 5-0. They found out I had got a job working here and leant on my boyfriend for information."

Vasara fully relaxed her finger and Neville instantly looked the happiest he had since Annie was bending over a few days earlier.

"So why did you want the job in the first place?" interrupted Kelly.

"Because you took over the pub and ruined it, and a little old lady asked us to get rid of you!"

"Get rid of me? How?"

"I don't know. We were working on that before the

police got involved. Maybe get the health inspectors in and replace all your drugs with Shake n' Vac?"

"Wouldn't I have noticed the fresh floral fragrance?"

"I'm clearly under pressure. I just blurted out the first powdery thing I thought of!"

"Well, baby formula would have been a better bet."

"Or the stuff you put on after a shower," offered Vasara.

"What, deodorant?"

"No, the dusty stuff."

"Athlete's foot powder?" mumbled fungus-footed Neville, and consequently everyone else ignored him.

"Oh, you mean talcum powder?"

"Yes, talcum powder!"

"Do people still use that?" queried Annie.

"They do in my country," exclaimed Vasara.

"Where's that, Transylvania?" guessed Annie.

"It's good, but it's not right." Kelly laughed in the style of Roy Walker.

"Do you want another kick in the head, you fat bitch? You think I come from fucking vampire land?"

"Fat shaming is a crime!" exclaimed chubby chaser Neville.

"It's not in my country!" screamed Vasara.

Annie deduced that further nationality-related speculation might be wholly unwise. Vasara was obviously a little touchy regarding her heritage, and at this point, Neville still had a full set of knees. She wasn't going home with a car, but given the stakes, that felt like a win of sorts.

"So what have you told the police?"

"Nothing yet, as I really hadn't found anything out! They only came round yesterday."

"I think your police are shit!"

"That gun entitles you to an opinion. What are the police like in your country?"

"They are amazing. They have guns, armoured cars and dress like RoboCop!"

"I sort of guessed you might say that. Is that why you break the law in this country instead of your own?"

"Can you blame me?"

"It's a fair point well made, but I think you're being a bit harsh. Our police are massively understaffed due to cuts in their funding…"

"As interesting as this all is, can you just get back to the questions? I've been tied to this chair for eleven hours and I can't feel my arse!" yelled Neville, whose mental health problems were also now revealing themselves.

"Neville is right, we should concentrate. So as yet, you have given the police no information and the only person that knows you are here is your boyfriend, yes?"

"Absolutely!" agreed Annie.

"Thank fuck for that!" lisped an utterly relieved Neville, who was wearing brand new Levis that he didn't need modifying by an Eastern European seamstress using a 9mm Glock.

Twenty minutes later, Neville fell flat on his face after being untied and attempting to walk. He and Annie were then zip-tied by their hands, facing each other around a thick wooden floor support in the cellar. Annie now had a shiner, and Neville's head resembled a dropped Easter egg.

"I love the smell of your body spray..." lisped Neville.

"You smell like a dirty bin that someone has pissed in and left out in the sun to dry!" responded Annie, who was in no mood at all for his swoony crap. "Exactly what did you say for this to happen?"

"Nothing. She heard us talking on the CCTV."

"What CCTV?"

"The CCTV I didn't know anything about..."

"How could you not know about the CCTV?"

"Because it was all wireless and hidden in stuff!"

"Didn't you see the screens?"

"There weren't any, she had it all on her phone!"

"I thought she was pretending to be his niece?"

"She was! I had no idea at all that she was the one in

charge!"

"That's understandable, I suppose. She didn't look like an international drug dealer to me when I saw her on the roof."

"There you go then. We both got it wrong!"

Neville had a point. Who would expect a teenage girl to be in charge of a well-run drug-dealing operation based in a run-down pub on the edge of the Black Country? Meanwhile, far, far away in a country very hard to pronounce at the other end of Europe, the man who did picked up his ringing satellite phone and cringed when he saw the number calling…

"Hello, Papa!" bawled Vasara.

"Hello, Vasara," replied Bogdan Snr, now manically massaging one temple with his free hand.

"Papa, we might have a problem…."

Oh, shit! thought Papa.

Bogdan was the largest dealer of illicit drugs in a country absolutely nowhere near Transylvania. He didn't grow or produce his narcotics; he was simply a very gifted wholesaler. By importing newly developed products from the East and introducing them to the West, he had created a powerful web that extended throughout Europe and beyond. He wasn't a violent man, nor was he particularly ruthless. He was honest, hard-working and at times rather more benevolent than you would expect a billionaire drug dealer to be. So nice, in fact, that for many years he lived openly without bodyguards or fear of assassination. But in recent years, all that had changed…

Vasara, his only daughter, was learning the trade, starting from the bottom. She had been educated in the finest schools that money could buy in France and Italy. Understandably, her father had hoped that one day she would make her living in high finance, politics or maybe the arts. But no, Vasara wanted to be just like her brothers and join the family business. In many ways, this was like any other enterprise involving profit and loss, products and customers. However, it was still not a business that any normal father would willingly choose for his daughter. But then, Vasara was no ordinary teenage girl. She was an absolute fucking liability! And so, following several death threats from rival outfits enraged by her audacious antics, he had wisely decided to send her to the opposite end of the continent, as far away from him as it was possible to get. So when the opportunity arose to open a Bogdan franchise in the back end of Birmingham, Vasara was booked on the first available flight with strict instructions to keep her head down and profits up. Bogdan and his sons breathed a deep sigh of relief and sent out a lot of free samples in a sincere attempt to soothe some ruffled feathers in the European drug-dealing community. After nearly a year, things had returned to near normal and Bogdan's bulletproof vest was back in the wardrobe. Now, within seconds, Vasara's father had his phone on 'hands-free' and was massaging his whole head as his psychopathic daughter ranted and raved about 'respect for da family'.

By the time two o'clock came and Annie hadn't returned from work, Jasper was getting nervous. He'd tried to text her several times but had not received a reply. As his anxiety increased, he dropped the cool approach and tried to ring instead, but it went straight to voicemail. She really didn't like the job, so she was hardly going to start working overtime. He even checked that she hadn't gone directly to the Eagle's Nest with urgent intelligence. But Bernd hadn't seen or heard from her at all that day. Then Jasper remembered their meeting from the previous afternoon, in particular, the footsie and minor hand brushing that his devious partner had mentioned in an attempt to secure a little takeaway action. Regrettably for Annie, she had forgotten that Jasper had seen Neville during their earlier reconnaissance mission at the New Inn and regarded him to be no more of a threat to their relationship than the Ebola virus. Her plan to secure an overpriced takeaway pizza and warm greasy cookies had therefore always been doomed to failure. But now his confidence in her devotion to him was being tested by her continuing absence. He decided that he would take the route he knew she used in the hope of meeting her halfway. No doubt there would be some entirely plausible explanation, and he supposed that he could use the exercise. By the time he was crossing the New Inn car park, he was a mess. In his head, they were frantically shagging their way through the 'Kama Sutra' on the pool table.

The front door was still bolted, which didn't help matters. Jasper relieved some of his pent-up aggression by booting the crap out of it until his toes finally sent urgent pain signals to his brain, much to the amusement of a group of regular customers who were cheerfully sharing the remainder of their dwindling stocks on the wall outside while they patiently waited to get re-supplied. When at last the door opened, Vasara invited him in. Jasper needed no encouragement, frantically hurrying towards the bar where he knew the pool table was. Relief quickly spread through him when he confirmed that the only gaping triangle experiencing any ball action there was the wooden one next to the cue ball in the front tray. This joy was short lived when he turned around and found Vasara pointing her Glock at him, now flanked by Mr Cable Tie.

"I'm looking for Annie!" he stammered.

"We know!" they said in unison.

Jasper felt foolish. He should have known that Annie would never do that to him. She would never betray him with another man. His language was awful when he reached the cellar at gunpoint and saw his beloved cable tied to a toothless athlete's foot sufferer. It was even worse once he gathered that they would soon be forming the world's worst-smelling ménage à trois.

As the evening drew on, it was Bernd's turn to get concerned. Since Jasper's early afternoon call, he hadn't been able to get through to either of them. Both numbers just went straight to voicemail, which wasn't surprising as by then they were both nestling in the U-bend of the gents at the New Inn. But being Spock to Jasper's Captain Kirk, he gave the issue far more thought before blundering in. Clearly, there had been a recent development in the case that he was not aware of, as neither of his colleagues was in the habit of turning their phone off. Therefore, he correctly assumed that they were somehow incapacitated, possibly being held captive, and that maybe this was beyond the skill set of an elderly German punk with a worsening prostitution habit. Bernd took out his phone and scrolled through his contacts. The call took a couple of seconds to go through before it was answered.

"Hello. It's me again," he said in German. "You know when you said if I ever needed any help...."

Back at the pub, things in the cellar were getting fraught. Annie was a bit put out that Jasper thought she might be carrying on with Neville. In turn, Neville was utterly miffed that she would consider such a thing a total non-starter, though he readily admitted his current fragrance and obvious lack of front teeth would now make any romance a big ask.

"She told me exactly what you did!" said Jasper.

"What did I do?"

"You brushed her hand and played footsie under the table."

"I did no such fucking thing! Besides, even if I had, she was clearly hot to trot because she didn't say she had a boyfriend."

"Partner!"

"What's wrong with 'boyfriend'?"

"Makes it sound like we're fifteen. People say partner these days."

"Well, I wouldn't know. It's a long time since I had one."

"I'm not entirely astounded by that fact. You smell like an orangutan's bidet!"

"I smelt fine until that teenage head case put a pistol against my knee and your 'partner' decided to be coy with the truth."

"Firstly, that's not strictly accurate. You're generally a bit whiffy, if I'm being honest," said Annie, who was not entirely enjoying being exposed as a stranger from the truth.

"A bit fucking whiffy? You weren't complaining when we were drinking tea and eating biscuits. I have a shower every day, change my clothes and wear deodorant."

"I was undercover," stated an indignant Annie.

"So you're saying those biscuits meant nothing to you? You cold-hearted cow!"

"I'm saying I had a job to do, and eating your biscuits was just part of that job."

"Looks to me like you might have had a long undercover career then!"

"Oh, so YOU'RE fat shaming me now?"

"Just saying what I see…"

"Kelly already did that gag!"

"What gag?"

"The Roy Walker catchphrase gag."

"Couldn't stand him and I never watched it!"

All three fell silent.

"So what do you reckon will happen to us?" pondered whiffy Neville.

"Bullet in the back of the head is my guess," replied Annie.

"Really?" said Neville, beginning to sob. "I still have so much left to achieve. Now I'm going to end my days in a crappy cellar."

"It's much worse for us," said Jasper.

"How come?" whined Neville.

"We're both going to die cable tied to an incontinent crybaby with recently diagnosed BO!"

"Maybe they'll make us take a lethal overdose?" suggested Annie.

"I'm really not keen on that!" spluttered Jasper.

"Why not? Sounds like a great way to go. As high as a kite and just step towards the light."

"That bit's OK. I just don't want my family finding out I died with a bellyful of jizz!"

Chapter 22

<u>Oldbury 1979</u>

Exhausted by the journey, Bernd had slept like a log in the little guest bedroom. As he slowly came to, he could hear fast breathing from the other bedroom and the faint sound of springs creaking. Fearful of accidentally overhearing another man's stress relief, it took him a couple of minutes to deduce that Gappy wasn't furiously gripping his gristle. He was working out with a Bullworker exercise machine in his bedroom. As he continued to reluctantly eavesdrop, there was a loud twang followed by a muffled thump and then it all went quiet. Eventually, the silence was broken by a weary moan. He waited for a few moments more before deciding that maybe he should go and see if everything was OK. He opened his bedroom door and stepped out onto the small landing, off which there was only one other door. Still wary of disturbing some bizarre sexual fetish, he knocked softly before entering. His knock was answered by the same weary moan. Bernd hesitantly pushed open the door, ready to quickly retreat at the first sign of leather or chains. Gappy was sitting on the bed with his hand covering his mouth, tears in his eyes and the Bullworker lying beside him. It was then that Bernd noticed the blood dripping from between Gappy's fingers, the look of total shock on his face and his fast-swelling upper lip. It didn't take a forensic pathologist to guess what had happened...

An hour later, Bernd was dropped off at school by the now aptly named Gappy, who had a mouthful of kitchen roll and an emergency appointment at the Dental Hospital in Birmingham city centre. On the back seat was a sandwich box of ice that now contained his front teeth that he had been 'lucky' not to swallow when the Bullworker had made a spirited break for freedom during his monthly workout, which had been solely designed to impress his imagined love rival and been done in the futile hope that he just might just mention it to Heidi. As Bernd walked through the twisted opal-green metal gates that hadn't moved since the 1960s, Gappy shot away with his tyres screaming like the tooth fairy on a shout.

Bernd had made a big effort with today's outfit, and he felt like a million dollars in his black Sta-Prest and trendy yellow Simon shirt. The brogues needed two pairs of socks to stay on his feet, but that was a small price to pay. Everything else fitted perfectly, as if he'd bought the clothes himself. He was clueless again about what the day ahead held, but seeing Hannah Klein waving him into her classroom through the window felt like a really good start. Finding his way in through the wired-glass double doors, he winced at the pong as he swiftly detected the boys' toilets, wisely rushing past them into the more fragrant corridor. He knocked politely for the second time that day on her classroom door before entering to find all the German kids and their teachers sitting patiently awaiting his arrival. Bernd gave his heartfelt apologies for his tardiness and helpfully explained the reason. The other teachers looked horrified, because of course they didn't generally discuss their colleagues' personal challenges in front of pupils. It's number one in the big book of teachers' rules, which is incidentally identical to the one given to trainee prison officers. But Bernd didn't know that, of course, and smiled as the kids roared with laughter at his intentionally comical explanation, complete with mimes. Heidi, sensing the dismay of her peers regarding Bernd's indiscretion, swiftly brought the matter to a close and began to explain the day's itinerary. Suddenly, another knock at the door interrupted proceedings, and a pupil entered with a note for Miss Klein. As she read it, she glanced nervously at Bernd and then again at Mr Comb-Over.

"The headmaster wants to see us in his office," she

said solemnly.

Bernd didn't like the sound of this at all. He had felt sure that his bogus teacher cover would eventually be blown and he would be arrested as a terrorist before being expedited back to Germany to stand trial. But he had expected more time to consider his position before any of that happened. Blanched by fear, he duly followed Heidi and Mr Comb-Over the short distance to the headmaster's office in the foyer of the school. The door was already open and Bernd could see no obvious evidence of any police officers, which frankly astonished him. Headmasters didn't tend to carry out citizens' arrests on terrorists in Germany, and he couldn't imagine that Britain would be any different. The trio trooped in and the headmaster got straight down to it, with Heidi naturally falling into the role of Bernd's translator.

"We have had a telephone call from a Mr Kunt Wiesel in Germany. He was ringing to apologise for missing the coach from Frankfurt as he was given the wrong departure time by the teaching agency. He was more than a little surprised when I confirmed that we already possessed a full complement of exchange teachers and that he must be mistaken. When I checked with the exchange coordinator here in England, I found that there was no Bernd Tost listed as an agency teacher for the trip. So, Mr Tost, might I hear your explanation, please?"

Bernd waited while Heidi translated the headmaster's statement and eventual question, which, as you would expect, took far longer than the English to say. He was further surprised by there being no mention of terrorism, the police, extradition or prison. Simone had either bravely kept her mouth shut or her rich father had smoothed the whole thing over. Either way, it seemed he was in the clear and his short involvement with Baader–Meinhof would remain his secret. Based wholly on that, he took the easy route and went straight for the sympathy angle.

"Headmaster, I am sorry for the deception, although I can assure you that I meant no harm. You are absolutely right. I am not a teacher. I am an East German citizen. I escaped across the border a couple of months ago and was being relentlessly pursued across Frankfurt by Stasi agents intent on returning me to the abject misery of the communist state. I, therefore, surrender to your custody and respectfully request that you notify the relevant authorities of my intention to claim asylum."

This statement of fact naturally made the room go a bit quiet when it was translated. Then Heidi laughed. The headmaster just looked shocked and Mr Comb-Over began to sweat rather profusely.

"I heard about the nipple twisting and the Chinese burn from the kids. They were terrified that they would get the same if there was any more misbehaviour. I couldn't see any teacher getting away with that, even in Germany. Plus, you haven't spoken a word of English since you got here!"

So that's the story of how Bernd Tost, the ex-Stasi operative and former Baader–Meinhof member, came to live quietly in a tower block in Oldbury after successfully applying for asylum and being granted indefinite leave to remain. Heidi helped him to learn English while they negotiated the application process together. They went on to have a three-year affair before, sadly, he lost her to illness – she ran off with the bloke in the next bed when she had her appendix out!

Gappy's teeth couldn't be saved, and he gave up speaking German not long after. Poorly fitting dentures and his comical surname made him a laughing stock amongst pupils. Eventually, he left teaching to pursue a career as a yoga instructor and was later credited for introducing tantric sex to wider audience. Sadly, hundreds of women later successfully sued him in a class action, citing his teachings as the root cause of their extensive vaginal erosion. He now lives in a caravan in Blackpool and makes his living selling candyfloss.

Bernd went on to teach guitar in schools all over Sandwell and was well regarded by both his colleagues and his pupils. He never returned to Germany despite the wall being torn down in 1989, ever fearful that doing so might somehow spark reprisals against his family for his disappearance during the 1970s. Instead, he became the quiet, thinking man of Derek Robinson House that people relied on for advice in times of crisis, living alone on the top floor with his German coffee, frozen strudel and some amazing memories until Jasper Skinner popped in to see him one day many years later…

Chapter 23

From down in the cellar, the world's worst-smelling ménage à trois could hear Vasara having her Al Pacino breakdown on the phone to her dad. She didn't sound happy at all, and whatever was being said to her on the other end wasn't improving her mood. When the call finished, she began raging at Kelly, and when you're cable tied to a post in a cellar, you know it's only a matter of time before you're next. Sure enough, a couple of minutes later, the cellar door flew open and Vasara stood at the top of the steps framed by the light. Her Glock was still in her hand and she was waving it around like a supermodel with a new hairdryer. Jasper didn't much like the way things were going. Why hadn't he just rung the police when Annie went missing?

Vasara stomped down the steps and sat on a beer keg surveying her captives. Jasper and Annie faced her and Neville glumly knelt on the floor with his back to her, smelling like a sewage worker's welly.

"If you're going to kill me, get it over with," he wailed.

"Why would I kill you when torture is far more fun!"

Neville wailed some more, but luckily hadn't had anything further to drink.

Annie noticed the powder on Vasara's face and started to laugh.

"What are you laughing at, Mrs Mop?"

"You've got jizz around your mouth."

"Maybe I put a gun in your mouth and pull the trigger? Still laughing now?"

Annie quickly stopped laughing. It just seemed sensible, given the escalating threat level.

"Why not just let us go?" asked Jasper in a voice he intended to be soothing. "We won't tell anyone about this. Neville just needs a few stitches and fresh underwear. We can go back to the old lady and tell her that you've agreed to keep the noise down a bit. You can just get a new cleaner and everyone is happy."

"What about the police? What will you tell them when they speak to you again?"

"I'll just say that we haven't found anything out and appeal to their better nature."

"And they will go away just like that?"

"I can't see why not. They're such very busy people and there's quite a lot of crime in this area."

"Want to hear my plan?"

"Am I going to like it?"

"Probably not, but anyway. I put a cable tie around Neville's neck, pull it nice and tight and you can all do… the err… you know… the kid's dancing thing…"

"Ring a ring o' roses?"

"Nope."

"Dancing around the maypole?"

"No, no, the party one…"

"'The Superman Song'?"

"The hokey-cokey," bellowed Neville, correct for once. "I loved the hokey-cokey in the children's home. We always used to play it when people came to choose kids to adopt."

"That must be a lovely memory," said Annie, smiling softly.

"Not really. I never got picked, and I looked a bit stupid still playing it when I was seventeen. But at least I'd mastered all the moves by then."

Upstairs, the pub phone began to ring and was eventually answered by Kelly.

"I've changed my mind," announced Vasara abruptly, and promptly shot Neville through the back of the head. He fell forward, face first, with the now very much more fluid state of his skull forming an excellent match for the rounded shape of the support post.

Annie and Jasper both stared in total horror at Neville's lifeless, kneeling, face-planted corpse, which was still cable tied to one of the wrists of each of them.

"That's so much better. I was so tired of his shit sad stories, weren't you?" With that, Vasara thundered up the cellar steps to see who was on the phone.

Detective Inspector Jim McClean was sitting alone in his car outside Derek Robinson House with a cheese and caramelised onion pasty he'd just microwaved in the newsagent's. It wasn't the most scenic venue for a meal, however basic. And as he prepared to demolish it, a used nappy thrown from a balcony high above landed twenty-five feet away with a plop on the grass. Warily, he peered upwards to ensure there wasn't a television following it, then took a steamy bite. For once he had a quiet day while his sidekick was on a course at the Police Training Centre, so he thought he'd pop round and put the wind up Jasper again, to see what he'd found out. Unfortunately, he didn't bank on the lift being broken or the lazy little tosser being out when he finally got up to the ninth floor. Now he was hot and mugged off. The pasty was his consolation prize, with the bonus of no young sergeant present to nag him about the calorie content or the long-term dangers of trans fats. His phone rang. He looked at the screen. No number was displayed and therefore he guessed exactly who it was.

"How is your wife?" enquired Bogdan. "Did she like her new caravan?"

"Hello, Mr Bogdan. Very much so, thank you. She is absolutely delighted with it," said McClean enthusiastically while juggling the hot pastry and molten cheese in his mouth.

"Did she approve of the optional extra coordinated scatter cushion pack that I surprised her with?"

"She did, sir. She's not put the home shopping catalogue down since. Everything has to match those cushions perfectly."

"Good, I am glad she is happy! Sadly, however, I am not!"

"Why is that, sir?"

"Because my crazy daughter, who I have bribed you handsomely to keep your eye on, now has three people held captive in the cellar of the pub. She also sounds to me like she might be indulging in the product, which as you might know is an unwelcome departure from the 'total dummies' guide to successful drug dealing'."

"I'm sorry to hear that, sir. I was totally unaware of both developments."

"Well, I find that disappointing, as I felt we had a clear understanding that it was your job to know what she was doing."

"But I had made contact with someone on the inside."

"Who?"

"The new cleaner's boyfriend."

"That would be the one in the cellar, along with the cleaner herself."

"Oh, that would explain why I am unable to find him. That is indeed unfortunate"

"I put it to you, detective inspector, that although you might be good at detecting crimes, you might not be very good at preventing them. I, however, am excellent at predicting future crimes. I can clearly see a burning caravan with a screaming woman inside it."

"Is she holding the catalogue, sir? I would prefer it if she was."

"Are you joking, detective inspector?"

"Yes, sir. That was an attempt to defuse the tension in the conversation."

"It didn't work. I need you to get down there and calm my daughter down. Release the hostages and smooth everything over. Am I clear?"

"As clear as the double-glazed windows in the wife's

six berth static, sir. I'll make it a priority."

"Don't make me have to call you again, detective inspector."

With that, the line went dead. McClean looked at the pasty. In a million cop films, he would have sighed and thrown it out of the window, stuck the red light on the roof and screamed off. But this was Oldbury, and he didn't give a shit. His wife was a nightmare and consequently he much preferred being at work. He'd been happy as a sergeant. But her relentless spending and generally materialistic attitude to life had forced him into climbing the career ladder. If she died in a flaming caravan clutching the devil's own home-shopping publication, it wouldn't be a problem for him. But the questions that would come afterwards regarding the benefactor of the said caravan probably would. So he decided reluctantly that he would finish eating, then make a move. Seconds later there was another loud plop, this time from the roof of his car, and a loud cheer rang out from above. Unmoved, he took another hot cheesy bite just as a mustard-coloured turd rolled down the windscreen.

When McClean's turd-splattered car with the now empty nappy swinging from the aerial pulled on to the deserted New Inn's car park, nothing he saw gave the impression that there was an ongoing hostage situation in the cellar. He reversed into a parking space a sensible distance away from the door and gave some thought to his next move. He hadn't personally had the pleasure of meeting Vasara, and as she now had a gun, he felt even less inclined to introduce himself in person. After considering the situation for more time than was strictly necessary, he decided that opening a line of communication with the pub was probably the obvious first step towards a successful siege conclusion. He lifted his phone and Googled the New Inn, but then got sidetracked for a moment by the terrible reviews.

There was so much sediment in my glass that when I lifted it to the light, it looked like shredded marmalade.

My wife went to the toilet and the seat had a crack in it which pinched her arse, and she had to phone me in the lounge to help get her free.

I asked the barman which of the draught ales he would recommend. He laughed and asked if I was stripping wood or metal?

He wasn't a trained siege negotiator, as those people tend to be parachuted in with their smooth-talking psychobabble and a calming manner. In reality, he had only ever attended one 'hostage' situation and oddly that was at Oldbury police station. An older officer had got a 'bit emotional' about a young female traffic warden at a Christmas party in the 1980s. What had started as a bit of slap and tickle in the toilets had quickly got out of hand when his wife rang. The office wag answered and told her that he was in the ladies 'getting mellow with some yellow'. His wife duly attended the station and the officer in question had to be coaxed out with firm guarantees of no domestic reprisals later.

He rang the listed number and opened his window while it rang. After around six rings, it was answered by Kelly.

"Good evening, New Inn."

"Hello, this is Detective Inspector Jim McClean of Oldbury CID. I understand that there might be an ongoing hostage situation on the premises. Is that correct?"

As those words left his lips, the unmistakable sound of a gun being fired travelled to his ears, both down the phone and live across the car park. Suddenly, parking a bit further from the door became infinitely more appealing.

"Was that a gunshot I just heard?"

"No, sir, that was a champagne cork."

"In a back street pub in Oldbury on a Thursday evening?"

"Thursday evenings are often very lively."

"So what's the occasion?"

"Somebody just got engaged."

"Somebody randomly got engaged at the New Inn, in Oldbury, on a Thursday evening? Not Paris by the Eiffel Tower, not next to the Hollywood sign in Los Angeles, but surrounded by junkies in some scabby shithole with a sticky carpet in a town famous for absolutely fucking nothing?"

"OK, fair play, you win. It was a gunshot."

McClean then heard a manic voice in the background and the phone forcibly being taken from Kelly.

"Who is this?" demanded Vasara.

"This is Detective Inspector Jim McClean of Oldbury CID."

"What does CID mean?"

"Criminal Investigation Department."

"So not the police then?"

"Yes, the police."

"So why not just say police?"

"Because most people know what CID means?"

"In my country, CID means sex disease."

"Really?"

"No, I just made that up to piss you off."

"So what was that shot all about?"

"I just shot the barman for telling shit sad stories."

"Dead or just wounded?"

"Very dead, I'm afraid."

"That seems a little unbalanced, if I'm honest."

"How many police are out there?"

"Just me at present. More on the way though," lied McClean. "What are your demands?"

"I think about it and you ring me back!" said Vasara, dumping the phone.

McClean closed the window again as the smell from the roof nappy was beginning to cloud his thinking. He wasn't 100% sure whom he should ring next or even how to explain how he became aware of the situation in the first place if he did. He was sure of two things, though. He was definitely moving further up the car park and he really wished he hadn't eaten that frigging pasty!

Chapter 24

Bernd quietly surveyed the scene at the New Inn from a discreet distance and hoped that he had given the correct GPS coordinates. He'd only downloaded the app that afternoon, and as it was free, naturally he had his doubts. Outwardly there was very little to suggest that anything untoward was happening at the pub apart from the fact it was closed. Just one lone car sat in the car park that appeared to have had the contents of a jar of piccalilli emptied over the roof. By now, the 'regular customers' on the wall had left to seek out other pharmaceutical suppliers, and the lack of activity didn't bode well. He felt reassured that his suspicion that Jasper and Annie were being held against their will was almost certainly correct, as throughout the afternoon he had continued to ring both their mobiles at regular intervals, without any response. The wheels he had set in motion would be difficult to stop, not to mention personally embarrassing. Events were now absolutely out of his hands, and he silently prayed for the welfare of his two prank-loving colleagues.

Thirty miles away, an NH90 German military helicopter with a team of ten KSK Kommandos was skimming over the rooftops of Leamington Spa on the last leg of a Black Ops mission designated to be of 'national importance'. Also aboard was a lone, highly classified principal trying very hard not to look queasy as the aircraft twisted and turned to allow for changes in the terrain. Their estimated time of arrival was 9 pm GMT. Being German, they were naturally fifteen minutes ahead of schedule!

"Time to target, seven minutes," announced the pilot over the intercom. This set in motion a flurry of checks, magazine clicks and night-vision goggle whines. The Kommandos eyed each other nervously. No one aboard wanted another Munich or even an

Oldbury. If this went well, they would become legends of the regiment. If it went badly, they might end their days in a rubbish-strewn car park and go home in a bag.

Staff Sergeant Willy Berninger peered down on the brightly lit West Midlands passing below him at lightning speed. He had been specifically chosen to lead the mission because of his fluent command of English. They had been briefed to expect a terrorist hostage situation, possibly multiple shooters and a well-defended urban building. The order and the information had come from the highest authority. His team had only half an hour to decide on their weapons and equipment before they were in the air. He was a soldier, and therefore he simply followed orders without dissent. But he was more than a little surprised to find that their target was in England and wondered why British special forces weren't being mobilised to deal with it.

In the cellar, Jasper and Annie listened while upstairs Vasara attempted to write a list of demands through a haze of jizz. Kelly watched nervously from across the lounge as she scribbled with a short red pencil in between muttering to herself. This wasn't what he'd signed up for at all. Dying with a police sniper's bullet between his ears had never figured in his vision of a successful drug-dealing landlord. Things had been going really well until the new cleaner arrived and Vasara had started self-medicating. He had strongly suspected from the start that she had 'issues'. But in order to secure a very favourable wholesale price from Bogdan, he had been persuaded to offer his daughter a work placement. Now he wished he'd just paid more for the drugs. He cursed himself for being so gullible. Another six months and he would have had enough to buy a bar in Spain and retire in the sunshine instead of sharing the upstairs of a pub with a massive dog and a crackpot teenager who was now free-writing her innermost thoughts onto the back of a bar tab.

McClean was stalling for time. He couldn't see the harm in waiting a few more minutes before calling in the cavalry. If this thing could be settled quietly, then he stood a far better chance of keeping his involvement with Bogdan under wraps. His fingers hovered over his phone. These were career-defining moments. Either he would retire with a decent pension and an exemplary record, or he would end his days on the force in disgrace. He needed to get it together and think calmly. How hard can it be to talk a drugged-up teen with a gun out of a pub? Heart pounding, he pressed the pub's number on his call log and it began to ring. Vasara answered after three rings…

"Hello. Is that Vasara?" was McClean's opener.

"How do you know my name?" demanded Vasara.

"Because it's my job to know. I'm a policeman. Have you decided what you need me to do for you?"

"Yes, I think so."

"Would you like some food sent in?"

"It's a pub, we have lots of food. Why would I want food, you idiot?"

"Sorry, it's a pretty standard question."

"I would like a helicopter and a pilot to take me to the airport. There I would like to be put on a plane back to my own country."

A helicopter? Shit!!!… thought McClean.

"That might be tricky. Would a car not be better?"

"If I wanted a car, I would have asked for a car! I want a helicopter, and if I don't get one, I'll shoot the cleaner next!"

This wasn't what McClean wanted to hear. He wanted a tearful, contrite teenager who opened the front door, threw the gun out and lay spread-eagled on ground in the car park while he handcuffed her. Then he could simply take her to the airport and stick her on a plane home to her dad. However, it didn't seem that this was going to be the case.

At that moment, he heard the sound of a helicopter in the distance. Perhaps someone had heard the gunshot and had rung it in? But if they had, the station would have sent officers to investigate. They wouldn't have scrambled the force helicopter first. The noise was now getting louder. Soon it was right overhead and descending as the pub's dog went mental on the roof.

"See what you can do if you try, Mr Policeman?" shouted an elated Vasara down the phone.

An utterly mystified McClean looked on as the helicopter landed, the side doors opened and heavily armed troops began to pour out, quickly taking up positions on the floor with their weapons pointing at the pub. Once he could work out exactly what was going on, he might call it in. But for now, it made better sense for him to wait in case, by some miracle, things worked themselves out in his favour.

Finally, Bernd summoned up enough courage to climb out of his elderly BMW estate and walk over to where the helicopter was now shutting down, wisely waiting for its blades to come to a total standstill before walking towards the open side door. His heart was pounding, and he felt sick. A familiar figure sat in the darkness, dressed in army fatigues and flanked by a single soldier. Now he was back in the bakery in Leipzig. She was older and definitely wider, but despite the years, still rocking the same crazy haircut that for some barmy reason was now dyed bright ginger.

"Hello, Strudel Boy," said Renate Redlinger.

"Hello, Fraulein Black Coffee. Long time no see."

"We're a long way from the old days in the bakery."

"A million years ago. I watch you on the news all the time. You still love an argument."

"Old habits die hard. Talking of which, the reason we are all here. Staff sergeant!"

Staff Sergeant Willy Berninger rose from his prone position on the asphalt and doubled over to the helicopter.

"Yes, Madam Chancellor."

"Willy, this is Bernd Tost, our contact on the ground. Bernd, please tell the staff sergeant all you know."

"Err, very little…"

"But you do have a line of communication with the pub?"

"I admit, I don't," said Bernd.

"So you're not 100% sure that this is a hostage situation then?"

"Er, no," said Bernd, fearing that he was beginning to

look a little stupid in front of Renate.

Back in the car, McClean peered at the black-and-white cross insignia on the side of the helicopter. He felt sure he recognised it from his Airfix modelling days, and unless he was very much mistaken, these were German armed forces. Bogdan clearly had more pull than he realised if he could mobilise the German army to a pub car park in Oldbury. He instantly felt the responsibility for the situation being lifted from his shoulders. As the only person present who had the faintest idea of what was going on, he thought he should at least brief them and formally hand over command of the situation. The last bit was probably a bit of an exaggeration, as until now, he had just sat in his shit-stained car and phoned the pub twice.

Creeping up on a bunch of twitchy, heavily armed soldiers didn't seem like the smartest move he could make. Nor did blowing the horn, which might lead to him convulsing in a hail of lead like Bonnie and Clyde. So he settled on flashing his interior light in the hope of attracting their attention rather than drawing their fire.

Staff Sergeant Willy Berninger was the first to notice the cack-decorated Audi flying the flag of Nappistan with its single occupant furiously flashing the interior light like a really shit kids' disco.

"Who's in the Audi?" inquired Willy.

"I honestly don't know," said Bernd, turning to look.

"Could be a dogger," said Madam Chancellor Renate Redlinger.

"A dogger?" said a puzzled Willy.

"Apparently, very popular in England. They drive to secluded areas and flash their interior lights to indicate they want sex with strangers."

"The English are really fucking strange. Don't they have any swingers' clubs?"

"I wouldn't know. When I come here, I just sit in a room full of people and argue about things that no one does anything about when I've gone."

"I've lived here for nearly forty years and I still don't understand everything they do. Putting minty vinegar on lamb is probably the worst of it." Bernd laughed.

"On lamb? Gott in Himmel! The pigs!" exclaimed Willy.

McClean now had four people looking at him, two of which had nasty-looking machine guns, so he thought he'd better introduce himself. Being careful not to make any sudden moves, he climbed out of the car then walked slowly across the car park with his hands clearly visible and his warrant card outstretched.

"Who are you?" said Willy in English, levelling his gun purposely.

"I am Detective Inspector Jim McClean of Oldbury Police. Who is in charge here?" McClean didn't fancy going through the CID thing again.

"I am!" said Renate Redlinger.

McClean gawped into the helicopter from where the female voice had come. The soft orange glow from the onboard lighting allowed him to make out the slightly familiar face staring back at him.

"Are you Renate Redlinger?" he stammered.

"The very same!" replied Renate, who thoroughly enjoyed surprising people and wasn't above farting at a G8 summit or calling the French frog-eating fucktards while on the phone to the Belgian prime minister.

Shit! thought McClean. *This thing goes even higher than I imagined!*

Then, trying hard to look the competent professional, he began to brief them on developments so far.

"OK, here's the situation as I see it. I have made contact with the pub and she's in the bar area."

"Who's in the bar area?" demanded Renate.

"Vasara, Bogdan's teenage daughter."

"Who is Bogdan?"

"Bogdan is a powerful Eastern European drug lord. Didn't he send you?"

"Are you suggesting that the chancellor of Germany would ride halfway across Europe in a helicopter on the orders of an Eastern European drug lord to collect his daughter?"

"Err, no, I suppose not. So why are you here?"

McClean hastily revised his earlier assumption that Bogdan had sent the German army to sort his daughter out. In reality, it was a bit of a stretch, but burning in a caravan or retiring in disgrace was making him a tad desperate to pass the buck.

"We have come to assist a very important German

citizen to free his associates, who are being held captive in this building."

Renate gave Bernd a little wink, and he blushed. Luckily, in the dark, no one could see.

"So how many shooters do we have?" probed Willy, who was becoming aware of a gathering crowd at the edge of the car park.

"Just one. Vasara has what I would guess is a handgun."

"So basically, then, we have a ten-strong team of heavily armed special forces troops without any authorisation whatsoever on another sovereign nation's soil and their aim is to defeat a lone teenage girl with one handgun?"

McClean was not only impressed with Willy's English turn of phrase but also with the sarcasm of his delivery. Renate looked a bit sheepish and Bernd had disappeared up his own arse.

"That about sums it up beautifully," replied McClean.

"OK, so how many hostages?"

"There were three, but now I suspect we're down to two."

"Why's that?"

"Well, I'm pretty sure she shot one. She said she did, but then she's a teenage girl, and in my experience, they tend to be a bit unreliable with regard to the truth."

"How do you know this?"

"I have the misfortune to deal with them and their adolescent lies nearly every day."

"No, I mean that she shot one."

"I was on the phone to the pub when she shot him."

"So you have a line of communication into the pub?"

"Yes, but it's only got 23% battery life unless I can plug my charger in to your helicopter."

Willy looked at McClean, aghast. Now the whole mission possibly hinged on someone having the right phone charger.

"So what else can you tell me about the situation?"

"The two remaining hostages are a man and a woman, the cleaner and her boyfriend! The building is a typical post-war British pub. Two main downstairs rooms; one is a bar, the other is a lounge, living quarters upstairs. In the basement, there is almost certainly a cellar where the beer is kept. Also on the premises is a man called Alan Kelly, who is the publican, and a large dog whose name I admit I don't know. But it's a noisy fucker, as you can hear!"

Chapter 25

In the New Inn's cellar, things were tense. Neither
Annie nor Jasper had ever been cable tied to a
corpse before. Admittedly, it did make talking
between themselves easier while Vasara and Kelly
were distracted by the helicopter.

"Wow, is that a helicopter I can hear?"

"Certainly sounds like one."

"And it's getting closer."

"Hopefully it's the police."

"Knowing our luck, it's Anneka Rice."

"Doubt they'd film 'Treasure Hunt' in Oldbury."

"I dunno, she'd fit right in with the shell suit, but she
definitely wouldn't hold on to her headphones for
long."

They both laughed. Jasper moved round slightly so
that his face was closer to Annie's. Neville's face
made a sucking sound as it was forced to twist on
the pole to allow him the movement. If he smelt bad
alive, he was certainly reaching new heights dead.

"You know I love you, don't you?"

"I sort of guessed, but as you'd never actually told
me, I couldn't be sure."

"Well, I do, and if we get out of this, I'll show you just
how much."

"Are we talking about a trip to the Dessert Shop and
a decent bottle of whiskey cream liqueur? Not that

Irish Fog stuff you bought last Christmas."

"No, I mean, will you marry me?"

Annie was taken aback. Although they were definitely in trouble, she hadn't considered that they wouldn't both come out of it alive. Admittedly, the circumstances might have been better and the venue a little more romantic. But if this is what it took to get Jasper to make an honest woman of her, then she was having it!

"Yes, of course I will. I would love to be Mrs Skinner. Can't be any worse than being called Weeny for the rest of my life!"

Jasper leaned in further for the kiss and Annie melted as their lips met. What was left of Neville's head made a noise like a fart pushing through a bowl of custard. Not a textbook proposal, but one she wouldn't forget all the same.

"Very touching…" said Vasara, looking down from the cellar steps. "Why don't we all celebrate in the bar?"

Kelly laughed. "I don't think Neville is going to be up for that."

"Let's bring him all the same."

Vasara covered Kelly with the gun from the steps while he cut Jasper and Annie free with his waiter's friend. Neville's arms immediately fell limply to his sides, and he slid off the pole and onto the floor, his now concave face giving him the appearance of a Mr Potato Head that had been left too close to the fire.

"Pick him up!" ordered Vasara.

"You pick him up!" said Annie defiantly.

Vasara climbed down the cellar steps and slowly walked over to Annie.

"I said pick him up!"

"And I said, YOU pick him up! You fucking shot him!"

Vasara raised the Glock to Annie's forehead. Annie didn't flinch, Kelly gulped, and Jasper wondered if this was going to be a Guinness record for the world's shortest-ever engagement.

After what seemed like an eternity, the stand-off was broken by Kelly.

"If you want to get out of this, we're going to need hostages, and two is far better than one!"

Vasara momentarily shifted her stare to Kelly. And that was all the opportunity Annie needed. Her right fist came up under Vasara's chin faster than a submarine with a serious water leak. Her head jerked back, and the pistol fell from her hand as Annie shoved away her arm with her other hand and Vasara crumpled and fell back. Now the scramble was on to get the pistol as it hit the concrete floor and bounced. Jasper shot forward and made a grab for it. But the hours he'd spent cable tied made his movement clumsy, and instead his foot connected with the gun, which inconveniently knocked it to Kelly's feet. This made it a simple matter of just picking it up, as he'd been characteristically slow off the mark.

"I think I'd better look after this," he said, brandishing the gun.

Vasara had been lucky. Had Annie's arms had the

usual amount of blood in them, she'd have had to stick her toothbrush up her nose to brush her teeth. But as it was, she just sat on the cellar floor rubbing her chin and trying not to cry like the daft kid that she was. When she'd had a few minutes to recover, Kelly indicated that they should all troop up to the bar. This time, he wisely decided that Neville should stop where he was for now, fast congealing on the cellar floor, and that he should retain the gun, as he didn't think Vasara should be left in charge of a penny rocket, let alone a Glock. Jasper and Annie were told to sit on bar stools in the middle of the floor, and they did so holding hands. That way, he could keep his distance from them and at the same time ensure they weren't plotting anything or picking up a weapon. Vasara sat in a booth sulking because she badly wanted to shoot Annie, but Kelly still wouldn't give her the gun.

Kelly positioned himself to the side of a window so that he could see out without becoming a target. He had no military training, and he'd never even fired a gun, but he'd seen similar sieges on a few films, so that helped. The problem was that they never ended well for the kidnappers. Usually, it was a bloodbath. Kelly needed to get creative or just surrender and blame it all on Vasara. He just needed time to think, which was the one thing that, unbeknown to him, he hadn't got much of. He could see the helicopter, but he could also see at least eight prone soldiers pointing weapons at the pub. He had one gun, a dog, and an unstable teenage girl. He didn't fancy his chances! By now the pub's dog was driving everyone mad with its barking, making it especially hard to think calmly.

Willy was another man who needed a plan, and fast. A large crowd had now gathered, and there was a danger that the whole operation would descend into farce. The risk that anyone else might discover that

Renate Redlinger was present was also increasing his need for a speedy closure.

"Are you a trained siege negotiator?" demanded Willy.

"I'm not even a trained first aider!" McClean said, laughing.

"OK, well you're all I've got, so ring them again and see what you can do."

McClean rang the pub again. After a few rings, Kelly answered…

"Just thought I'd ring back and see if you had any more demands."

"We're still thinking about it."

"OK. Well, we've got one. Any chance you could shut the dog up?"

"What, permanently?"

"No, just get it to stop barking."

"Is it driving your private army mad, then?"

"Not my private army. You wouldn't believe me if I told you."

"Try me!"

"What about ten German special forces troopers and Renate Redlinger, the chancellor of Germany."

"What is she doing here?"

"Search me!"

"So no demands then?"

"How about you all go away?"

"I don't think that's an option. What about you surrender instead and we all go home?"

"I don't think that I would end up going home though."

"Fair point. Anything else you need?"

"Have you got any more hostages? We've only got two."

"Ha! Good one!"

Kelly cut the line, and Willy looked at his clueless negotiator in disgust.

"Why did you tell him that Renate Redlinger is here?"

"Well, I was busting to tell someone!"

Back in the pub, the balance of power had firmly shifted to Kelly.

"Go upstairs and bring the dog down, then it will stop barking."

"Why have I got to do it?" whined Vasara.

"Because it likes you and you can't be trusted not to shoot the cleaner while I'm gone."

Vasara couldn't fault Kelly's thinking. She would definitely make Annie into Mrs Potato Head if she got half a chance. Reluctantly, she rose from the booth, went behind the bar and climbed the stairs to the living quarters. The flat was freezing as the patio door that opened onto the roof was wide open and the cold night air was making a good job of overwhelming the ancient central heating system. The dog didn't acknowledge her entrance because it was busy barking at the intruders from the edge of the roof. So she picked up its lead and called it.

"Gretta, come on Gretta...."

The dog looked back defiantly from the edge of the roof and then continued to bark.

"Gretta! Come on, Gretta...."

Out in the car park, one of the soldiers sniggered. Willy knew straight away why he was laughing, but stoically ignored him. He was used to needling from the lads. Being a member of the special forces wasn't like being in the regular army. Despite his rank, they were a team, and with that special understanding came banter.

Gretta was having none of it. Her job was to guard the pub against intruders. A helicopter, several soldiers, a policeman and the chancellor of Germany added up to a fairly hefty intrusion, so it was going to take something really interesting to break her concentration. Vasara remembered that there were some gravy bone biscuits under the sink and went over to get a few. Gretta heard the creak of the cupboard door and stopped barking, understandably deciding that her hunger took precedence over duty, and she happily trotted back into the flat to receive a biscuit or two. As Gretta ate her fill, Vasara slipped the lead over the head of the eight-stone Rottweiler and wound the leather strap at the other end tightly around her wrist. Then, being very careful not to create a silhouette in the patio window, she crept around the edge of the room with Gretta in tow, intending to shut out intruders without accidentally becoming a target.

Just as she reached for the handle of the patio door, a shrill whistle cut through the air and a laughing voice shouted "Gretta!" from the car park. On hearing its name, the dog decided on an immediate return to duty at the edge of the roof. Vasara realised her mistake in that split second and desperately tried to free her wrist from the strap. Regrettably, the enormous hound was far too powerful for her weedy frame and she exploded out of the patio door right arm first after the dog in the slapstick style of Norman Wisdom. Instantly, eight red laser dots lit her up like a neon ladybird and the firing began. Special forces are allowed to make their own choice of weapon, so it was quite a duck shoot. In those short seconds, Vasara experienced la crème de la crème of the world's arms manufacturers. From Swiss ones to Israeli ones, she got to try them all before finally performing a perfectly executed forward roll and falling off the roof, dragging the now stunned mutt after her.

Renate was the first to speak as the enormous cloud of gun smoke slowly drifted off towards Blackheath.

"Bugger me, lads, tell me no one shot the dog?"

Her query was swiftly answered by a bark from Gretta, who was slowly dragging Vasara's gelatinous remains across the car park towards them seemingly no worse the wear for her recent crash course in free-running and now thoroughly intent on reaching safety behind German lines.

"Hold your fire!" ordered Renate, pushing past her bewildered bodyguard and jumping down from the helicopter. Walking towards the enormous dog, she held out her hand in greeting. Gretta stopped pulling and sat down, tilting her head and looking puzzled.

As Renate reached out to her, everyone held their breath. No one had a problem shooting an unhinged teenage girl, but they all drew the line at unnecessarily killing a dumb animal. With her other hand, Renate slowly unwound the blood-spattered lead from what was left of Vasara's and held it firmly in her own. Gretta seemed unperturbed by the unexpected change in management and happily sat waiting while Renate did this, before obediently walking beside the chancellor of Germany to the helicopter and jumping in to nestle happily by her feet.

Kelly watched Vasara's gruesome passing from beside the window with growing alarm. This wasn't a rescue team, it was a death squad. But from a positive angle, at least the dog had finally quietened down. When the shooting had started, all three had flung themselves to the floor in a joint attempt to stay alive. That had been the catalyst for a bond of sorts, and Kelly suddenly felt the urge to unburden himself.

"Look, folks, none of this was my idea. I didn't set out to be Oldbury's answer to Pablo Escobar. I was happy to just sell a bit of draw and things got out of hand when she arrived. I'm not a hardened drug dealer. I just fell into it by accident."

He walked over to the bar and put the gun down. He was visibly far paler now, which made his teeth seem all the yellower.

"How do you fall into drug dealing by accident?" said the newly betrothed Annie, who wasn't swallowing any sob-story bullshit.

"I used to have an honest job as the night manager in a hotel. People ask for all sorts of things at three o'clock in the morning, and it's your job to find them. They don't tell you that at the interview. You think it's all going to be condoms, toasted sandwiches and the odd bottle of wine. But it's a slippery slope. Next thing you know, you're on first-name terms with the local pimps and drug dealers are offering you bulk-buy discounts.

"Then one time we have a rock band in. Who, for some reason best known to themselves, wanted a dwarf to throw. Luckily, it's Christmas. So I get on the blower to the local theatre, as they are doing Snow White and are knee-deep in midgets, if you'll forgive the pun. No problem, they send a little fella over in a taxi. I tell the band it's a ton fifty. I give him the ton, naturally keeping fifty myself. The band has already had a snowman's worth of coke and there are enough barely legal girls up there to start a ballet class. He's cool, he's been thrown before and knows exactly what to expect. So I stick him in the lift and take him up to their suite on the ninth floor. I make sure he's happy and everything is sweet. I get back in the lift and go down to the front desk, just in time to hear a loud bang in the car park and a shitload of screaming. I go out to see what's happened and find that they'd chucked the little fucker through the window and he's lying dead on the roof of the foyer. The theatre are raging because he's got lines in the panto and his missus won't perform without him. So they end up with five dwarfs instead of seven and have to get two agency midgets in, which apparently are quite expensive.

"Then, as you can imagine at the inquest, things that seem fairly reasonable in the wee small hours sound completely different in the cold light of day. So, penniless and out of a job, I start managing pubs out of desperation. One day, a dealer I used to use at the hotel walks in. We get talking over a few drinks. I confess that running pubs is a lot of work for not that much money, and the rest you can probably guess."

"So you ended up here selling shandy and jizz?"

"Well, more jizz than shandy, to be fair, but that's about the strength of it."

"So what are you saying, then, that you surrender?"

"Well, in preference to becoming a human tea strainer, that seems like a sensible move to me."

"How long do you reckon you'll get for drug dealing, false imprisonment and murder?"

"Drug dealing fair enough, but I don't think, strictly speaking, I did any false imprisonment or murder. She shot him and I certainly didn't tell her to. I wasn't even aware she had a gun till this morning. She just produced it from nowhere, and I wasn't about to try to take it off her. I'm as much of a victim in all this as you. Plus, if I hadn't picked up the gun and sent her upstairs, you would be lying next to Neville. If you need me to sweeten the deal, I have a couple of multipacks behind the bar."

"This is no time for cheap own-brand crisps," raged Annie, without managing to find that statement in any way ridiculous. "We need to get out of here before the blokes outside with the guns decide to become the blokes inside with the guns!"

"OK, I'll ring McClean and let him know that we're coming out," said Jasper, who had located the pub's phone and was now dialling 1471 for the number and furiously searching for something to write it down on.

Chapter 26

Outside in the car park, Renate was getting tired of the waiting game. The crowd was getting bigger, and she knew it was only a matter of time until someone realised that they weren't actually the police and it all started to get really complicated.

"Ring them again!"

"What's the special word?"

"Fucking now!"

"That's two!" replied McClean, who continued to be astounded by Renate's firm grip of Anglo Saxon. Taking out his phone, he redialled the last number.

"It's engaged."

"For God's sake, who do you ring in the middle of an armed siege?"

"Maybe he's ringing his family to say goodbye before he goes all Scarface?"

"Right. Fuck it. If that's the case, we're going in!" said Renate.

"We?" enquired Willy.

"Well 'you' then…" Renate sighed.

"Right, lads, the chancellor says we're going in," commanded Willy, pressing his throat microphone.

No one moved a muscle. No guns were cocked. No response of any type.

"Might you be better saying it in German?" said

McClean gently.

Willy reddened, pressed his throat mike again and barked far more words in German than McClean felt might be an accurate translation. He didn't understand German, but it would seem that they didn't have a German equivalent to 'frontal assault'. Therefore, he had a fair idea of what was about to happen. This time the response was instant. Magazines were clipped and unclipped, safety catches clicked off, and lucky charms were kissed. Then, finally, everyone was poised to go, like at the start of Mike Reid's 'Runaround'.

"We go on my count of three," ordered Willy, who wasn't wearing square glasses or any chunky gold jewellery but clearly remembered the show.

"Eins, zwei…"

Inconveniently, the front door of the pub opened and Kelly gingerly stepped out with his hands aloft and his pot belly fully on display due to another poorly fitting promotional T-shirt. A wave of disappointment spread around the trigger-happy soldiers, who were keenly anticipating another opportunity to let off some steam. These days, far too many operations ended with no shots fired due to much-improved siege negotiation. Life had been far more exciting before everyone started talking about 'how they felt' and the underlying unhappiness leading to them taking hostages. Abseiling, throwing thunder flashes and double-tapping people in the head was a great deal of fun and was sorely missed by everyone in the wider special forces community.

All eyes were now on the yellow-toothed pub manager, and everyone was desperately hoping for the tiniest flicker of a hand movement. Even a cheeky bum scratch could be seen as justification for making him dance like an epileptic Michael Jackson tribute. But he just stood there motionless, clearly unsure of what to do next.

It was Renate that eventually broke the silence by speaking through the loudhailer on the helicopter.

"OK, on your knees."

Kelly instantly complied without hesitation.

"Right then, Leave or Remain?"

Kelly looked puzzled.

"Sorry?" he replied.

"What did you vote Englander? Leave or Remain?"

"What do you want to know that for?"

"Just thought I'd make it more interesting…"

"Remain!" shouted Kelly, clearly looking a bit shifty.

"Bollocks. You've got 'Leave' written all over you. Do you know the trouble you've caused me? I've been to more frigging summits than Sherpa Tenzing and eaten more crap buffets and dried up vol-au-vents in the last two years than in the previous twenty. I've had to go back to Fat Dodgers because of you lot!"

"I honestly didn't know what to vote. It was nothing personal. I just hate the energy-efficient light bulbs you lot made us have. They're utter crap! Have you tried Kalorie Kutters, though? It's a far easier plan. We used to have a group here. There are still a couple of recipe books behind the bar if you want them."

"Can't stand quark in everything and I always found the coloured days thing confusing!"

"They don't do that anymore. It's all super simple now."

"Oh, I wasn't aware of that. Thanks. I might have a look then."

"Madam Chancellor, might it be possible to return to the job in hand?" prompted Willy wearily. He was growing impatient with the Renate Redlinger Roadshow.

"OK! Face down on the ground with your hands behind you," said Renate, pretending that was what she had been going to say next anyway.

Kelly misunderstood the command and tried unsuccessfully to move to a lying position with his hands behind his back. Predictably, he overbalanced forwards and head-butted the tarmac loudly in doing so. Two soldiers rushed forward and secured his hands before frogmarching him over to the helicopter, still chuckling at his utter stupidity. Annie and Jasper watched, laughing, from the window, and once they were sure the coast was clear, they too nervously stepped from the front door.

"Hands up!" shouted Renate, who was getting into her new role as siege compère.

Jasper happily raised his hands to comply, but Annie steadfastly refused. Instead, she just glared in the general direction of the helicopter.

"Hands up!" shouted Renate again angrily, who was more than a little used to getting her own way without asking twice.

"We're hostages, not terrorists!" Annie bawled back.

"How do we know that?"

"When did you last see a fat terrorist?"

"It's a fair point, Madam Chancellor," said Willy. "Can't recall ever seeing a fat one. Being that angry about something must naturally make you thin."

"OK, jog over here then," replied a disappointed Renate, who had been looking forward to another two rounds of the tarmac headbutt game.

A grateful Jasper did as he was told and happily trotted over to the helicopter. Annie wasn't big on being told what to do, even if the woman who was doing the asking had single-handedly transformed German politics. So she meandered over in her own time, not forgetting to thoroughly check out the still-prone army crumpet as she did so.

Satisfied that their mission was now complete, the soldiers began collecting up their gear ready to move out, along with high-fiving each other and laughing loudly amongst themselves at Kelly's tarmac-textured forehead that was now swelling nicely.

McClean stood quietly, thinking about how to gain closure from his point of view. He wasn't sure how Bogdan was going to take the unexpected gymnastic death of his daughter in a hail of German special forces gunfire. Or even if he would believe it when he told him.

"So where do we all go from here?" said Bernd.

"Well, obviously we go back to Germany. Job done!" replied Willy.

"Just like that, then? What about Vasara's body over there? Won't that create some awkward questions when the pathologist starts pulling out all the bullets? I'm sure that some of them might be so special that they lead back to you lads," reasoned McClean, who was still grasping for an angle that left him in the clear.

"OK, we'll take her with us and drop her out over the North Sea! No body, no death, no questions!" said Willy.

"Then there's poor Neville's body in the cellar? Naturally, they'll want to know who shot him. As that was Vasara and soon she'll be swimming with the fishes, won't that raise suspicions too?" interjected Annie, who was extremely sad that Neville had ended his days reminiscing about his unhappy childhood, but she was managing to hide it rather well.

"OK, we take the other body too," declared Willy helpfully, who just wanted to get far away from all these mad Tommies as quickly as he could. He turned and jumped into the helicopter and rummaged about in a locker, returning seconds later with two black zip-up body bags and ordering his soldiers to collect up the bodies.

"What about me?"

By now, Kelly was looking very dejected. It didn't take a fortune teller to know that all he had in his future was a very long stay in a big house with bars on the windows. McClean looked hard at him and thought about an alternative solution that would suit all parties. If he took him in and charged him with anything, he had a good story to tell. A story that may well result in them sharing a cell and serious disruption to his fast-approaching retirement plan.

"OK, what if you just go back to running this like the pub it used to be? No drugs or junkies. Just lager tops and crisps. Keeping regular hours. Roast dinners on a Sunday. Birthday parties and discos at the weekend."

"Suppose I could if I had some help," replied Kelly, brightening slightly.

"Well, I know a good cleaner and her bloke might make you a decent barman once you've shown him the ropes." Annie laughed.

"Well, all's well that ends well," said Renate from inside the helicopter, who was irritated that solution-based negotiations were clearly going well without her input. "Can I keep the dog then?"

"You might as well," replied Kelly. "It hates me. Vasara was the only one that could ever do anything with it."

"So that's settled then. You run the pub properly with your new pals. I keep the dog. Dead bodies go in the sea on the way home! Wunderbar! If only Brexit had been this easy!"

"There is just one last thing," piped up Bernd bashfully.

"Oh, Strudel Boy. Don't go all mushy on me. That was all a long time ago. I'm an old married lady now…"

Bernd laughed. "That's not what I meant." He was more than happy with his arrangement with Candy and amused that Renate had flattered herself. "I want to visit my family back home. Would there be any problem with that?"

"None whatsoever. Visit any time you like. The new Germany welcomes everyone, including ex-Stasi agents!"

Minutes later, the helicopter lifted into the air. Renate turned to Willy as the waving figures in the car park below slowly disappeared into the darkness.

"Exactly why did your men laugh when Vasara called the dog?"

"My wife's called Gretta, and she's well known to be a bit of a Rottweiler," chuckled Willy, who was going to try some mint sauce on his lamb dinner that Sunday.

Epilogue

Six months later, the New Inn was a very different pub altogether. The sticky carpet and horse brasses had been replaced by modern laminate flooring and bright new décor, and there was a fully operational condom machine in the gents. Iris McKenzie was the guest of honour at the reopening, and this time the old lady shed tears of joy. Soon the faithful regulars began to return, as the little back street boozer once again became what it had once been, the social hub of the community and a place where nice people were always welcome.

Not long after, Kelly moved on to realise his dream of running a bar in Spain, swapping bags of jizz for jugs of cheap sangria and a lifetime of English breakfasts in sunny Benidorm. He missed Neville and always regretted the way things had worked out for his old friend, so he named the bar's cat after him and they spoke every day.

McClean retired from the force with an unblemished service record and spent his days enduring his wife's scatter-cushion addiction in a caravan park just outside Bewdley. He never heard from Bogdan again, mainly because Bogdan didn't hear from Vasara, and quite honestly that was the way they both liked it.

Annie and Jasper took over management of the pub, and she started a Kalorie Kutters group on Wednesdays, eventually losing five stone by limiting her crisp addiction to a single packet a week. When they tied the knot, they held their reception at the New Inn, and all the friends they had made along the way were in attendance. Naturally, the Right Reverend Richard Morris presided over their nuptials and Mucky Barry produced the wedding video. They still play tricks, but only on each other.

Bernd made an emotional trip to meet his sister, Frieda, her husband and their three kids. He marvelled at how much Germany had changed in the nearly forty years he had been absent. The old bakery was still there, but now it sold mass-produced cakes delivered daily by van. Nonetheless, he sat and drank a coffee there with a dear friend for old times' sake, surrounded by the memories of his parents and the old days when they had spent so much time baking in the back. She didn't tell her husband. It didn't seem wise, as after all, somebody needed to look after the dog…

Other Books by Eddie Lancaster

The Sardinian Job

Charlie Stroker's Mini Centre lies in the backstreets of a small Black Country town just a short distance from the gates of the factory that built them. But now with the best years of the business behind him, his dream of making a fortune from a lifelong passion is quickly fading away. Straining relations still further with his discontented wife and their antisocial teenager. Both already disenchanted by a decade of wilful neglect and a tankerload of cooking sauce!

Following a chance encounter of the deep-fried kind, he learns of a long-forgotten stash of valuable Mini spares languishing on a remote Mediterranean island. Recognising the chance to change his fortunes, he embarks on a quest to bring them home. For Britain! For glory! But most of all for the money!

Will this barmy enterprise be the making of Charlie? Or will his first ever foreign holiday finish off both his marriage and his business? It's a bawdy comic caper, but only a chancer named Stroker could pull off The Sardinian Job!

The Cheesy Dips

Middle-aged Martin has a sexless meal-for-one life and a boring job at a DIY superstore in Halesowen. Following a chance reunion, he persuades his old pal Craig to form a covers band and save him from an unwelcome bromance with Nigel, his nerdy supervisor. Who has a thing for irritable Polish women but still lives at home with his elderly mother and a fridge full of soft cheese.

Meanwhile, down in London, the Dafoe twins are busy wrecking their once stellar musical career with a rock-and-roll lifestyle guaranteed to finish them too. Until their exasperated manager stages a furious last-ditch intervention. Forcing them to quit London and record on a North Sea island hideaway. Safely tucked away from everything that turned his lucrative cash cow into an absolute nightmare!

When these two worlds collide, a hilarious tale of sex, violence and chicken curry unfolds. Resulting in a meteoric rise, right from the bottom, straight to the very top, as the laughs just keep coming!

Printed in Great Britain
by Amazon